The Basic Book of
Organically Grown Foods

The Basic Book of Organically Grown Foods

by the staff of
Organic Gardening and Farming
Edited by
M. C. Goldman *and* William H. Hylton

T.M. REGD.

Rodale Press Book Division
Emmaus, Pa. 18049

The text is based on material which has appeared in
Organic Gardening and Farming, Prevention and
Organic Food Marketing

Standard Book Number 0–87857–044–6
Library of Congress Card Number 72–83364

MANUFACTURED IN THE UNITED STATES OF AMERICA
Book Designer: J. Schuman
OB-133

FIRST PRINTING—November 1972

Contents

Part Five 🐞 Looking at The Big Picture

Part One

Introducing Organically Grown Foods

1

What's It All About?

"Organic"

The word "organic" is a hot property these days. It's appearing on more and more foods each year. It's appearing on items that aren't foods, too. Articles and books centering on the word are flooding the market.

But people are still confused. People are still puzzled. What's it all about? What does the word "organic," as applied to foods, gardening and even a style of life, really mean? It does have, after all, a lot of established food experts in a real dither. Some purport to be puzzled. Others speak volubly on the subject, generally expressing their hostility to it, demonstrating that they have considerable information but very little understanding.

The usual puzzlement stems from an association with "organic" as it's applied to chemistry. In chemistry, "organic" signifies any substance containing carbon molecules. Thus, a desk, a rubber tire and even DDT are chemically "organic."

But we're talking about "organic" as it relates to living things. We're talking about "organic" as it relates to organic materials—plant residues, animal wastes and just plain garbage. At the very beginning of the "organic movement"—the one that's sparked all this puzzlement and that's sparked this book—"organic" referred to a method of agriculture. Sir Albert Howard wrote a book or two about it, as did J. I. Rodale. Sir Albert didn't call his agricultural technique organic, but J. I. did. The foods produced through this method of agriculture are properly called organically grown or organically raised or organically produced.

But common usage has given us the term "organic foods." And common usage has broadened the definition of organic foods beyond the strictures of a method of agriculture to include as well methods of processing and distribution, methods that are as related to living things as Sir Albert's method of farming. Foods raised, processed and distributed according to these "organic" methods are what this book is about.

The book provides information. It'll tell you about the special qualities of organically produced foods, how they're grown and how they're moved to the consumer. It'll tell you how to grow your own foods and how to use them. And it'll give you some insight into the relationships between a deteriorating society and a blighted food production and distribution system. The information is here.

The understanding must come from you.

"Organic Foods"

"Organic food" is grown in soil rich in organic matter. Organic matter —or humus—is the living part of the soil. In that moist, woodsy part of the soil exist the uncountable billions of bacteria, fungi and other minute organisms which give soil remarkable powers to feed tremendous amounts of minerals, and other nutrients to plant roots.

When American land was virgin, before the days of commercial agriculture, our soil contained a significant amount of organic matter. Each growing season a small amount was consumed by plants, then in the fall as leaves fell and annual plants died, the humus was built up again. Insects, earthworms and other small animals burrowed in the soil, sometimes carrying the humus to depths of several feet.

The past 150 years of large-scale farming have depleted soil organic matter. Now, many soils contain less than 1 per cent humus. Manure is spread on fields less often, and the stalks or other waste portions of plants are often removed from the land. Many soils are therefore less alive than they used to be, and the crops they produce are less healthy and sometimes are lower in nutritional value.

A steadily growing number of gardeners and farmers are working to restore the organic quality of the soil. Using old, time-tested methods, they're restoring humus to the soil. They're eschewing artificial fertiliz ers and poisons, because they contaminate soil or plant and simply aren't in tune with the idea of producing food that is natural and of high quality.

Organically grown food is handled differently after it is harvested. It is not refined, chemically treated or processed beyond the dictates of bare necessity. There is no such thing as organically produced white bread, for example, because by refining the wheat you would destroy its "organic" quality. You can see that the word organic has grown beyond its original farm and garden meaning and has become a matter of interest and concern to all people.

Organically grown food varies in quality according to the area in which it is grown, but almost always it has a recognizable good, old-fashioned taste which is sadly lacking in supermarket food. An organically raised chicken, for example, is fed no drugs to stimulate growth and is allowed to scratch in the ground and eat the worms, bugs and the other critters that are delicacies to a chicken. As a result, the meat of the bird has a hearty flavor. A member of the older generation fed an organic chicken will suddenly remember how white meat used to taste.

Blemishes can actually be a mark of quality in organically grown fruit. An apple, for example, will almost always have a few nicks and scars to show that somewhere along the line the bugs got at it. While those marks limit the beauty of the apple according to most standards, to an organically oriented person they mean the fruit is pure. An unmarked apple will most always have been sprayed a dozen times to keep the bugs away.

THE AGRICULTURAL CRAFTSMAN

Of course, producing food by the organic method isn't easy. This type of agriculture isn't one of machines and magic potions. It's one of thought, care and lots of hard work. The farmer must be intelligent and conscientious. He must be concerned about tomorrow as much as he's concerned about today. He must be concerned about his primary resource—his farm's soil—and his product—the food raised on his farm.

For the organic farmer is a craftsman. He works hard, taking pride in the fruits of his labor. His product took time to produce, and it requires extra care in handling. It's a better product because of the farmer's unusual attitude, philosophy and techniques. And it costs more.

To many, the extra cost isn't a barrier. They know that organically grown foods are less expensive in the long run. They know they're getting extra value and don't mind the extra cost.

But there's another factor in the extra cost, a factor stemming from the fact that "organic" is a hot property. There's virtually unlimited demand but a very limited supply. There are only a limited number of organic farms in this country, yet there are millions of people who want to start eating organic food. There won't be enough to go around, unless many people start growing their own. Fortunately, hundreds of thousands of people are doing just that.

What we must all be particularly alert for is the possibility that some ordinary food will be palmed off as organically grown. Even a chemical test for pesticide residues only determines if the produce has been sprayed. It's not a guarantee that the total organic method has been used. So your best defense is to know your store owner and your organic farm supplier well enough to be able to trust them.

First, though, be sure the people you deal with really know what organically grown means! One health food trade journal took the editorial position that health foods, natural foods and organic foods are one and the same thing. That's absolutely untrue.

Health food is an umbrella term covering all kinds of food that are in a general way more healthful than the plastic sort widely sold in supermarkets. For example, unsulphured dried figs are health food, whether they are grown organically or not. Whole grains and dried beans are health food. Corn oil margarine is also a kind of health food. So is safflower seed oil.

But the term health food is also applied to a wide range of foods marketed for people on special or restricted diets. Foods under this section of the health food umbrella contain salt and sugar substitutes and many contain chemical additives and preservatives. The list of health foods is very large indeed, and individual items on the list aren't necessarily unmixed blessings.

The phrase natural food, less widely used, helps us tell the difference between good and bad types of the same food. Mom's chicken soup is a natural food, but dehydrated chicken soup is not. Honey, especially the raw kind, is a natural food, while refined sugar is not. A fresh fruit salad is natural, while the canned, sugared kind is not.

Organically grown food is the most precise term of all, referring specifically to food that has been grown on a certain kind of farm, using special methods. No chemical fertilizers are used in growing organic food. No toxic pesticides are used, and weed killers are avoided, too. Most important, organic matter is added to the soil of an organic farm to increase the humus content and thereby create a much healthier soil condition. In most cases, the process of converting a farm from chemical to organic takes about three years, allowing time for the chemical residues in the soil to dissipate.

THE ORGANIC PHONIES

Needless to say, much health food that has been sold and is being sold is not grown organically. That is not a bad thing and does not mean that health food is not really productive of health in the person eating it. What is bad is to sell regular food and call it organic food or to try to confuse people about what the phrase organically grown really means.

The way food is produced is of vital concern to a growing number of shoppers. Sensitized by pollution and by such "accidents" as botulism scares, food buyers are suspicious of agribusiness and of the food processing companies and have declining faith in the food regulatory agencies. They are looking for a new quality in food—ecological purity. Only a few years ago, few people even thought there was such a thing.

The word organic is crucial to the appreciation of the concept of ecological purity in food. Organically grown is a label that is easily understood by city people, who, after all, know very little about farming. Organically grown means food as it used to be grown, without the latest chemical aids that have backfired on the environment in so many ways. Organically grown means food that helps the land and the bodies of people, instead of tearing them down. Organic is power to people who were just manipulated into thinking that food like fat, drugged beef is "quality."

The enemies of organic farming realize, to their great disgust, the tremendous value of the word organic. They see how it has caused food consumers to wonder about all that chemical junk they are eating. Even more important, the chemical proponents sense in the popularity of the word organic the seeds of a genuine revolution, which will eventually deprive them of their markets for food additives and chemical fertilizers. The chemical salesmen know the word organic is telling the public that the ordinary food they eat is not quite as natural or as pure as it could be.

The chemical people are alerted to the coming organic food revolution. In self-defense, they are trying to kill it. One of the spokesmen for that effort is Dr. Emil Mrak, chancellor emeritus of the University of California at Davis and long associated with agricultural science at the highest levels. Dr. Mrak has helped to build chemical farming and now sees it threatened by the crazy idea that food should be grown naturally, as it was 50 years ago.

"Dr. Mrak firmly believes there is no such thing as organic fruits, vegetables, and grain products," says Jeanne Voltz, food editor of the *Los Angeles Times.* She told how Dr. Mrak wrote to the FDA and said that the public is getting fleeced by sellers of organically grown foods. "I had hoped that the FDA would say that there is no such thing," he told Mrs. Voltz.

The Food and Drug Administration has taken almost a hands-off attitude toward organically grown foods up to now, but if enough people like Dr. Mrak keep writing them, they could change. At present, they're leaving organic food regulation to state governments.

Dr. Mrak gives many specific reasons why he is against organically grown food. He thinks people don't know what the word organic means when it is used to describe food. He thinks there is considerable fraud in the marketplace, with much conventional food being labeled as organic when it really has been sprayed and grown on chemically fertilized soil.

Another person fighting organic foods is R. A. Seelig, information consultant for the United Fresh Fruit and Vegetable Association. In a booklet called "Selection and Care of Fresh Fruits and Vegetables," he calls organic food a "fraud," and says that claims of superiority for organic foods are just "talk."

Dr. Mrak and Seelig are only two of the people trying to kill the word organic. There are others. Sometimes they say that "organic is no good," without giving a reason. Other times they pick one arguable point about some organic foods and dwell on that, without giving a balanced picture. Almost always, the anti-organic people are closely connected with the chemical industry. Although they may wear the white coats of scientific researchers, they are getting grant money or other support from producers of pesticides, chemical fertilizers or synthetic food additives. They are simply biased.

The word organic is also under attack from within the organic movement. It is being underminded. Farmers—both large and small—who sell conventional food and call it organic are spoiling the whole moral basis of the organic system of agriculture. They're giving it a reputation for being phony because they see in organic farming a quick way to get extra money for ordinary food. If that situation is not corrected soon, our chance of ever getting food in the hands of the majority of consumers will be destroyed.

There's a scandal coming in organic foods, says marketing columnist E. B. Weiss in *Advertising Age.* "I now predict that organic food will before long get the attention of the highly articulate and powerfully organized consumer groups," he forecasts. There will be Congressional hearings, he says, and "these hearings will produce sensational testimony about malpractice in organic foods." The end result will be a tight federal inspection system for organic food producers, with jail penalties for violators, says Weiss. But that won't kill organic food. Far from it. "Out of all this organic food will eventually emerge as a strong mass-marketing factor," Weiss says. He believes that "organic foods are almost urgently needed."

Weiss is trying to do organic people a favor by pointing his finger at the scandal he thinks is coming. But it's already here. The New York City Department of Consumer Affairs held a public hearing in December 1971 that dealt mainly with misrepresentation and unreasonably high prices of organic and health foods. The hearing attracted the attention of many newspapers, radio and even television stations. We are likely to see more such hearings.

All the brouhaha may just mark the coming of age of organically grown foods. It certainly demonstrates that organically grown foods represent a concept in sustenance that simply can't be ignored any longer.

THE BIG BENEFITS

People are becoming increasingly aware of the benefits of organic foods. The following five reasons probably best explain why.

1. There are no chemicals used in growing or processing the food.

The lack of chemical residues ranks as the number one benefit because it is the one people think of first. It is the advantage that convinces most people to start eating organically grown food.

Only a few years ago, you didn't have to worry about weed killer residues in food, because no one used weed killers. Only a few years ago, you could eat a ham without wondering what was used to cure it. But now you know that your ham probably contains calgon, the same water-softening chemical you use in your laundry. There is a chemical to make ice cream hold its shape as it melts. There are hundreds of different chemicals to kill insects and to cure plant diseases, some of them so poisonous that only one drop on your skin is enough to cause serious illness and even death.

The average person knows something about the chemicals in his food and would choose not to eat them if he had an alternative. The steady growth of interest in organic gardening and farming is a measure of the desire of more people to eat pure food.

2. Organic food has superior quality as the result of growth on fertile soil.

The expanded use of chemicals in food has perhaps caused some people to overlook the fact that the original reason for growing foods organically was to get more nutritional value. The birth of the organic idea can be traced to very near the time of Sir Albert Howard's experiment with the diets of two groups of children at a boys' boarding school in England. One group was fed the usual food and the other was given organically grown foods—the actual menus of each group being the same. The group fed organic foods showed dramatically better health than the group fed ordinary fare. They had fewer colds, better teeth and greater resistance to infectious diseases. It was that experiment which stimulated J. I. Rodale's interest in the organic method and inspired him to found *Organic Gardening and Farming* magazine.

Humus-rich soil improves the food value of plants by providing them with all the nutrients they need in the proper balance. Balance is the key word. When artificial fertilizers are used, the plants' roots are often saturated with an abundance of one nutrient, making it difficult for them to pick up others they need just as much. Since artificial fertilizers present their food in soluble form, the plant can't be selective and you can almost say it is forced to use whatever is given to it.

There are some scientists, though, who still claim that the soil has no effect on the nutrient value of plants. They say that no matter how poor or how fertile a soil is, the crops grown on it contain the same balance of nutrients. Most of the scientists holding that view are the ones most closely allied with agribusiness. They don't want to believe it is their responsibility to provide proper food balance in plants; they're just interested in high yields. Fortunately, that outlook is not uncontested.

3. Organic food is not debased by unnecessary processing.

You can't call a loaf of white bread organic even if it is made from organically grown wheat. Having taken the life from the grain, you have eliminated its right to bear the label "organic." Fortunately, most growers and suppliers of organic foods appreciate that users want a product natural in all respects, and they strive to treat their food naturally. And when you grow your own organic food you have control over it every step of the way. Most important, the average organic gardener doesn't have the knowledge or the means to over-process food. It usually takes a lot of skill and expensive equipment.

4. Better varieties of plants are used in organic cultivation than are used by commercial farmers.

When you buy tomatoes in the store, you are getting the fruit of a plant that meets the farmer's requirements but not necessarily yours. The same could be said of almost every fruit, vegetable or grain. When a farmer grows tomatoes, for example, he wants plants whose fruit will ripen in unison, be easy to pick, stand up under shipment and yield the maximum number of bushels or tons per acre. Your wishes as a consumer are observed only so long as they don't conflict with his production problems. But when you grow tomatoes in your own garden, you can pick the variety that fully meets your needs. If you want high vitamin C content you can grow DOUBLERICH or HIGH-C tomatoes. If you want plenty of vitamin A you can select CARO-RED. The day may come when supermarkets will handle superior varieties of plants because their customers are demanding them.

5. Growing food organically saves the land.

Any reckoning of the reasons why organically grown food is good must include consideration of the state of our soil. For it is from the soil that the true strength of America springs.

Commercial farmers today are too concerned with events of today and are making excuses for the failures they are breeding for tomorrow. They know organic matter is essential to the health of the soil, and they know their farming methods are draining that organic matter away little by little each year. But they have to pay off loans on their big, new machines, so they use methods they know are unsound to get highest yields. Tomorrow is time enough to put back the humus, they figure.

Even though the farmer is the custodian of the soil, you can't blame him entirely for slowly wearing it out. In our modern agricultural establishment there are hordes of people who are helping him with that job. The chemical companies are spending millions of dollars to get new pesticides cleared for farm use, but they spend practically nothing to find out what the pesticide residues are doing as they accumulate in the soil. About a third of all the research done by the state experiment stations is directly financed by companies with some product to sell to the farmer. Many new farm scientists graduating each year have had their educations paid for by chemical company scholarships and grants.

As you read on in this book, you'll learn more and more about organically grown foods and about why we think they're so important. You'll get an idea of why organic gardening is more than just a way to raise food in your backyard and why organic foods are more than just tastier eating. You'll get an inkling of how food relates to a better quality of life.

Organic Living

Long before the technological world became as oppressive as it is today, the organic gardening idea was a full-grown philosophy. In fact, the unpleasant conditions of pollution which we are experiencing now were predicted almost 40 years ago by the founders of the organic method. They could see evidence then of trouble on a small scale, and knew that the isolated, eroded fields and polluted crops of that time would mushroom eventually into a pall of illness across all of society.

Sir Albert Howard, an English agricultural advisor to the Indian state of Indore, first thought out the concept of growing plants and husbanding animals without using synthetic chemicals. Partly, his development of natural gardening and farming was a reaction to necessity. The area of India where he worked was so poor that local farmers couldn't afford to buy fertilizers imported from other areas. So Sir Albert had to devise ways to recycle the natural nutrients available locally—the manure of animals and the waste plant materials that would otherwise be burned or ignored.

There was more to Sir Albert's thinking than just a solution to an immediate practical problem, however. He was disturbed by the trend of the scientific community toward advocating synthetic substitutes for many natural commodities, using the discoveries of the 19th-century German chemist, Justus von Leibig. Hailed as a pioneer of a new age of science, von Leibig had demonstrated the chemical simplicity of plant matter simply by burning it and then analyzing the ash for nitrogen (N), phosphorus (P) and potash (K), ignoring the organic portion of the plant. The chemical fertilizer industry was created out of the ash of von Leibig's experiment.

Sir Albert perceived in von Leibig's doctrine something extremely dangerous—the rupture of the cycle of life. Under the "scientific" system of farming, soil became primarily something to hold up the plants so that they could be fed with artificial solutions. The age-old rhythms of nature which had built the soil were violated. Sir Albert began preaching that it was possible for thinking farmers to preserve the cycle of life by returning plant and animal wastes to the soil, by countering insects by non-poisonous means and by avoiding the synthetic, soluble fertilizers with their burden of toxic residues. If the cycle of life wasn't preserved, said Sir Albert, future generations would be faced with an increase of hunger, disease and pollution.

J. I. Rodale first read about Sir Albert Howard's ideas in the late 1930's. Even then, the United States was so industrialized and technologically "advanced" that it was possible to see that what Sir Albert was predicting could easily happen. The American Dust Bowl experience of the Depression years was graphic evidence of the disruption of the cycle of life. But there were signs of trouble everywhere. Food quality was low. Pollution was intruding on our lives. Disease caused by physical degeneration—not just by microbes—was increasing. J. I. Rodale noted with dismay that the grim harvest predicted by Sir Albert and other philosophers of the conservation school was about to be reaped.

J. I. first used the word "organic" to describe the natural method of gardening and farming, mainly because compost, humus and the organic fraction of the soil were emphasized so strongly. However, even in 1942, when *Organic Gardening and Farming* was born, J. I. Rodale saw that this method was more than just a way to husband the soil and grow plants and animals. He proclaimed that to be "organic" was to know and to understand the lessons of nature in all ways, and to use that knowledge to evaluate all of the "blessings" of science and technology. What good was it, he said, to grow food without using chemical fertilizers or pesticides, and then to process that food so that its content of vitamins and minerals would be depleted seriously? In fact, not caring whether he was called an extremist or a crackpot, J. I. Rodale created what might now be called a "strict constructionist" interpretation of natural life under the banner of organiculture. If it is synthetic, avoid it, he said. If it goes through a factory, examine it with special care. Follow the dictates of the cycle of life when growing things, he advised, and you will be blessed with foods of surpassing taste and quality that are less troubled by insects or disease.

Of course, there was originally much objection to the organic idea from the scientific community. Anyone who said that all artificial fertilizers, pesticides and foods were bad simply was not living in the 20th century, they felt. Strangely, many "chemical" people who expressed violent disagreement with organic gardening and farming as a practical technique, admitted that it made sense theoretically. "Humus in the soil is important," they said, "but there isn't enough compost to go around." Almost everyone agreed that old-fashioned, natural ways of growing things produced tastier foods, but few would admit that it was possible to grow them now on a large scale.

A NEW WORLD

Events of the past few years have changed a lot of minds. Many people can now see the direct result of the misuse of our environment, and of the failure of industry and agriculture to understand the importance of the cycle of life. You no longer have to be a prophet or a visionary to perceive that the way our world is being abused is leading to trouble.

Let's face facts. Things are going to get a lot worse before they get better.

America is going to continue to grow—in population, in housing, in number of automobiles, in miles of highways and in generation of electric power. But growth no longer means progress. As our country grows it will become more polluted. Growth itself is becoming pollution.

People are now beginning to realize the urgent necessity of slowing growth and of stopping pollution, but our leaders seem ineffectual. Most of the anti-pollution measures enacted so far are just token steps. They don't close the cycle of resource use, they simply make wastes less noticeable. Our accumulated scientific and technological experience seems to be of little use in trying to solve current environmental problems.

Up at the Massachusetts Institute of Technology, a computer was fed data which would help to indicate what our future world will be like if we increase our spending to reverse the decline in the quality of life by 20 per cent. According to *The Limits to Growth* a book reporting the project, the computer fed back the depressing answer that pollution and quality of life would become so bad in the next few generations that large numbers of Americans would die. Only after that tragedy would the quality of life again rise for the much smaller human population then occupying this country.

The message of the MIT computer is clear. Spending more to fight pollution but going about the business of life as usual will lead to cataclysmic disaster. To thwart the inexorable downward trend of the quality of life, we must do more than just increase spending for "improvements" on an ill-conceived, planned and developed way of life.

AN ORGANIC AMERICA

There is only one way to make America more natural, more reasonable in its burden on the ecosphere. That is the organic method. If everyone became organic-minded and backed it up with organic actions, the dire predictions for America's future could surely be thwarted. In an organic America, the sales of chemical pollutants would end. There would be no problem with additives in food and no DDT to worry about. Garbage would be less of a problem because almost everyone would be sure that organic wastes were being composted. Sewage would enrich farm fields instead of polluting rivers, lakes and harbors. Automobile smog would be minimized because more people would be living on small home-steads, raising much of their own food instead of commuting into large cities to work. Pollution would be virtually eliminated in an organic world.

Can you accept that? Or do you think we're going too far in saying that a method of gardening and farming can save the world? Well, the organic method is more than just a way to garden and farm. It is a natural philosophy of living, outlining a way for people to complete the cycle of resource use which is now broken completely in almost every city and town and home in this country. When you are organic you use the energy of the sun and the fertility of the soil to produce food and even clothing for your family, without expecting the aid of powerful chemicals which cause pollution. Far more important, however, an organic person puts what is used back into the resource bank upon which future generations will depend. When garbage and sewage and crop wastes are returned to the soil, we are making life a complete cycle instead of a drain down which the world's accumulated resources are flushed.

We organic people thus hold in our hands the key to the survival of America as a workable, sensible place to live. No one can overestimate today the importance of the organic method to human survival. Suddenly, the organic movement is growing faster than ever.

ORGANIC ACTION

But the trend toward organic awareness has to grow much faster, how-ever, if the environmental disaster predicted in *The Limits to Growth* is to be averted. All of us who are now organic in the way we think and act must accept the responsibility of working to extend the impact of organic awareness into all phases of life. We have to show other people what we have learned about organic living for one simple reason: the organic method is a method of *doing*. Almost all other approaches to the pollution problem are 98 per cent conversation, 1 per cent regula-tion and only 1 per cent action. The standard approaches to environ-mental problems will not work until they, like the organic method, complete the cycle of life. When that happens, these other methods will also be organic.

Already you see the word "organic" cropping up more and more frequently in the writings of people who are truly ahead of their time.

Many years ago Frank Lloyd Wright planted an important seed with his idea of organic architecture. He thought buildings should blend with and reflect the true nature of their sites. At least in a symbolic way that concept foretold the closing of the broken link of the cycle of life, which is the essence of the organic method of growing plants and animals.

More recently, Lewis Mumford's powerful book, *The Myth of the Machine: The Pentagon of Power,* concludes with a plea for a form of science and technology that is more organic than present forms. The human variability and the spirituality of man has been overlooked through the centuries by the leaders of scientific thought, he says. We are being recreated by our technology as clockwork automatons, because that is the direction machine-building has taken. Only a new organic way of organizing industry will allow us to retain a true human character.

As appealing as these high-type organic ideas are, they provide little place for the average person to grab on—no handle on which individual people can exert leverage. But we can all bury our garbage in the earth. We can all pick the bugs off our potato plants, instead of using poison sprays. And we can grow much of our own food—and food of the finest, purest quality—instead of using the plastic food sold in supermarkets. The organic method of gardening and farming is therefore a place to start, which is what we desperately need. I firmly believe that the organic way of living points down the right road, even though that road might have a few bumps and some hills to climb. Let's hope that everyone will start understanding the world as organic people have been understanding it for 30 years.

—Robert Rodale

2

The Food Industry

A Pretty Bleak Picture

Several years ago an official of the U.S. Interior Department's Bureau of Commercial Fisheries told a group of food industry executives that a good deal of the frozen haddock and breaded shrimp being sold in American supermarkets were not fit to eat. He reported that two out of every five consumers buying these items were getting food of substandard quality. Harold B. Allen, chief of the branch of technology of the Bureau of Commercial Fisheries, was telling about the results of a three-year study of the quality of frozen fish sold in supermarkets. His general conclusion was that the study presented "a pretty bleak picture."

Taste was the main factor which concerned Allen. Although some of the fish examined contained filth, he did not say that frozen fish was a health problem or that many people were getting sick from eating it. The government study primarily showed that large quantities of frozen haddock and breaded shrimp just tasted inferior. The main cause of the problem was overlong storage. Although the Interior Department investigators confined their purchases only to supermarkets to get the freshest possible stock, they found that some samples of fish they purchased had been in storage for four years. Even two-year-old frozen fish is too old, Allen told his audience. Kept under ideal conditions, frozen fish stays in top quality for six months or perhaps a year.

Fish isn't the only food with quality problems. It's easy to draw up a long list of items which fail to tickle the palate. Who can get excited about the taste of an instant potato, or be pleased with a real potato that has been treated with anti-sprouting chemicals and stored too long? How often do you buy an apple pre-packaged in plastic that has a real, fresh taste? Do people buy frozen, pre-cooked dinners by the millions because they are pleased with their taste, or because of the savings in preparation time they offer?

Unfortunately, most people can't do much about the declining quality of American food. Unless you garden—preferably organically—and grow some of your food yourself, you are even likely to forget what real, natural food tastes like. The basic reason for this decline in flavor of food is the fact that our food supply is now almost completely industrialized. It starts with the farms, which are mechanized and chemically oriented. But most of the dirty work is done when food gets into factories for conversion to powders, pastes, gums or frozen bits and pieces that can stand shipment over thousands of miles and will still look presentable years later when the American housewife picks up the attractively printed box the food is in. Anyone who has to live on convenience foods knows what that kind of stuff tastes like.

More food is going to factories for processing now than ever before. People want—or at least are told they want—pre-cooked, instantized or otherwise prepared foods that can be taken right out of the box and eaten. Manufacturers of food products are continually figuring out ways to do more food processing, because more processing means more profits for the processor. It's in the food companies' interest to use advertising and other promotion methods to encourage the public to want more convenience foods.

THE PROCESSOR'S MAGIC

To compete in this market, food manufacturers must process their food products. They may process food to give it a long shelf life, dye it an attractive, ripe color, sweeten it, emulsify it, cure it, stabilize it, salt it, irradiate it, bleach it, blanch it, polish it, de-germ it, de-bran it. And it's possible the farmer's already gassed it (to delay ripening), sprayed it with insecticides, nematocides, rodenticides and fungicides, or treated it with sex hormones, antibiotics, tranquilizers, disinfectants, anti-spoilants, anti-sprouting agents, desiccants and sex-sterilants.

By the time some of this food reaches your mouth, it's loaded with chemicals, many of which are of proven high toxicity, some of them carcinogenic and almost all insufficiently tested to allow their effects to be known. Moreover, the positive qualities of these foods have been destroyed. Their vitamins could not have survived. If the food's nutritional value has not totally disintegrated, it certainly has been diminished.

Let's look at some random examples. Apples, for instance. A three and a half ounce ripe raw apple will give you 90 international units of vitamin A. Make it into apple sauce and the count is 30. Strain this apple sauce and the count drops to 20. Rice. Three and a half ounces of brown rice will give you 303 milligrams of phosphorus. Remove the bran, changing it into fluffy white rice and you have only 136 mgs. Puff up this rice and you're down to 40. Three and a half ounces of fresh ripe blueberries have 280 I.U.'s of vitamin A, but can them with heavy syrup and all you have is 40.

Yet our mass production agriculture harvests crops while they are still immature, stores them for months in warehouses and finally sells a flavorless, unenjoyable food. The nutrient content, like the flavor, is lacking. We need all the vitamins found in a food to help our bodies detoxify themselves.

Every poison, swallowed or breathed, if not immediately excreted, must be detoxified by the body. This puts a severe burden on the liver in particular and other organs in general. Detoxification means using up large quantities of vitamin B complex and C. The liver is obliged to steal these vitamins from other parts of the body for they are essential aids in detoxification. The liver thus depletes the body of vitamin security.

How serious is our toxic intake through foods? How much poison—the air and water pollution aside—are we really swallowing? Are we just ringing alarm bells or is it fact?

Let's really investigate and examine some typical dinner foods. In addition to the food, this is what you get:

Fruit juice: All canned, commercial juice contains benzoic acid, a slightly toxic preservative to give it longer shelf life. It also contains dimethyl polysiloxane, an anti-foaming agent that is a mild depressant.

The fruit from which the juice was made was probably sprayed with DDT, parathion or dieldrin. According to *Clinical Toxicology of Commercial Products,* a standard reference work on poisons, DDT has a toxicity rating of 4, which means it is "very toxic, more than a teaspoon will kill." Parathion and dieldrin have toxicity ratings of 6 and 5 respectively. A 5 rating means a substance is "extremely toxic, over seven drops will kill." A substance rated 6 is considered "supertoxic." A taste will kill.

In addition, practically every canned or bottled juice used dyes ranging from mild to strong toxicity. Usually, either sugar (if you're lucky) or saccharin (if you're not) is added to sweeten the drink.

Roast Beef: The steer from which it came was fed corn and hay, both of which were sprayed repeatedly with chlordane, heptachlor, lindane or aldrin, which have a toxicity rating of 5. The steer probably also was treated with diethylstilbestrol (DES), a hormone, and an antibiotic, usually aureomycin, both to increase bulk weight. DES is a carcinogen.

Government inspectors concede that some DES is reaching the consumer. One of every 200 cattle checked by agriculture department inspectors shows some residues of the hormone, but there isn't enough money for manpower to check every animal.

Besides its potentially harmful effects on health, DES-treated beef has poor texture. Even meat packers, who usually espouse the use of additives, are unhappy.

Cal Santare of the Western States Meat Packers Association complains that "the meat is very soft and mushy." Chester Calvert, a former USDA grader and now a consultant for independent Los Angeles meat packers, puts it this way: "DES is a help for growers but a disaster for packers. The buyer goes into the feed lot and sees a fat animal and assumes it's choice grade, but many times the fat will be all outside the beef instead of marbled within it. Buyers have purchased it for a choice animal and then have to sell it for a grade lower."

Antibiotics in meat can cause trouble, too. As far back as 1963, the World Health Organization warned, "Individuals not previously sensitized as a result of medical treatment with an antibiotic might develop reactions of hypersensitivity" from eating treated meat.

Bread: This one is a chemist's dream. As a starter, the seed from which the wheat was grown was probably treated with bichloride of mercury—a dangerous poison with a rating of 5. As it grew the grain was sprayed with a variety of pesticides with toxicity ratings between 4 and 5. The flour was then bleached with agene, nitrogen trichloride, or chlorine dioxide. Agene was used for 25 years until the University of Aberdeen in Scotland discovered that it caused running fits in dogs. But dogs are not humans, said the millers. Further investigations, however, showed that it also deranged the human mind. The U.S. government finally proscribed it. The millers have gone back to chlorine dioxide, once abandoned as a dangerous, toxic explosive. A dough conditioner is now added, ammonium chloride, which has a simple poison rating of 3. Then polyoxyethylene is added, a softener. This is an intense skin irritant which has sickened rats and killed hamsters in experiments conducted by Dr. Edward Eagle of Swift and Company but it's not considered a serious poison. The softener is used because people like to squeeze the bread they buy, believing that if it's soft it's also fresh.

An antioxidant, ditertiary-butyl-para-cresol, poison rating of 4, is added. To improve the gluten quality of the flour, a little bromate, toxicity rating of 5, is added. Bromate tends to destroy the kidneys and cause liver necrosis. Finally, calcium propionate is added, an antifungal compound to keep the bread from becoming moldy. This is commercial bread.

Butter: Contains diacetyl, a synthetic flavoring agent, which smells like butter and any of the strong yellow dyes, most of which are made from coal tars. Butter may also contain traces of the hormones, antibiotics and pesticides ingested by the cows with their feed.

Apple Pie: If you buy this pie, or any pie, ready-made in the bakery or grocery, you're buying one of the most highly chemical-laden foods on the market. It contains potassium sorbate, an antifungal agent, toxic rating of 2; butylated hydroxyanisole, an antioxidant, toxic rating of 4; sodium phenylphenate, a preservative and fungicide, toxic rating of 3. Other sprays used are benzene hexachloride, malathion, parathion, demeton or lead arsenate and even nicotine—all with a rating between 5 and 6! These pesticides are sprayed on the fruit as often as six or seven times.

Ice Cream: You would expect this simple dessert, made of cream, flavoring, sweetener and eggs, to be free of chemicals. But a visit to an ice cream factory will dispel that notion. Ice cream makers use stabilizers, emulsifiers, artificial colors and artificial flavorings.

If an ice cream maker is not selling his product outside his state, he is not subject to federal control. His product can—and often does—contain chemicals banned by the FDA.

In addition, residues of pesticides and antibiotics are likely to be found.

Pickles: Surprisingly, pickles are practically chemical-free. Pickles contain only alum, aluminum sulfate, a firming agent made from distillation of coal, and sodium nitrate, a texturizer with a toxicity rating of 4.

Salt: This seasoning contains calcium hydroxide, or caustic soda, a violent corrosive poison not listed under the poison index since it can't be swallowed because of its intense, burning pain. But it can be ingested in tiny quantities as mixed with salt. Calcium silicate—one of the basic ingredients of portland cement—is also added to keep the salt from caking.

Milk, Coffee: The milk would have the residues of pesticides and antibiotics, as would the cream for the coffee.

Any other dinner, from food bought from the market and supermarket, would show a similar array of toxic additives. The average shopper buys food on the basis of smell and color, indications of vitamin content under natural conditions. The food manufacturers knows this. That's why he adds synthetic smell and color.

Thus we face the fact that we are constantly being deluged with tiny bits of poison, coming to us from every conceivable purchase of food, some so stated on the label, most of them hidden and unmentioned. Most of these poisons are excreted, straining the liver and other organs with a serious depletion of our inner vitamin stock. But some of these poisons are not excretory. They accumulate in the body, increasing even further the work of the liver and destroying even more of our vitamin stock.

THE PROCESSOR'S PROBLEM

Strange as it might seem, the greatest barrier to increasing factory treatment of food is not the public's taste. Apparently people can get used to eating low-grade food. (Harold Allen's complaint about the bad-tasting breaded shrimp and haddock didn't originate with consumers but with professional food tasters.) The biggest problem facing the food industry now is evidence that food poisoning bacteria is able to find a friendly home in many of the most modern types of processed foods. New methods of preservation use low heat, so all of the salmonella, staphylococci, clostridium and other organisms capable of causing both mild and serious illnesses are not killed. Another factor contributing to the problem is the mixing of large quantities of food together before processing. When that is done, a small lot of food that is "loaded" with bacteria will be mixed throughout an entire large batch, causing the whole lot to be at least slightly contaminated. Stomach upset and diarrhea can be the symptoms of such mild forms of food poisoning. But there can be serious results from improper food processing. Botulism is now causing concern in the food factories. A U.S. Public Health Service scientist recently disclosed that botulism in very small amounts can be found in some foods sold in American supermarkets. "This shows how we are on the borderline of a hazard," Wesley E. Gilbertson told the House Health, Education and Welfare Appropriations subcommittee.

Health experts feel helpless in trying to cope with poisoning in processed foods because people eat so many different types of foods these days that it would be extremely time-consuming to trace the source of the infection. Cases usually don't crop up in groups, but tend to be isolated. The chief of Richmond, Virginia's Public Health Laboratories commented some time ago that the large number of processing plants makes it difficult to find the source of food contamination. "In the Richmond area alone, there are several hundred food plants putting out several thousand products—it's impossible to check them all," William A. Dorsey said. "We're groping in the dark." The Food and Drug Administration is working on a test that can spot food-poisoning toxins before they get out to the public and cause illness, but it isn't in wide use yet.

Although food law enforcement agents do have a responsibility to keep clean and wholesome, they can't be blamed entirely for the gradual lowering of the standards of taste and flavor that we have experienced. The trouble is that flavor is a delicate thing, which can't be described or regulated with complete accuracy. Food that actually smells bad can be prohibited, of course, but the slight difference in flavor that is caused by almost each new processing method is usually considered acceptable. It's up to the buyer of food to give his approval to the flavor standard, which then becomes acceptable in the marketplace. Unfortunately, the consumer has not been alerted to notice the gradual changes in flavor of food or to protest those changes in effective ways.

Peanut butter is an example. There was a time when it was made only of ground up peanuts and salt. Then the large food companies got interested in peanut butter. Gradually, they began to change the formula to lower their cost but at the same time offer an apparent advantage to the consumer. Lower-cost cottonseed oil was added, for example, so the peanut butter wouldn't stick to the roofs of children's mouths. Sugar was added as the public became interested in more sweet foods. As a result of this trend, most peanut butter now sold contains only 90 per cent peanuts. Efforts to change the situation by having the Food and Drug Administration require a higher level of peanuts in the product run against the argument that "the public likes it that way, because that is what they are buying." Could it be the other way around? Perhaps the public buys it because that is what they are offered and sold on with continual advertising.

Food Through Chemistry

Most people know that many brand-name foods are loaded with additives, but they don't realize the extent to which chemicals are used by the food industry.

An opportunity to read a journal, *Food Product Development*, edited for the people who are creating new kinds of food, would really open their eyes and maybe boost them out of their ruts. It has articles on such things as how to make imitation cheese and why people are eating so much ready-to-eat pudding. There are articles on how to use food additives and unintentionally funny stories pointing out that real foods are so loaded with naturally occurring poisons that people can't be safe unless what they eat is made of chemicals. But the ads! In page after page, promoters for the chemical companies let loose their trade secrets. They tell the fellows making new foods how to use chemicals to make more money by fooling people into thinking that the food coming out of envelopes and plastic packs is really better than what nature makes.

SMOOTHNESS

An Eastman-Kodak ad provides a good introduction. "Enrich it with vitamins, smooth it with monoesters," says the headline. "Today's dehydrated potatoes are even better than the homemade kind," says the body of the ad. "Eastman products play a big part. Our monoesters serve as processing aids and assure a smooth, mouthwatering consistency. And our vitamins can boost health-giving value." The vitamins are o.k., but what about the monoesters? Did you know that the smoothness of those powdered potatoes comes not from nature but from chemistry?

Next comes a very revealing ad by Corn Industrial, a division of CPC International, Inc. "Only Bossie knows for sure," says the headline. Then: "It's getting more and more difficult to tell the difference between natural and formulated dairy products. And just as difficult to keep abreast of the growing flow of new, formulated co-dairy products, products that are meeting their ultimate test of success: acceptance in the market-place."

Let's stop there a moment. Note that these fellows judge their success by rather selfish standards. They try to copy food formulas that nature developed, then say the ultimate test of their success is whether people will buy their imitations. Not a word about nutritional quality, which is sadly defective in some synthetic dairy products. The Corn Industrial ad lists the products they are tinkering with: "Filled and imitation milks, coffee whiteners, toppings, whips, cheeses, frozen desserts." The ingredients they seek to use in those imitation dairy products include sweeteners, oils, starches, and hydrolized cereal solids.

MOUTH-FEEL AND COLOR

Hercules, the people who make blasting powder, are also funneling synthetics into your food. "Nearly 200 types of Hercules Cellulose Gum ® to solve your food problems," the headline says, "Keeps bakery products fresh longer. Improves the taste and mouth-feel of juice and dietetic foods. Thickens soups, gravies and sauces. Holds moisture in pet foods."

That word "mouth-feel" is really irritating. Many of the ads and articles in *Food Products Development* brag about the wonderful "mouth-feel" that will be created if food makers use this or that chemical. Natural food is inherently pleasing to the mouth. Only when processing goes beyond the limits of good practice does your mouth tell you that something has gone wrong in the food factory. The constant desire of these food tinkerers to add chemicals to mask that danger signal is a clear warning that they are going too far.

Another thing the food developers worry about too much is color. "No matter how nutritious, flavorful or well textured a food is, it will never be eaten unless it is the right color," an article contends. "Never" is a strong word for a scientist to use, but they use it anyway. Chemical coloring is not essential to the marketing of food; it's a gimmick to fool people into thinking that something is fresh when it isn't. The deep, orange cheese you like is usually white before processing. You would eat white cheese if that was the only kind you could get, but the doctored orange kind turns some people on. They think they are getting a richer food. You would also eat green oranges if people had the chance to learn that oranges can be ripe and green at the same time. But the food people won't run the risk of letting us find that out. They pour on the color.

FLAVOR AND MORE

Flavor is another quality we are fooled about. "New Pfizer Chicken Corral is the tastiest imitation chicken flavor you've ever tasted," says another ad in *Food Product Development.* "Chicken Corral, like our Beef Corral, is a complete flavoring system. The result of new flavor technology pioneered by Pfizer, based on reaction flavor chemistry. Pfizer Chicken or Beef Corral can be used alone as the flavor base in foods like soups, gravies and prepared dinners."

These fellows have grabbed the flavor ball and are running with it. The poor farmer with his need to plow and cultivate and harvest and feed the chickens and carry out the manure is working with a ball and chain around his leg. Sure, the chicken factories and the feed lot managers pump drugs into their animals to try to keep pace with the imitation meat flavor people, but in the long run the animal raisers just aren't in the same league.

The chemical additive people are like the Arab who gets his hand in the tent, then his arm, and finally his camel. They realize that most people won't switch directly to full artificial food, so they begin by infiltrating some chemicals to make a real food product partly fake.

We are what we eat. We are eating food that is increasingly laden with chemicals and is of decreasing actual nutritional value. Sadly, we appear to be a people on the downgrade: unstable, drugged, unsure of our national purpose. The food companies and the chemical makers aren't directly responsible for what is happening, but they have fostered the deterioration in our traditions and our standards of quality.

How can this trend toward artificial and unsatisfying groceries be stemmed? The best way is to grow as much of your own food as possible. Do your own food processing by canning and freezing whatever surplus food you grow. The work involved will be worth it when you compare the quality of your own food with what you would have to buy in the store.

When you do have to buy food, try to do it selectively. Patronize people who are selling their own, home-grown organic foods in your area. When you venture into the store for food, give some thought to the amount of processing that is needed for the type of food you want. Often you have a choice between a product like instant potatoes and the real thing. Take the real thing. Buy the freshest food possible. There's little doubt that the trend toward factory treatment of food has gone too far to be reversed completely, but it may be stemmed if enough people show by their actions that they prefer real, fresh quality to magic food gimmicks in a box. Not only will you be getting better-tasting and healthier food, but you'll be avoiding a whole host of chemical additives put in food whenever it gets inside the doors of a factory.

3

For Better Nutrition and Health

The Mysteries of Nutrition

The idea that we are what we eat has been popular for many years. It has been a keystone in the philosophy of those who see the very real connection between nutrition and health and act on it. The problem has been that not enough people understand the idea and are willing to act on it.

People talk about coffee nerves, espouse the need for a balanced diet and joke about the legendary medicinal qualities of chicken soup. Mothers counsel their children against all sorts of foods because they're "not good for you." They accept the idea that a lack of vitamin C causes health problems and include some citrus fruit in their diet. High school health classes reveal that pellagra and beriberi are dreadful nutritional deficiency diseases.

People *know* their health is affected by what they eat, but they don't let that fact affect what they eat.

Instead, with the support and even the encouragement of medical and nutritional experts they slop down whatever the food industry puts before them. And the food industry, with all the backing that carefully developed marketing and merchandising techniques can provide (and a visit to any supermarket and exposure to any communications media will demonstrate that that's a lot of backing), puts whatever is technologically profitable before the public. It takes foods force-grown on depleted soils and processes, mixes, precooks, enriches, candies, preserves and, most important, nutritionally destroys them. The diet centered on these "engineered" foods undermines constitutions and does little to sustain health. This is becoming more and more clear.

The government has designed and mobilized program after program to improve the nutritional state of every American . . . and has failed to achieve its goal. In spite of all the talk, the fact remains that you are what you eat, and the average American simply should not be what he eats.

What does he eat? Manufactured, synthetic, convenience foods derived from crops raised on soils permeated unnaturally with chemicals, crops sometimes lacking the vital complex trace nutrients. How's his health? About as good as medical technology, drugs and good luck will permit.

But the idea, the "food faddist" idea, that you are what you eat is beginning to take root with the nutrition establishment. The supportive evidence is becoming harder to ignore. You must eat well to live well.

Primitive men undoubtedly understood this. The earliest medicine men focused in their research and practice on diet. The connection between food and health was so obvious that it was *the* logical starting point for explorations into health and disease.

UNCOVERING NUTRITION'S MYSTERIES

Although many men tried to uncover the mysteries of nutrition hundreds of years ago, they lacked the necessary understanding of chemistry and biology. As advances were made in these sciences and others, though, man applied them to his studies of nutrition and gained fuller understanding of the relationships between food and health or the lack of it.

Back in the days of the Greeks, science consisted of a belief that the universe consisted of four elements—earth, air, fire and water—and four qualities—dry,wet, hot and cold—and that four humors—blood phlegm, black bile and yellow bile—were all there was to the human body. Hippocrates, the father of medicine, was one of the first to suggest that we are what we eat. He taught the value of diet.

PROTEINS

But in the hundreds of years since, a great deal has been learned. The 20th century opened with general acceptance of the idea that proteins, fats, carbohydrates and minerals were the sole necessities for proper nutrition. Dr. Wilbur O. Atwater, the father of American nutrition science, had spread the idea that green and leafy vegetables were merely expensive luxuries. He wrote a bulletin in 1896 for the U.S. Dept. of Agriculture which established the first extensive table of food values prepared in this country and pressed the case for his protein-centered, fat-, carbohydrate-, and mineral-supported diet. Protein thus occupied much attention as the century turned. Slowly, scientists learned that protein isn't just protein, but that there are many different proteins in food. It was learned that not all proteins are equally efficient in promoting growth or maintaining nitrogen equilibrium. Cambridge University's Dr. Frederick G. Hopkins was a pioneer in this area of study. He fed mice a diet with casein as the sole nitrogen-containing constituent, and the animals flourished. He replaced the casein with zein, a protein from corn, and the mice died. When tryptophan was added to the zein the mice lived but did not grow.

Eventually, protein came to be described as being "complete" —adequate to maintain life and promote growth—and "incomplete" —lacking certain amino acids. Amino acids are the basic constituents of proteins. The presence of certain "essential" amino acids determines the completeness of a protein.

As more amino acids were discovered—there are 22 known to occur in food proteins—work was begun to determine whether each was essential in the diet. Patiently and persistently, the work continued. Finally, in 1955, recommendations for the daily intake of amino acids were made, based on available data. Work on this problem, including the nutritive value of individual proteins and the specific functions of individual amino acids, has involved many workers in many laboratories since 1930, and the work is continuing.

Protein thus far has been found to be the material for building muscle and body tissue and to be a part of the hemoglobin molecule in red blood cells. Enzymes and hormones have been crystallized and found to be derived from proteins. Enzyme systems contain proteins. Antibodies present in the blood stream, an aid in resistance to infection, are protein in nature.

FATS AND OILS

Fats and oils have always been foods, but not until 1814 was it discovered that fats are made up of fatty acid and glycerol. By the beginning of the 20th century, it was accepted that fats and carbohydrates could be used interchangeably in the diet. Thus, the accepted concept was that fats—not being essential in the diet—were consumed in large amounts only because of their flavor and satiety value and energy value.

They aroused new interest in 1929 when scientists observed that rats kept on a fat-free, but otherwise adequate, diet did not maintain health. The animals lost hair from the body, developed a skin disease and necrosis of the tail, conditions that could be prevented by feeding highly saturated fatty acids. Linoleic acid was identified as the essential fatty acid.

The high content of fatty substances in the thickened artery walls often associated with heart ailments, has again focused interest on dietary fats. The amount and chemical nature of the fats and the fatty acids that should form part of man's daily diet are still being investigated. Perhaps there is yet to be found a pattern of the kind and amount of fatty acids needed in the diet, as was the case with amino acids.

MINERALS

Minerals—or inorganic elements, ash or inorganic salts, as they have been called—were known a century ago to be essential for plant-life. Farm animals did not thrive if common salt was omitted from their diet.

At the beginning of the century, calcium, phosphorus, sulfur and iron were recognized as essential in the diet, and many experiments were focused on just how much of each was needed, exactly how they functioned in the body and how they were affected by food preparation. Some of these questions are not yet satisfactorily answered. By 1930, as newer techniques and apparatus made it possible for chemists to measure minute amounts of certain inorganic substances, the significance of the trace elements in nutrition was recognized.

Iodine, for example, had been identified a century earlier. In the 1920's it was identified as an essential nutrient. Without iodine, the thyroid gland, located at the base of the neck, enlarges to form what is known as the simple goiter. In the Great Lakes area, where iodine deficiencies in the soil led to iodine deficiencies in food, goiter was a common occurrence among children, especially girls.

One of the earliest large-scale controlled human experiments—using 6,000 Akron, Ohio, school children—was conducted in 1921 by Drs. David Marine and O. P. Kimball. It demonstrated that children given iodine did not develop goiter. The researchers fed the children iodine in drinking water, but a more effective way of providing iodine was developed later by adding potassium iodide to table salt.

The list of essential trace minerals grew when investigators at the University of Wisconsin in 1928 found that pure iron salts were ineffective in curing anemia in rats and that small amounts of copper had to be present in the diet before iron could be utilized. Manganese, magnesium, chromium and zinc were added, too. Cobalt was found necessary to prevent disease in cattle and sheep and has since been proven essential for people. The list goes on.

VITAMINS

Probably the major nutritional discovery of the 20th century is the vitamin. Captain James Lind, two centuries earlier, had shown that because lemon juice would cure scurvy, there must be something besides proteins and the other, accepted constituents to food. Other investigators had unusual results in dietary experiments. Dutch army surgeon Christiaan Eijkman discovered that a chicken fed polished rice developed a neuritis, like beriberi, which he could prevent or cure by feeding brown rice. He was the first person to produce a dietary deficiency disease experimentally. In Japan, Kanekiro Takaki had found that he could prevent beriberi, which took the lives of many Japanese sailors, by increasing the amount of meat and fish in their diets.

These findings attracted little attention in a world that was making rapid progress in chemistry and bacteriology, though. Louis Pasteur's research in the 1870's had established the germ theory firmly in the minds of scientists and this fixation served as the basis for resistance to the vitamin theory as it developed in the early 1900's. The resistance continues today as many medical men refuse to acknowledge the importance of nutrition in preventing and curing disease.

Vitamin is now a household word, but it was only coined in 1912. Dr. Casimir Funk, a Pole working in the Lister Institute in London, was trying to isolate from rice polishings a substance—he thought it was an amine compound—which would cure or prevent beriberi. He reasoned that if there indeed was something in foods which prevented deficiency diseases like beriberi, that something was vital to life. The name he applied to the substance he isolated was vitamine—"vita" for life and "amine" for the group of chemical compounds his was related to. In later years, when vitamins were clearly distinguished from the amine compounds, the "e" was dropped from the word's end.

Support for Dr. Funk's theory was offered by the work of Cambridge's Dr. Hopkins, who conducted dietary experiments with rats which suggested that there were unsuspected dietetic facts or accessory food substances that were essential for health. Experiments with cows at the University of Wisconsin also seemed to confirm the vitamin theory. One of the assistants on the latter experiments was Dr. Elmer V. McCollum, who pursued them using rats.

By 1913 he had found an artificial diet of protein, lactose, starch and minerals that, with butterfat, gave good growth. If he used the same diet, but replaced the butterfat with olive oil or lard, the rats failed in growth and health. Some essential unknown factor was thus shown to be present in butterfat. It was first called fat-soluble A, and later vitamin A.

Further study of the purified diets then being used disclosed that the lactose was not pure. Further purification produced polyneuritis or beriberi in the rats. By feeding a water extract of the rice polish—water-soluble B or vitamin B—the rats were cured.

Two Norwegian investigators—Axel Holst and Theodor Frölich—applied the lesson of the vitamin studies to their work on "ship beriberi", a common ailment among Norwegian sailors, and realized that the "unknown" in fruits and vegetables which prevented and cured the disease must be another vitamin, vitamin C. More factors believed to be vitamins were discovered and labeled as the research continued. By 1926, what had been called vitamin B was found to be at least two factors. Each new discovery made it possible to prepare more highly purified diets and thus lead to more new discoveries. Vitamin B is now known to be a whole complex of factors.

Eventually, vitamins were isolated and identified chemically, their functions and food sources studied and the amount required daily for maintenance of health and vigor determined. The old terms of antiberiberi, antiscorbutic and the like were dropped when it became apparent that vitamins did more than prevent disease. They were essential for health and well-being and functioned as part of many systems of the body.

NUTRITION AND INDIVIDUALITY

The story of nutrition is more than one of discoveries of new compounds needed by the body. It is one of research into the close interrelationships between many of the nutrients and the numerous factors affecting the availability of the different nutrients as they exist in food. The biochemical individuality of each person must be kept in focus in providing for man's nutritional needs.

Dietary studies on man have been conducted throughout the centuries, but most have used animals, chiefly because man can't deliberately be deprived of essential foods. History, geographical circumstances and economic verisimilitudes, however, have provided opportunities for experimental studies on humans. James Lind's classic experiment was the first clinically controlled one.

The inquiring mind of Dr. H. C. Corry Mann, an English physician who was in charge of a boy's home, led him to wonder if he could improve what was considered by all standards of the day to be an adequate diet. He could, and he did, And in the process he demonstrated the value of the concept that biological investigation provides information that cannot be obtained by chemical analysis.

Another study was that of Lord Boyd-Orr and his coworkers of the health of two African tribes living in the same area but with different food customs. Physical and medical examinations, blood analyses and careful examination of food intakes were made on several thousand tribesman. The Masai tribe was a pastoral group that lived mainly on milk, meat and raw blood—a diet relatively high in protein, fat and calcium. The Akikiyu were agriculturalists living on cereals, roots and fruits—a diet low in calcium. The Akikiyu had a higher incidence of bone deformities, dental caries, anemia, pulmonary conditions, and tropical ulcer. The full-grown Masai males averaged five inches taller and 23 pounds heavier and had greater muscular strength than their neighbors.

Further emphasis of the importance of nutrition was given by the studies of Dr. Frederick Tisdall and coworkers in Toronto, who in 1941 found that the physical condition of infants at birth was markedly superior when the mothers had received an adequate diet during pregnancy.

These findings were verified in 1943 by Dr. Harold Stuart and Mrs.

Bertha Burke in Boston. They took records of 216 pregnant women whose diets could be classified as good, fair, poor and very poor. The health of each baby reflected the quality of the mother's diet. Most of the infants born to mothers who had good or excellent diets during pregnancy were in good or excellent physical condition at birth. Infants born to mothers on poor diets were mostly in fair or poor condition, stillborn or prematurely born. The poor diet during pregnancy did not appear to affect the mother's health, but it did affect the health of the infant. The amount of protein in the mother's diet also was correlated with the weight and length of the infant at birth.

Scientists have wondered for a long time whether nutrition affects the length of a person's life. If results from rat experiments can be applied to man, and there is evidence that they can, then the experiments of Dr. Henry C. Sherman at Columbia University have provided an answer.

Beginning in 1920, Dr. Sherman started two series of rats on different diets, with succeeding generations from the original animals maintained on the same two diets. By 1949, the 70th generations were still thriving. Those on the better diet showed differences which were statistically significant: A more rapid and efficient growth, earlier maturity, longer duration of reproductive life, greater success in rearing of young and increasing length of life.

The depression years provided the clinical material for the study of nutritional deficiencies in man. They also aroused nationwide concern that our people be adequately fed. Yet recent studies have indicated that, despite massive government effort, Americans are nutritionally no better off than before, [1] largely because of modern chemical methods of agriculture and modern food processing technology. An Associated Press release of June 17, 1971, reported: "The diet of affluent Americans able to afford any foods they choose is less nutritious than it was a decade ago. The problem: we are overfed but remain undernourished. As a result, experts say, 10 per cent of the population may be anemic and 25 per cent overweight."

TECHNOLOGY AND NUTRITION

As noted in the previous chapter, the modern food technologist is virtu-

---

[1] Mayer, J.: *Science 176:* 237-241, 1972.

ally able to concoct food. Chemistry has duplicated food textures, smells and flavors. And to some degree, it has duplicated nourishment. That, at least, is what many respectable, responsible scientists would have us believe.

A key development, and a good one only from the standpoint of the food industry, in the story of nutrition was the synthesis of nutrients. Biochemists have for many years been breaking down the structure of nature into its elemental bits and pieces. It's nothing new. Men have been looking at the trees rather than the woods since the very beginning.

But the biochemist has probed into the organs, and deeper, into the cells, and deeper, into the chemical constituents of all living things. It's both good and bad.

For the biochemist has been instrumental in the discovery of all the nutrients necessary to keep us going. He's uncovering more and more of them and learning more about them. It appears that he's even able, chemically, to duplicate them. Thus synthetic vitamins are available and widely used.

Since the technology to "manufacture" vitamins in an industrial system existed, it was only a matter of time until it was used. World War II offered the impetus. While European countries were curtailing the refining of wheat to retain the grain's nutrients, the United States embarked on a massive program to "enrich" flour by treating it with synthetic nutrients to replace *some* of the nutrients removed and destroyed by the milling process.

The program was foolish on its face. Common sense should have demonstrated that removing a complex of vital nutrients and replacing them with replicas, and replacing only a few of them at that, lacked merit. Common sense should have dictated that a processing system that would retain the nutrients be instituted.

But, of course, the industrial process had to be served. The economics dictated that we all should suffer. The nutrients came out. Chemicals went in. And the curious process became known as "enrichment." It was an unfortunate milestone in the story of nutrition, marking a second crucial misstep in man's striving for better health.

The first, of course, had been the over-application of Pasteur's germ theory. "At the very time when the relationship between nutrition and disease might have come to the fore," says Dr. Roger J. Williams in his book *Nutrition Against Disease,* "medical science experienced a revolution and became intoxicated with the success of treatments that derived from Louis Pasteur's dramatic discovery that microbes cause disease." But, Williams notes, "Pasteur had never said that *all* diseases are microbial in origin . . ."

Because of the broad acceptance of Pasteur's theory by the medical profession, the relationship between nutrition and health has been given short shrift. Ask your doctor about diet and if he's like most doctors, he'll tell you to eat a balanced diet but offer little sound dietary advice. He cares little about nutrition and knows less.

Matching these two failures in nutrition was the failure to comprehend that fertility of soil and agricultural methodology play an important role in the nutritional quality of the foods grown on them.

There have always been a few who saw the unhealthy effects of industrial food. They could see that it filled stomachs, but didn't meet the body's nutritional needs. As in most instances of economic change conflicting with established social values, however, those who defended the purity of food were hooted down as unprogressive, ill-informed, inexpert, crackpot, irresponsible, and irrational. And the economics of the situation prevailed.

Nutrition and Disease

The economics don't change the facts, nevertheless. Recent studies among the Eskimos offer compelling evidence of food's effect on health, and the effect of modern American foods can hardly be construed as beneficial. Because the shift in Eskimo life style has been so abrupt, the medical consequences are vividly revealed. It took thousands of years for the tribes of Western Europe to reach today's urban style of life and develop the pattern of disease now typical of Western industrial countries. The cause-effect relationship between diet and disease was blurred. But the transformation in Eskimo communities took place for the most part since the mid-1950's, providing what Dr. Otto Schaefer calls "a textbook-perfect example of what happens to people when their eating habits change."

Dr. Schaefer, who has practiced medicine among the Eskimos for more than two decades, incriminates the Western diet—and particularly the increased consumption of sugar—for the rapid increase in the incidence of diabetes, atherosclerosis, abnormal serum cholesterol levels, obesity, gall bladder disease, dental caries and acne. "We have discovered more new cases of diabetes in one group of Eskimos living in the Canadian western Arctic than occurred in Eskimos in all of Canada a few years ago," He reported in *Nutrition Today* (Nov.-Dec. 1971).

With urbanization, the Eskimo's consumption of protein has plummeted. Studies show a 318-gram average daily ingestion of protein by tribesmen still living traditionally by hunting and fishing, while Eskimos living near white settlements and buying from the trading post consume just over 100 grams of protein a day. Sugar consumption, including candies and soft drinks, has risen sharply. In one large trading district studied by Dr. Schaefer's research team, sugar consumption quadrupled in eight years.

Besides the increased incidence of "civilized" disease, growth of the young has been accelerated, and young people are arriving at puberty at a much earlier age than ever before. A similar phenomenon was noted in Japanese school children following World War II—the generally accepted explanation being the increased protein (for example, milk) of the Westernized diet that was introduced.

The Eskimo experience, however, in which protein consumption has sharply declined, points rather to increased sugar as the cause. "One must wonder just how beneficial—perhaps a better work would be 'healthy'—this phenomenon of modern man really is," Dr. Schaefer said, "since earlier puberty and more rapid growth are both so closely linked to the epidemiology of civilization afflictions like diabetes, atherosclerotic cardiovascular diseases and obesity."

He concludes: "The Eskimos' experience presents further evidence that behind many medical phenomena with which every practitioner in the Western world is now confronted lies a nutritional factor. How important we do not know. But important it certainly is."

Similar, earlier evidence is found in Dr. Weston A. Price's *Nutrition and Physical Degeneration.* Like Dr. Schaefer's research, Dr. Price's work focused on the changes wrought in primitive peoples by "civilized" diets. The changes were marked and undesirable. Dental deformities, for example, were non-existent amongst those on "primitive" diets and widespread amongst those on "civilized" diets.

THE UNAVOIDABLE CONCLUSION

As the research continues and the evidence piles up, the conclusion that diet and health are intimately related becomes unavoidable. Indeed, in a report *(An Evaluation of Research in the United States on Human Nutrition)* released in mid-1971, the U. S. Department of Agriculture acknowledges this conclusion.

The purpose of the report is to inventory the existing information on the relationships of diet and disease and to develop recommendations for areas of potentially fruitful research. The body of it is peppered with commentary on what we do and don't know about the relationships between the various prevalent diseases and diet.

On cardiovascular disease, the number one cause of death in the U.S.—"Substantive data have not been obtained on the role of diet prior to or during the development of cardiovascular problems. Overweight is a problem because of the frequent association with high blood pressure and diabetes. In addition, additional body mass puts an added weight on the heart. The relationship between high blood sugar levels and stroke is clearly established although the reason is not. Depending on the individual, the blood cholesterol level may be reduced by one or more of these dietary changes; reduction in the amount of fat, increasing the proportion of fat occurring as polyunsaturated fatty acids, or changing the type of carbohydrate. Very likely other nutrients can and do exert an effect. For example, an increased intake of chromium may increase the glucose tolerance of many individuals and thus might reduce the risk of heart disease for some persons.

"There is no proof, but considerable evidence, that to be effective, any change in dietary patterns should begin at an early age in order to delay the onset of these diseases. . . . Good nutrition, including control of weight and diabetes by those having a family history of heart disease, should be encouraged from birth."

On respiratory and infectious diseases, the most frequent cause of illness in the U.S.—"Diet and nutritional state of the individual involved are clearly associated with the incidence, duration and severity of respiratory and infectious diseases. . . . Individuals in good nutritional state are less likely to succumb to the disease and those with high levels of nutrient reserves are more likely to recover quickly."

On infant mortality and reproduction—"There is considerable evidence relating to the relevance of birth defects [second only to heart disease as a cause of death] to poor nutrition. . . . Malnourishment in the mother usually results in the birth of a baby who is underweight. These babies are more likely to have birth defects."

"The increased nutritional needs of women during pregnancy has been recognized for many years. Yet information from human metabolic studies on the nutritional requirements of this important group is only fragmentary, and few new studies have been made in the past 15 years."

On dental health—"Diet serves three major roles in the maintenance of good dental health. Adequate nutrition is essential for the proper development of tooth structure before eruption and later for the maintenance of a firm, healthy tooth surface and resistance to the cariogenic organisms in the mouth . . . The third critical area for diet in dental health is in the maintenance of healthy gums and teeth in adults to prevent or modify the onset of periodontal disease."

On diabetes and carbohydrate disorders—"Diabetes has been known for some time to be a hereditary disorder which can be controlled by insulin therapy and diet management. During the past decade, the trace mineral chromium has been shown to improve the body's ability to use carbohydrate, particularly when the reduction in glucose tolerance is associated with aging. It has been postulated that the decreasing ability to handle glucose with age may reflect chronic marginal intake of chromium throughout life. It is known that the original content of chromium or its biologically available form, as of other trace elements, is markedly reduced by refining and processing of foods."

On anemia and other nutrient deficiencies—"Nutritional anemia is one of the most widely occurring deficiencies. These anemias are most likely to develop during periods of rapid growth, such as infancy and adolescence, and during the childbearing years in women. During these stress periods, it is difficult to select diets to meet the increased needs for iron. Anemia due to iron deficiency is presently recognized as the most common type of nutritional anemia. Folic acid, vitamin B_{12}, and protein often are involved."

"It is important to recognize that individuals vary in the amount of nutrients needed, and that in some cases, clinical and biochemical deficiencies may appear in spite of a diet which would be adequate for most persons. Very little is known of the upper limits of nutrient requirement or the incidence of persons having unusually high needs.

"There may be a number of chronic dietary deficiencies which have not been identified. Some of these may be trace elements which have been provided in the past in adequate amounts, or nearly so, by diet. Changes in food technology, including formulation of foods, may result in chronic marginal intakes of some nutrients with the development of subclinical deficiencies not recognized at this time as nutritionally caused."

"Changes in environment also may contribute to the problem of excesses. For example, the fertilization of the soil may increase the nitrate and cadmium levels to the point where the foods produced may contain high enough levels of these nutrients to be adverse in infant feeding. Increasing levels of lead, carbon dioxide and ozone in highly populated areas may stress individuals consuming diets borderline in nutrients."

On eyesight—"The eye is particularly sensitive to nutritional inadequacy. Vision is one of man's most precious faculties. Good nutrition and intact vision are inextricably linked together throughout all phases of life."

"Lack of vitamin A is responsible for the most widespread form of blindness of nutritional origin in the world today."

"Deficiencies of the B-complex vitamins, thiamine, niacin, riboflavin and vitamin B_{12} are associated with impaired vision. In some instances, adverse changes in vision thought to be due to vitamin A have responded to vitamin B therapy but not to additional vitamin A."

"Problems of eyesight also are associated with other diet-based problems. It is not uncommon to find cataracts in diabetics and in galactosemia. The latter condition occurs as a result of the inability to metabolize galactose from milk sugar."

On cosmetic ailments—"A clear, soft, unblemished skin and glossy hair have long been considered indices of good health. Changes in the skin and hair are often the first indication of nutritional deficiency."

"There are no statistics on the numbers of persons in the U.S. having adverse changes in the skin and hair because of nutritional deficiency nor of the extent to which improvement in appearance might be brought about by change of diet."

On allergies—"The actual incidence of food allergy is difficult to determine. Estimates are controversial because a large number of persons suspected of having food allergies have not been identified. . . Some allergists believe that food is frequently a cause of allergic symptoms. Most agree that the incidence seems greatest in infants."

On cancer, second only to cardiovascular disease as a cause of death—"There is no diet that prevents cancer in man. However, individuals in good nutritional state are less likely to develop cancer."

"The major known causes of cancer are felt to be viruses and cancer-producing chemicals in food and the environment. The food we eat may contain preservatives and other purposefully introduced additives; chemicals may be altered by heating and other processes; or contamination by bacteria, mold, fungi and other organisms may produce cancer-producing metabolites. Some cancer-producing chemicals occur naturally in food."

"There is a small but growing body of data suggesting that chronic low-level intake of some nutrients is a factor in the incidence of cancer in man."

"Data relating nutrition to the incidence and control of cancer are still too fragmentary and hypothetical to provide a basis for estimating benefits from diet management. The results of ongoing research may justify appreciable benefit claims from regulation of diet in the avoidance and management of cancer."

The report's summary, prepared by Dr. C. Edith Weir, assistant director of the human nutrition research division of the USDA and a member of the team that prepared the report, is as striking as the commentary. We are, she says, what we eat.

"Major health problems are diet related," Dr. Weir says. "Most all of the health problems underlying the leading causes of death in the United States could be modified by improvements in diet . . . Death rates for many of these conditions are higher in the U.S. than in other countries of comparable economic development. Expenditures for health care in the U.S. are skyrocketing, accounting for 67.2 billion dollars in 1970—or 7 percent of the entire gross national product.

"The real potential for improved diet is preventive . . . in that it may defer or modify the development of a disease state so that a clinical condition does not develop. The major research thrust, nation-wide, has been on the role of diet in treating health problems after they have developed. This approach has had limited success. USDA research emphasis has been placed on food needs of normal, healthy persons. . ."

"Major health benefits are long-range," Dr. Weir continues. "The human body is a complex and very adaptive mechanism. For most essential metabolic processes alternate pathways exist which can be utilized in response to physiological, diet or other stress. Frequently, a series of adjustments take place and the ultimate result does not become apparent for a long time, even years, when a metabolite such as cholesterol accumulates. Early adjustments of diet could prevent the development of undesirable long-range effects. Minor changes in diet and food habits instituted at an early age might well avoid the need for major changes, difficult to adopt later in life."

The body of evidence is becoming too great to ignore. The connection cannot be denied. Though the brunt of medical and biochemical research has been based on the premise that microbes are the dominant threat to health, the threat posed by improper nutrition is becoming too obvious to avoid. And the failure of our foods to provide the nutrients essential to health—either because they weren't provided by the soil as the plant grew or because they were removed or destroyed in processing—becomes abundantly clear.

Nutrition and Organically Grown Foods

The pertinent question at this point is: How do I best get nutrition?

The answer is: By eating organically grown foods.

Organically grown foods have none of the additives and residues of conventional commercial foods to debilitate their health-giving qualities. Organically grown food is, according to the definition being used in conjunction with *Organic Gardening* and *Farming's* Organic Farmer Certification Program, "food grown without pesticides; grown without artificial fertilizers; grown in soil whose humus content is increased by the additions of organic matter; grown in soil whose mineral content is increased with applications of natural mineral fertilizers; and food that has not been treated with preservatives, hormones, antibiotics or other synthetic additives.

That really isn't too difficult to understand. Organic food is ecological food. It's been nurtured in a natural system. The food production won't impinge on surrounding ecosystems. Biologically, organic foods provide you safer nutrition.

It's very important to remember that your body is a carefully balanced, complex system evolved over many centuries. It's a system that's a part of a greater but similarly carefully balanced, complex system. Anyone with a degree of ecological awareness knows that changing parts and processes in natural systems can wreak havoc; even seemingly small changes can disrupt or destroy the whole works.

Thus, the use of pesticides in conventional, commercial agriculture, poses a threat not simply to the garden pest but to the pest's natural predators and anyone who eats the chemically tainted produce. The avoidance of pesticides means not only that the food produced will be free of poisonous residues, but that the earth and waters adjacent to the growing site will be residue free, too. It means that insect predators will be safe from poisoning and that their predators will likewise be safe from poisoning. If practiced on a wide-enough scale, avoidance of pesticides could mean a reduced impingement on ecosystems by the pesticide manufacturing process.

The other elements of the definition involve other, similarly ecologically sound principles and practices, all of them a matter of working with nature, rather than working against nature. But a major ecological benefit of organically grown foods that's generally overlooked is their nutritional value. This is an ecological benefit—as well as a biological benefit—because proper nutrition is vital to the maintenance of the human system. That we've seen.

ELEMENTS OF PROPER NUTRITION

Basically, proper nutrition involves getting vitamins, minerals, proteins, fats and carbohydrates in sufficient quantities and proper balance. The specific required quantities of these nutrients vary from individual to individual; no two people are alike, so no two people have the same nutritional needs. Now the way most people gain their nutrition is through the food they eat. If their diets contain the nutrients necessary to them, they're properly nourished; if the diet has shortcomings, their biology—their health—will suffer.

What you should do is avoid all those industry-contrived, sugar-based goodies. The supermarket shelves are crammed with them, and more are being devised and marketed. There're breakfast cereals, pastries, baked goods, pasta products, snacks and all sorts of other nutritionally deficient manufactured foods available. And none of them are worth the money they cost.

Get your nutrients from fresh produce, meats, dairy products and whole-grain cereal products; these, of course, are the so-called four basic food groups. There's a fifth group being advanced, the so-called Fifth Dimension, which harbors all the nutritionally valueless, manufactured foods. Stick with the basic four, and try to balance your dependence on each of the groups in coordination with the nutrient intake you need.

Remember, for example, that you needn't eat bread to get carbohydrates. They're found in many fruits and vegetables and in more complex forms that are more easily assimilated by your system. Remember that you can get necessary food energy from any foods with proteins, fats or carbohydrates. And remember that "enrichment" of foods doesn't mean much. Despite the old saw—"Bread is the staff of life" —grain products are probably the most expendable items in any diet.

Dr. Roger J. Williams, the eminent biochemist, fed ordinary enriched bread—the kind on your grocer's shelf—to weanling rats. Most of them died before the 90-day test was concluded. Since the results of that experiment were challenged—people don't eat only bread; the results would have been the same on any single-food diet—he conducted more 90-day tests with weanling rats. Some got only eggs for 90 days, others got only milk, only hamburger, only breakfast cereal and so on.

The results, reported Dr. Williams, were that "eggs alone proved to be an exceptionally good food for the young rats during the test period. Milk alone showed up nearly as well, except that after about two months the deficiency of iron (and copper) began to be exhibited and an iron-copper supplement was given. Hamburger meat, frankfurters and tuna fish showed up well for 40-50 days . . . None of the other human foods—including those designated 'enriched'—at any time showed promise of sustaining growth even remotely approaching 'normal.' " The foods that failed were roasted peanuts, enriched macaroni, enriched wheat flakes, shredded wheat and enriched puffed rice.

"Diversity in nutrition is recommended," said Dr. Williams, "but it must be done in such a way that the sum total of the diet yields everything needed. An assortment of foods which are largely stripped of everything except energy-yielding constituents will not suffice."

He continued, "If guarding our internal environments is important, then these observations are valuable. Only if we take the position that cells and tissues thrive equally well in good and poor environments can we ignore the quality of the foods we eat."

Thus, you need the best quality foods in a reasonable balance to provide all the nutrients necessary, not just to sustain life, but to nurture good health. Organically grown foods are the best quality foods because of the way in which they're produced and handled. Because preservatives don't stretch their shelf-life, you're assured of their freshness. Because they haven't been processed or "enriched," you know the natural nutrients are all there. Because they're grown using nature's methods, you know there's no poisonous residues on them and they've not been prettied up with phony colors nor artificially ballooned to impressive sizes.

FARMING AND HEALTH

The effects of DDT, PCB and other pesticides on our environment— from death in man to the development of cancer in animals—are pretty thoroughly documented. The use of arsenic-compound insecticides has had an adverse effect on the quality and quantity of crops.[2]

But insecticides aren't the only poisons used on foods. Fumigants are used all over the world to control insects in stored cereal grain. The commonly used fumigants are halogenated hydrocarbons, and since all these compounds are poisonous to men and farm animals, any intake in the food or feed may be harmful. Fumigant residues are present in cereals and may have poisoning effects even at low concentration.

It's known they are poisonous when administered at 0.1 to about 4 grams per kilogram of body weight, yet very little is known about chronic poisoning with smaller amounts over extended periods. The fumigant studied most extensively is probably ethylene dibromide (EDB). Mash containing 10 parts per million of it was found to cause decreased egg size and egg production after several weeks.[3,4]

Wheat fumigated under commercial conditions retained 6 to 8 ppm carbon tetrachloride, even after airing for 2 to 3 months, and this

[2] Jacobs, Keeney, and Walch: *Agron, J. 62*, 1970.
[3] Bondi, Olomuchi, and Calderon: *J. Sci. Food Agr. 6:* 600, 1955.
[4] Fuller and Morris: *Poultry Sci. 41:* 645, 1962.

amount decreased only by 30 per cent after grinding to flour. Residues of carbon tetrachloride in bread baked from fumigated wheat are being investigated.[5]

The poisoning action of carbon tetrachloride—a model for all the chlorinated hydrocarbons—is under continuous study and recently was reviewed in depth.[6] The known symptoms of carbon tetrachloride poisoning are fatty and necrotic livers. Trichlorethylene is known to be metabolized by the liver enzymes of rats, forming chloral hydrate, a substance used in the manufacture of DDT.

But the health threats of chemicals in foods aren't limited to those man uses to control plant pests and diseases.

Over the past decade there has been significantly increased use of nitrogen-containing chemical fertilizers. It has resulted in an increase in nitrogen compounds entering lakes and rivers, with the subsequent fouling of both recreational and municipal water supply facilities and an increase in the nitrate content of plant material.[7,8]

Studies on this matter have been made.[9,10] In one, the use of fertilizer nitrogen in excess of 50 pounds per acre caused nitrate accumulation in red and icicle radishes, turnip roots, kale and leaves of turnips and mustard.[11] (For example, 250 pounds per acre of 20–20–20 is equivalent to 50 pounds of nitrate per acre. The usual application recommendation is 500 pounds per acre, or 100 pounds of nitrate per acre.) In general, heavy applications of nitrogen will decrease the calcium and phosphorus content of plants.[12]

There's a great deal of concern, too, over the possible health hazard of high levels of nitrates found in some foods, particularly baby foods.[13] The symptoms of "nitrate toxicity" actually result from the reduction of nitrate to nitrite by microbial action either prior to ingestion or within the gastro-intestinal tract. The nitrate content of the food is thus only an index of the amount of nitrite which might be formed. Both

[5] Bielorai and Alumat: *J. Agr. Food Chem. 14:* 622, 1966.
[6] Rechnagel, R. O.: *Pharmacol. Rev. 19:* 145, 1067.
[7] Bodiphala and Orarod: *Can. Inst. Food Technol. J. 4:* 6, 1971.
[8] *Wall Street Journal,* November 10, 1971, p. 38.
[9] Richardson, W. D.: *Journal Anv. Chem. Sec.* 29: 1757, 1907.
[10] Wilson, J. Kin: *Agron. J. 41:* 20, 1949.
[11] Brown and Smith: *Agron. J. 58:* 1966.
[12] Sheets, O. A. et al: *J. of Agron. Res.* 68: 1945, 1944.
[13] USDA, *An Evaluation of Research in the U. S. on Human Nutrition,* Ag. Res. Svc. Report No. 2, August, 1971.

nitrate and nitrite freely traverse the gastro-intestinal wall into the blood stream. Nitrite—but not nitrate—oxidizes the ferrous iron of the red blood pigment hemoglobin and causes an reduced availability of oxygen to the tissues called methemoglobinemia.[14] Nitrates can interfere with normal iodine metabolism of the thyroid gland and result in a reduction in the liver storage of vitamin A.[15] Cases of nitrate poisoning are well known where the livestock have consumed forages containing high nitrate levels.[16] The hazard of high nitrate concentrations in drinking water has also been recognized. Water which contains 10 or more milligrams of nitrate nitrogen per liter is considered potentially hazardous to infants who are especially sensitive to high concentrations. During an 18-month period, 139 cases of infant cyanosis or "idiopathic methemoglobinemia" were found in Iowa which were attributed to a high concentration of nitrates in well water. Ten per cent of these cases were fatal.[17]

Tumors have been induced in animal experiments by nitrosamines or nitrosamides by Dr. Johnnes Sander of the Hygiene Institute of Tubingen University in West Germany. "There is no big difference between the amount of nitrite which is allowed to be present in nitrite-treated food and the dosage which was necessary to induce tumors in the animal experiments," he warned in the May 17, 1971, *Journal of the American Medical Association.* According to the March 22, 1971 *Chemical and Engineering News,* Dr. William Lyinsky of the University of Nebraska Medical Center says there is a potential hazard in the possible formation of carcinogenic nitrosamines in the stomach from the amines and nitrites. Clearly, nitrate consumption represents a serious environmental health problem, one which concerns the food technologist and nutritionist as well as the agronomist and soil microbiologist.

But such considerations don't enter the organic foods picture. Pesticides and highly soluble chemical fertilizers with heavy concentrations of nitrogen aren't used in organic farming or gardening. Nature's methods are used, so you know the food is naturally safe.

[14] Wright and Davidson: *Adv. in Agron.* 16: 197, 1964.
[15] Bloomfield and Welsch: *Science* 134: 1690, 1961.
[16] Brown and Smith: *Agron. J. 58,* 1966.
[17] Federal Security Agency. *Environment and Health, Public Health Service in "Drinking Water,"* 1951, p. 6.

The Soil and Health

Organically grown foods are raised on soils rich in nutrients. There's been a great deal of haggling over the nutritional difference between organically grown foods and foods grown by chemocultural methods. But at best, there has been very little formal, scientific investigation into the difference. No one, for example, has analysed the nutritional constituents of a field-fresh cabbage grown conventionally and of a field-fresh cabbage grown organically and compared the results.

But the food industry contends no difference exists. Establishmentarian writer James Trager says, for example, "Soil fertility will determine how many plants will grow, but for all practical purposes of human nutrition, the content of the soil will have little if any effect on the composition of plant foods grown on that soil."

According to Dr. Mark Schwartz, *Prevention*'s director of research and development, "The evidence is clear. The soil serves as more than a medium of physical support for plants. Our well-being depends on the growth of nutritionally balanced crops. And organically grown food serves to assure that."

In a carefully documented report on the nutritional aspects of organically grown foods, Dr. Schwartz showed the definite connection between the fertility of the soil and the nutrient content of produce. "Intensively farmed land just can't keep on supplying the amounts of zinc, manganese, iron, copper and other trace minerals necessary to prevent dietary deficiencies," he said.

Recent years have witnessed an increased awareness of the indispensability of micronutrients to the maintenance of health in man, animal and plant. The prolonged cultivation of the land and modern agricultural practices, such as double cropping, use of high yielding hybrids and heavy applications of concentrated chemical fertilizers have reduced the supply of many of these elements. There are even instances of reduced yield traceable to these missing micronutrients.[18]

Scientists generally agree that the mineral balance of foods are contingent upon the mineral quality of the soil on which they're grown.[19]

[18] Univ. of Georgia, Plant Nutrient Survey, *Expt. Sta. Res. Rept. 102* May, 1971.
[19] Hopkins, et al: *Am. J. of Clinical Nutr. 18:* 390–394, 1966.

Studies by Dr. Firman E. Bear in the late 1940's demonstrated this.[20] In comparing tomatoes, for example, it was found that the sample with the highest phosphorus content had double the amount of the sample with the lowest content. Variations in other elements were even greater. The tomato highest in calcium had five times the amount of that having the lowest content. The highest in potassium had three times the lowest; in sodium, boron and cobalt, more than six times; and in iron, 1,938 times.

Corn from fertile soil was observed to have a higher protein content and was a better hog feed than corn raised on poor, though highly fertilized, soil.[21]

THE HOPKINS MEMO

In 1965 Dr. Homer T. Hopkins of the U. S. Food and Drug Administration reported on the relation of soils and fertilizers to the quantity and chemical composition of foods and plant origin to Dr. Phillip L. Harris, director of the division of nutrition. While working for the U.S. Department of Agriculture previously, Dr. Hopkins had studied the mineral elements in fresh vegetables from different geographic areas and found a considerable divergence.[22] He reviewed the literature on this subject for Dr. Harris and concluded that the statement that "The nutritional values of our crops are not significantly affected by either the soil or kind of fertilizer used" could not be defended.[23]

Dr. Hopkins cited the following as the basis for his conclusions: Application of 40 tons of barnyard manure to potato soils on Long Island, N.Y., resulted in doubling the iron content of potatoes grown there.[24] Composition of roughages may be affected greatly by the amount of plant food in the soil.[25] Hypomagnesemia, or grass tetany, occurred in animals fed on grasslands heavily fertilized with potassium fertilizer.[26] The chemical composition of forages may be altered by

[20] Bear, F. E. et al: *Soil Sci. Soc. Proc. 13:* 380, 1948.
[21] Kohnke and Vestal: *Soil Sci. Soc. Proc. 13:* 385, 1948.
[22] Hopkins and Eisen: *J. of Ag. & Food Chem. 7:* 633, 1959.
[23] FDA, DHEW, *2nd Nat'l Congress on Medical Quackery,* Washington, DC, Oct. 25-26, 1963, p. 11.
[24] Belson, D. C.: *Michigan St. U. Centennial Symposium on Nutrition of Plants, Animals, Man,* 1955, p. 45.
[25] Morrison, F. B.: *Foods and Feeding,* 21st. Ed., 1951.
[26] T'Hart, M. L.: Proc. 7th Int. Grasslands Congress, 1956.

fertilization of soil. Application of a plant nutrient to soils in quantities greater than those required for maximum yield response usually resulted in luxury (excessive) consumption of the nutrient by the plant. Biological assays showed that forages grown on sandy soils, when fed to guinea pigs, had lower biological value than forages grown on clay soils.[27] Further, it has been demonstrated that the amounts of trace elements added to the soil as "contaminants" in chemical fertilizer supplying nitrogen, phosphorus and potassium are inconsequential.[28]

Scientific effort in the study of soil quality's effect on nutrition has been given a very low priority. Neither has there been much research into methods of producing food of better-than-normal nutritional value through the use of superior methods. It's widely known, for example, that the genetic makeup of plants is a very significant factor in the nutritional value of the food those plants produce. Genetic factors, however, have been manipulated primarily to produce plants of uniform size, uniform date of ripening and other benefits to mechanized agriculture. Nutritional factors have been sacrificed as a result.[29]

That the addition of organic matter to the soil improves its water-holding capacity, increases its drought resistance and reduces the activity and movement of pesticides is well-known. The effect of organic matter in the soil serves as an important reserve source of certain nutrients for plants, and in many cases it helps to keep important nutrients available to the plant.[30,31] The importance of organic matter and its effect on available nutrients has been demonstrated. It increases both calcium and phosphorous content in turnip greens.[32] The results of an extensive and comprehensive experiment demonstrated a highly significant positive relationship between soil organic matter and iron content of this vegetable.[33] A recent report by the U.S.D.A.,[34] indicated

---

[27] Ward, G. M.: *Jour. Dairy Sci. 42:* 277. *1959.*
[28] Bear, F. E. *Chemistry of the Soil.* 2nd Ed. New York: Reinhold Publishing Co., 1964.
[29] Harris, R. S. *Nutritional Evaluation of Food Processing.* New York: Wiley & Sons, 1960.
[30] USDA. *Agricultural Information Bulletin* #299, October, 1965.
[31] Adams, R. S. *Effect of Soil Organic Matter on the Movement and Activity of Pesticides in the Environment.* Paper presented at the 5th annual Conference on Trace Elements in Environmental Health. June 29-July 1, Columbia, Mo.
[32] Sheets, O. A. et al: *J. of Agron. Res.* 68: 1945, 1944.
[33] Belson, D. C.: *Michigan St. U. Centennial Symposium on Nutrition of Plants, Animals, Men,* 1955, p. 45.
[34] USDA, *An Evaluation of Research in the U.S. on Human Nutrition,* Ag. Res. Suc. Report No. 2, August, 1971.

that the highest death rate areas in the United States generally correspond to those where agriculturalists have recognized the soil as being depleted for several years.

MINERAL ASSIMILATION

By fertilizing their soil with natural materials, organic gardeners and farmers not only assure their plants proper nutrition, they ensure it for whoever eats the foods they raise, for there is now good reason to believe that minerals from organically grown foods are more easily assimilated by the body than the same kinds of minerals from equal portions of inorganic substances.

Evidence of this discovery was reported in the *Journal of Applied Nutrition* (July, 1970) by Harvey Ashmead, Ph.G., Ph.D., the founder of Albion Laboratories, a research organization in Ogden, Utah. Dr. Ashmead, a pioneer in research into organically chelated trace minerals (minerals held together and completely surrounded by organic materials), has experimented with over 200,000 animals, using both organically and inorganically chelated trace minerals.

In nature most minerals occur as chelates. Gold, for example, is almost always found as an earth ore in combination with other substances, rather than in pure form. Dr. Ashmead has explored the dietary difference between chelates that occur in foods naturally and inorganic chelates that are made synthetically from minerals which just occur in the ground itself, and which are often used in fertilizer, animal feeds and pharmaceutical mineral supplements.

After analyzing the effects of organically chelated minerals on hair, feathers, eggs, sperm and tissue, he reported, "In most every case mineral levels were favorably increased. The beneficial effects of increased assimilation and of better mineral balance within the animal were noted in better growth of the young, better production and in some cases reduction of disease."

The importance of this disclosure to human beings is twofold. Organically fed animals will provide more minerals to whoever eats the meats that come from them. In turn, people who maintain a diet of organic foods will receive and assimilate a higher and more balanced mineral content from their foods than if they were eating equal portions of inorganically produced foods.

The importance of trace minerals has been noted. The body's enzymes for example, depend on a minute, but essential, amount of trace minerals to carry out their functions. And the best way to get your trace minerals is through the foods you eat. Organically grown foods will fill your mineral needs best.

In organic gardening, every possible natural mineral should be made available to the nutrition of the plants, and therefore available to the people—or the animals—who eat those plants. Organic fertilizers are made up of natural materials, such as composted garbage, manure, blood, sawdust, shavings and leaves. Organic gardeners and farmers return to the soil naturally what has already been taken out of the soil by other plants and keep it "alive." Mineral content therefore, never is depleted.

THE ASHMEAD TESTS

Dr. Ashmead's tests help us to understand why organically grown foods should be more effective than those raised by the chemocultural method. He experimented with both plants and animals and got similar results.

Two lots of corn were planted in white silica sand which itself contained no trace minerals. Organic zinc chelate was put into one lot, and inorganic zinc sulfate chelate into the other. The corn to which the organic mineral was added germinated faster and grew taller than that planted in the inorganic zinc. When iron was tried, the organic iron chelate from fish meal scored best, while inorganic iron sulfate prevented growth!

Next, grains were grown under controlled conditions to protect them from external contamination from pesticides and insects. The same proportion of organic and inorganic metals were added to two separate lots of grain, and the roots and stems were tested for mineral content. Once again the organic minerals were absorbed far better than the same, but inorganic, ones.

Dr. Ashmead had satisfied his contentions about the superiority of organic over inorganic metals in plants with these tests, and many others like them, so he next applied the same kind of procedure to animals. In one test for absorption, copper, magnesium, iron and zinc were each chelated organically with fish meal, soybean meal and whey. These organic chelates were tested on the intestines of rats which showed no signs of mineral deficiency. The inorganic carbonates, sulfates and oxides of the same metals were also tested. The results showed that under normal conditions, the organic trace minerals were absorbed far better than the inorganic minerals.

The experiments with specially protected plants and laboratory animals proved organic minerals more effective than inorganic ones when absorbed by living tissues. But laboratory findings become meaningful only when they can be applied to present needs. So Dr. Ashmead tested his findings successfully against one of the immediate problems plaguing our minerally depleted environment.

Today most baby pigs are anemic when they are born, and to prevent death they must be given supplemental iron. The hemoglobin level averages 5 grams per cent. However, when pregnant sow pigs were fed organically chelated iron, zinc, copper, cobalt and magnesium 30 days before they gave birth, their piglets were born with hemoglobin levels averaging 11 gm. per cent. Pigs fed the same proportions of inorganic metals delivered piglets of the same weight, but the baby pig's hemoglobin levels ranged from 5 to 9 gm. per cent. They would have died if they hadn't received additional iron injections. On the other hand, the pigs born from mothers fed organic feeds didn't require additional iron to keep them alive until they could feed themselves 14 days later.

"At weaning, the dramatic results of our organic-chelated minerals were truly seen. The average weight of the piglets coming from the treated mothers was 2.65 pounds more than those coming from the controlled (inorganically fed) mothers," said Dr. Ashmead. "Thus not only was the baby pig anemia prevented by feeding the sows our organic chelated minerals, but we got the extra bonus of increased weight gains."

Further evidence of the ability of living tissue to assimilate organic minerals with greater ease than inorganic ones comes from a director of a Utah State Fishery Division. He reported a high ratio of one pound of fish for every 1.36 pounds of feed containing organic zinc. He added that the treated fish grew more rapidly than those which were untreated and "their texture approximated the texture of fish in a natural environment."

While we can appreciate the benefits of organic minerals in making healthier pigs and fatter fish, we still want to know what these minerals can do for you and me. This was Dr. Ashmead's main concern in his experiments. His findings throw valuable light on the relationship of organic minerals to human beings.

To use minerals effectively, the human body must be able to remove the trace mineral from food. It does this within the bounds of what scientists call the stability constant range, and for the human body the constant is 12, plus or minus a few decimal points. What this means is that as long as a substance is bonded weakly enough, or has a stability constant less than 12, the metal that it contains is easily removed from the chelate and can be used by the body.

The comparison between organically and inorganically chelated minerals according to stability constants shows that the body can benefit much more from organically chelated minerals. The stability constant of the organic-chelated minerals used in the experiments was about 9-11, as compared with the inorganic chelates' stability constant rating of 16 or more.

"We have found that only under extreme cellular mineral depletions can the body cells compete with such a stable mineral constant as presented by EDTA metal chelates and remove the metal from the chelates for enzyme metabolism," Dr. Ashmead said. "Metals from organic metals chelates are easily removed." (EDTA is a synthetically produced material commonly used for bonding minerals into chelates.)

The obvious conclusion of these various findings is that the best source of nutrition is food grown organically. You'll get the greatest variety of nutrients essential for good health, and you'll get them in forms tailor-made for your body's use. This conclusion, of course, isn't new; research done in the early 1900's by Sir Albert Howard, Sir Robert McCarrison, Dr. Ehrenfried Pfeiffer and others pointed, without the detailed sophistication of, for example, Dr. Ashmead's experiments, in this direction. The work of these men, unfortunately, wasn't as widely heralded and accepted as it should have been.

THE ORGANIC PIONEERS

Sir Albert Howard is generally regarded as the founder of the organic method of agriculture. He developed the Indore process of composting and did the essential practical research basic to the organic method. He told of his work first in *An Agricultural Testament* and later in *The Soil and Health*. And J. I. Rodale told of Sir Albert's work in *Pay Dirt*.

"In 1905 Howard was appointed Imperial Economic Botanist to the Government of India and was stationed at Pusa," wrote Rodale. "He was now in a position to put into practice the ideas that he had developed in the West Indies and at Wye for combatting plant diseases. His program was simply to allow plants to become strong through methods as close to those of Nature as possible. They would thus, he thought, be in an excellent position to resist disease and insect infestations. At the outset, he noticed that crops in the regions surrounding Pusa were practically free of both. The natives had never heard of insecticides or fungicides, nor did they use any chemical or artificial fertilizers, but they always made sure to return to the soil every bit of plant and animal matter that originated on and near their farms.

"Howard refused to follow the usual scientific laboratory procedure by placing investigators in separate cubbyholes, and assigning specialized lines of research to each, for he believed that scientific research was far too fragmentized. He obtained 75 acres of land, a grant of money, and the power to test out his ideas on a practical scale. His method of experimenting was to run his farm as a farm. For five years he imitated the methods of Pusa. By 1910 he had learned how to grow crops almost free of disease without chemical fertilizers or sprays. In his mind he established the principle that *'Insects and fungi are not the real cause of plant disease but only attack unsuitable varieties or crops imperfectly grown.* Their true role is that of censors, pointing out the crops that are improperly nourished . . . in other words, the pests must be looked upon as Nature's professors of agriculture.'

"By applying the same principles to oxen he developed in them a remarkable resistance to disease. They were given food raised on land not abused by caustic chemicals. 'They were not given inoculations, even though they frequently came in contact with diseased stock. As my small farm-yard at Pusa was only separated by a low hedge from one of the large cattle-sheds on the Pusa estate, in which outbreaks of foot-and-mouth disease often occurred, I have several times seen my oxen rubbing noses with foot-and-mouth cases. Nothing happened. The healthy, well-fed animals reacted to this disease exactly as suitable varieties of crops, when properly grown, did to insect and fungus pests—no infection took place.' This experiment was duplicated later in many parts of India, always with the same good results."

PFEIFFER'S WORK

The late Dr. Ehrenfried Pfeiffer, an advocate of the bio-dynamic method, a variation of the organic method which places more emphasis on the making of compost, conducted experiments which demonstrated the superiority of foods raised by natural methods, too. In his book *Bio-Dynamic Farming and Gardening,* Pfeiffer referred to an experiment with mice in which some were fed bio-dynamically grown wheat and milk, as against the control group that subsisted on wheat grown with commercial fertilizers and milk. At the end of the experiment, the amount of mice in the commercially fertilized batch averaged 6.2 mice per litter—the bio-dynamic group averaged 6.7 or about 8 per cent more.

However, at the age of nine weeks 16.9 per cent of the control group had died, whereas in the bio-dynamic group only 8.6 per cent had died, or about one-half. The experiment was done in three generations of the mice with a total of 164 animals.

Then an experiment was made with White Leghorn chickens which continued for a year, one group getting bio-dynamically raised feed, the other food grown with the conventional commercial fertilizers. The average total weight of the daily production of 10 hens was:

> Commercial   427.2 grams
> Bio-dynamic   464.5 grams

"In the bio-dynamic pens," wrote Pfeiffer, "the chickens stayed outside in the sun from one to two hours longer in the evening; which shows that their vitality was increased. In rainy weather, the birds in the commercial pen sought the shelter of the chicken house sooner than those of the bio-dynamic pens."

Total egg production of 10 birds for nine months:

> Commercial   1,495
> Bio-dynamic   1,916

The experiment was repeated the next year, 1933, with approximately the same results. Then a hatching test was made. Of the commercial batch of eggs, 35 per cent hatched. Of the bio-dynamic eggs, 68 per cent hatched.

Then the eggs were tested for keeping qualities. After six months 60 per cent of the commercial eggs spoiled—of the bio-dynamic only 27 per cent.

"That an overbalance of salts, in the case of mineral (chemical) fertilizing, can have a harmful effect on the food, has been shown from various studies," wrote Pfeiffer.

Dr. Pfeiffer also drew on research by G. Tallarico, who reported on his experiments which demonstrated the influence of fertilizing on the quality and the nutritional properties of foods.

Tallarico used turkeys to establish evidence of the superior health qualities of crops raised with natural fertilizers.

"The food was raised on three parcels of land. The first parcel was fertilized with mineral (chemical) fertilizer each year for two years with 180 lbs. of ammonium sulphonitrate per acre, spread during the time of cultivating the field, also 90 lbs. of potassium per acre and 350 lbs. of super-phosphate per acre which was spread after seeding.

"The second parcel was fertilized each year for two years with rotted stable manure, in a proportion of 1,000 lbs. per acre.

"The third parcel was used in its natural state without mineral or animal fertilizer.

"On these three parcels, the most important foods for the raising of the turkeys were grown in separate beds. In the second year, a portion of the produce grown on the same parcel the first year was used as seed."

As the experiment continued, the foods grown were fed to four groups of poultry over the first six months of their lives in the form of mash, supplemented with egg yolk and ground meat.

"In order to determine the organic capacity for resisting disease the following phenomena were observed and considered: the number of sick animals, the beginning of the crisis (the time when the characteristic red growth appear on the head and neck) for each animal, its length and its termination, whether in death, cure or stunting. From these results the mean percentage was then determined for each group and each test series, taking into consideration the unavoidable accidental losses in raising them—such as death through cold, injuries or birds of prey.

"From this it is plain that the turkeys which were fed in the first two months with grains or green feed from plants grown on stable-manured soil show, when they are attacked by the crisis, a smaller number of cases of sickness, a shorter duration of it, and a lesser number of cases ending fatally in comparison with the corresponding group of turkeys which under the same conditions of life and environment are fed with green feed or grains from plants that were fertilized with mineral (chemical) fertilizer."

McCARRISON IN HUNZA

Sir Robert McCarrison was another pioneer of the organic method. The crops he and his co-workers grew gave greater yields with organic than with chemical fertilizer. [35] In the case of a crop of *Panicum miliacoum,* the organic method brought an increase of 100.7 per cent in yield, in contrast to the yield without fertilizing, whereas with chemical fertilizers the increase in yield was only 32.8 per cent.

In a feeding experiment with pigeons, the group that was fed a basic ration, plus plants grown on stable manure as the fertilizer, lost 22.4 per cent of their body weight during the days of the test, whereas those fed with chemically fertilized plants lost 37.4 per cent of their body weight.

In an experiment with the feeding of barley, in terms of loss of body weight, stable-manured barley showed 15 per cent better results than the chemically fertilized barley.

In another experiment with oats, the organic group gained 114 per cent in weight, whereas the chemically fertilized group gained 89 per cent.

But McCarrison's most familiar work centered on the ten years he spent with the Hunzukuts of northern India around the second decade of this century.

He discovered that the people of Hunza had an excellent diet which made them extremely healthy.

"McCarrison decided to find out if rats could be endowed with health equal to that enjoyed by the Hunzas through feeding them on a similar diet," J. I. Rodale explained. "He worked with three groups of rats—one group fed on the same diet as the Hunzas; a second group on the diet of the southern India rice-eaters; and a third group that was subjected to the diet of the lower classes of England, containing white bread, margarine, sugar-sweetened tea, a little boiled milk, cabbage, potatoes, canned meats and sugared jam.

[35] Pfeiffer, E. *Bio-Dynamic Farming and Gardening.* New York: Anthroposophic Press, 1943, pp. 193-5.

"McCarrison found the Hunza group quite healthy, but group number two suffered from a wide variety of diseases.

"The third group, the British rats, not only developed those diseases, but were nervous and apt to bite their attendants. They lived unhappily together and by the sixtieth day of the experiment began to kill and eat the weaker ones amongst them." McCarrison's evidence, like that of many researchers since, seemed to indicate clearly that diet is associated with health.

ORGANICALLY GROWN FOODS FOR HEALTH

Moreover, McCarrison's evidence and the evidence of many others all points to the fertility of the soil as the source of the nutritional qualities of food. And this is the whole point of organically grown foods. Husband the soil, and the soil will husband the crops, and the crops will husband your health.

Dr. Barry Commoner, in *The Closing Circle,* cities four informal laws of ecology, one of which is "Nature knows best." Commenting on this law he says, "One of the most pervasive features of modern technology is the notion that it is intended to 'improve on nature'—to provide food, clothing, shelter, and means of communication and expression which are superior to those available to man in nature. Stated baldly, the third law of ecology holds that any major man-made change in a natural system is likely to be detrimental to that system."

Thus the ecology of nutrition starts to become clear. The natural system of nutrition has evolved over millions of years. The best soils grew the best plants. The best plants returned the largest amounts of the best nutrients to the soil. Thus evolved a cycle of fertile soil nurturing nutritious crops which in turn maintained the soil's fertility. What the organic method has done is come to terms with this ecological system.

The adherent to the organic method has always been somehow cognizant of the threat to the natural, ecological system that agribusiness' major man-made changes represent. He knows the effects of the changes may not become immediately clear and may be difficult to trace to a single cause. Moreover, when the disastrous effect of the man-made changes really becomes clear, it may be too late to reverse the system's deterioration.

The organic method is a coming to terms with nature. The organic way has always been the natural way. The organic farmer depends on natural fertilizers; he depends on biological pest controls; he depends on a fertile soil to nourish healthy crops. The organic farmer knows that properly fertilized crops need a balance of plant nutrients, and he provides them, naturally.

Likewise, the people who eat organically grown foods have come to terms with nature. They know their systems have evolved over the centuries and that any major man-made change is likely to be detrimental to the system. The best way to health is proper nutrition and good nutrition comes from organically grown foods. They provide a proper balance of nutrients, naturally. This is the ecology of nutrition. This is the organic way.

—William Hylton

4

From the Farm and Garden

Crisis In Agriculture

There has never been a civilization that produced as much food with so little human energy. Our technology, together with abundant resources of land, water, a favorable climate, and abundant fossil fuels, make it possible. We have become experts in exploiting the available natural resources. Very little thought has been given to replenishing and/or recycling any wastes.

Agriculture has moved from what was substantially a self-renewing industry to one that is almost completely dependent on outside sources for its operation. As a result, farming has moved from a way of life to a factory-in-the-field concept. The effects of these changes on the biology of agriculture is, indeed, significant and far-reaching.

We point with pride to the fact that one man can now produce the food requirements for himself and about 30 and more other people. Although this may be true to a large extent, it is not altogether the whole story, because of the number of people and resources that are used in industry to supply this one farmer's needs. Again we are replacing human energy with the stored energy of the fossil fuels.

The machinery, inorganic fertilizers, and other products produced by industry for the farmer are, of course, using up some of our natural resources. Again the stored fossil fuels which are not inexhaustible, the precious oxygen which scientists tell us we are using faster than it is being produced, and the various mineral stores are being depleted in

63

this process. In many cases use of these products is obviously becoming a major source of soil and water pollution. It is quite generally known, for example, that almost all the streams and rivers in Illinois are carrying high levels of nitrates. The city of Bloomington, Illinois, gets its water from a lake now contaminated to such an extent that doctors recommend not using this water for babies. Contamination of wells in the Midwest—from organic wastes as well as chemical fertilizers—is also well-known.

The insect pests that always result from a monoculture are becoming more of a problem every year. New and apparently more toxic materials must continually be used. The monoculture becomes attractive, of course, because of industrialized agriculture and, indeed, becomes a necessity because of the tremendous investment the farmer has in his machines.

Meanwhile, the livestock that has been for centuries an integral part of the traditional methods of agriculture, is also moving from the farms. Livestock, like people, have been concentrated in small areas. Again our drive for efficiency and our industrial concepts of producing a given product for the least amount of cost, is our only yardstick for measuring success. Disease is becoming a greater problem as a result of high concentrations of animals.

Waste disposal problems have in fact reached such proportions that even the urban dweller is well aware of them. Mountains of manure have become a real source of pollution, while back on the farm, where the substitute is used, it also has become a source of pollution. Again the nitrogen cycle, that every high-school biology student learns about, has been broken. Soils are rapidly losing their nitrogen-fixing bacteria. Indeed, some have largely lost their ability to properly nourish the growing plant. They have become like the dope addict who needs his "shot" to function at all.

The industrialization of agriculture has so speeded up the biological functions of the soil that they simply cannot maintain a healthy environment for the growing plant. Trace mineral problems have become very common largely because of the reduced microbial action in the soil. There is roughly a 50 per cent loss of organic matter in our soils—so very necessary to maintain their tilth, water-absorbing capability, and active biological life. Only a healthy soil can produce a healthy plant. Only a healthy plant can survive in nature's domain, and our attempts to fight insects and fungi that attack our plants should be tempered by this fact, and serve notice for us to proceed with caution.

NATURAL LAW ON THE FARM

Agriculture will perhaps never again become the totally self-renewing industry that it once was. But if we are to observe the laws of biology and adhere to nature's law that all things must operate in a cycle, how are we going to accomplish this with 94 per cent of the population living in the cities, and only 6 per cent left on the farms? How can we recycle the tremendous concentrations of food which, of course, becomes "waste" when the centers of population are so far removed from the source of food? How can we recycle the tremendous amounts of waste from our feedlots and poultry houses when they are so far removed from the land?

Now we are getting to the real gut issue and the real test as to whether or not we really *can* or *will* obey the biological laws that we have been ignoring since the beginning of the industrial revolution and especially since the beginning of modern agricultural practices. This is the real crisis in agriculture, for that matter, the crisis for all of the so-called developed countries. We have become accustomed to an abundance of cheap food that is the result of our taking shortcuts in nature's biological cycle. We have accumulated a huge debt, and nature will have her due in one way or another. She is very patient, but very demanding. A century is but a moment in her web of life. If we choose not to pay the debt, she may have to wait until man disappears from the scene, when she will once again, in her own way, restore the earth as we found it. Remember the tremendous fertility we found in the North American continent was not the work of man.

So the question needs to be answered. Do we really want to start living as though we want to remain on this earth as a species? Do we really have the technology that will enable us to continue to ignore the biological laws? This is the key question on which our very survival may hinge. Can we continue to take from our fields and gardens the very essence of life, century after century, in exchange for a small portion of sterile mineral matter, and feel we are paying our due?

In our consumption of a plant as food, we utilize only about 25 per cent of the fertility of the soil used in producing that food. In other words, in the route from soil to plant to animal and/or man, 75 per cent of the fertility of the soil is retained in the part of the plant or animal that we refer to as waste. This is what we bury in our garbage dumps and flush down the sewers. Yet this is material that nature does not consider waste, but in her way of doing things, would return to the earth to replenish new life. In nature's pattern, the end of one life is the beginning of another. But our wastes are buried, burned and dumped into the rivers or destroyed.

A CRISIS FOR ALL

The crisis in agriculture is not just the farmer's problem. I'm afraid we are all involved. He can only begin to pay this huge debt to nature if we all insist, and if we make it possible. It is going to demand a complete rethinking of our agricultural policy. It may involve a reversal of the population migration, a decentralization of populations, and all the resulting re-evaluation of our priorities. The problems facing the cities in the '70's may help force this reappraisal of our goals. The cities are rapidly becoming unfit for human life. We need to take a good hard look at where we are heading, and whether or not this ever-increasing gap between man and his earth is really what we want.

Such broad implications may very well leave you feeling overwhelmed and helpless as to what can be done. You are not alone in this plight. It has bothered many of us for many years. But I can tell you this: The current widespread interest in ecology is not just a passing fad. The science of ecology can help us because it does put man in his proper place in the web of life. We simply must try to understand more of God's laws of nature, act accordingly, and all things will begin to fall into place. It will require much study from all of us. Young people are not burdened with orthodox methods and traditions, but they must remember that traditions do provide the framework—and often the only framework—within which our society knows how to function.

We can make the changes needed, within the existing framework, but the picture that needs to emerge is quite different from the one I can see today. We need to develop what we may refer to as an intermediate technology in agriculture. I'm sure we cannot and will not go back to the traditional peasant's way of farming, and all the hand labor involved. But we do need to study his methods and adopt what we can to this new technology. The technology we develop must be governed by ecological principles. The monoculture that results from vast areas of cash crops must once again be broken up by crop rotations. Field sizes can and will be larger and better and adapted to modern machinery. But grass and legumes must once again take their place in our rotations.

Farms certainly can be larger than they have been, but they can also be small and operate efficiently if some of the larger machines are owned jointly or by cooperatives. The number of people involved in the production of our food will be greater when food requirements go up. And when one considers the number of urban people engaged in so many non-productive and service-oriented occupations, there should be no trouble in finding the people who really never wanted to leave the farms in the first place. And if the consumer wants to assure himself of an adequate supply of high-quality food in the years to come, he will have to pay for it, through either greater effort on his part or a willingness to reward those who do it for him. Somehow all of us must come to the realization that there is really nothing free. As the ecologist reminds us again and again: everything is connected to everything else. This includes the price tags.

—Robert Steffen

The Organic Farmer

Wendell Lundberg pushes his straw hat to the back of his head as he looks up. His face is lined and serious as he speaks.

"You're standing on our entire bankroll," he says, letting a handful of rich, black soil sift through his fingers. "If we want the land to support us, we have to take care of it. Build it up. Invest in it. But if you ever get careless, and start to live off of your capital, then what you leave behind won't be worth much—either to your kids or to the earth.

"We feel that we should leave the land in better condition than we found it," he says, standing up and brushing the dirt from his hands. "That would be a real legacy."

Wehah Farm's land taxes were about $28,000 last year, and being faced with this kind of a bill, whether your crop is a success or a failure is a staggering responsibility. But Lundberg's apprehensions go well beyond the traditional fears about the weather, prices, and rising taxes. Not long ago, he and his three brothers decided to convert their 3000-acre rice farm to organics. Today, they are organic farmers—part of a growing movement in rural America that is returning to some of yesterday's methods to produce today's food—but their future is far from assured.

The Lundbergs' decision to go organic was a courageous, but difficult one. Modern rice farming is so sophisticated and chemical that the prospect of abandoning the synthetic fertilizers, soil conditioners, chemical herbicides and pesticides and growth stimulants was frightening. There were many problems and many risks involved. For example, in the soil of the rice paddies there is a small pest called the tadpole shrimp. When the paddies are flooded, the tadpole shrimp are activated; in a week or more the paddies are filled with tiny, wiggling creatures which churn up fine silt and turn the water a cloudy consistency. Sunlight and heat are blocked out and germination is critically hindered. Tadpole shrimp will also feed on the tiny shoots of germinated rice before the small plants have developed chlorophyll. The more silt, the less sunlight, and the less chlorophyll.

Some years are worse than other years. Modern rice growers as a general practice assume that there will be a heavy tadpole infestation and the standard procedure is to spray the paddies with parathion or carbaryl (Sevin) or the soil with copper sulfate crystals.

To prevent various seedling diseases, seeds are treated with Captan or Arasan 42S (Thiram). *The soak water from treated seeds is so toxic (poisonous) that it is supposed to be retained in settling basins and not allowed to return to intake or drainage ditches.* Molinate and/or Propanil are either worked into the soil before flooding or later applied to the flooded paddies in order to control a water grass called barnyard grass. Carbo Furadan is applied on the soil prior to flooding to control rice water weevil. Copper sulfate is applied in the water to control algae. Parathion is sprayed on growing crops to control mosquitoes. Malathion or parathion is used on seedling rice to destroy the eggs and larvae of the rice leafminer. Leafhoppers and armyworms are controlled by applications of Sevin.

Such a wide proliferation of chemicals in agriculture today is common . . . and it was just this situation that greatly influenced the Lundbergs' decision to make the switch.

A RISKY BUSINESS

Farming, in general, is risky business. Take away the "insurance" that many chemical fertilizers and sprays provide, and those risks multiply . . . as does the amount of work needed to compensate for the functions these chemicals once performed and yet, with all the risk and labor involved, the organic farmer must satisfy himself with a yield-per-acre that is less than that of the conventional farmer. (The Lundbergs, for instance, are only producing about 50 per cent as much rice per acre as they did before they went organic.)

Still, this is the way most farmers — organic or otherwise — would *rather* raise their crops.

For 4000 years, the primary function of every farmer has been one of maintaining soil fertility. This is not so much tradition as it is plain common sense. Fertile soil produces healthy plants and animals . . . and consequently, healthy humans. An imbalanced or deficient soil condition produces a deficiency throughout the entire length of the food chain. Harsh chemicals destroy necessary soil bacteria. Supernutrients rob the soil of bacteria-sustaining humus and also destroy the soil's structure.

As conventional farming continues to move toward larger equipment and more chemicals—and toward techniques which are isolated from and in opposition to sound agricultural and ecological practices —it is not surprising to find farmers like the Lundbergs turning to the alternatives of organic farming. Organic farming is basically a practice of soil conservation and improvement . . . and it is this distinction that separates the sheep from the wolves.

But vitamin- and mineral-poor crops and depleted soil aren't the sole reasons farmers give for abandoning conventional methods. Many are unhappy with the changing nature of farming itself. For them, farming today vaguely resembles what it was just two generations ago. They have seen farming evolve from a fulfilling *way of life*—a life style in which they could take an active part in the natural life cycle—to a demanding, profit-oriented profession . . . and many are resisting that. Others admit that making the switch to organic methods is an economic necessity.

Not long ago in this country it was relatively easy for the family farmer to earn a living off the land. That, of course, was before America's technological explosion and long before farming was anything but a gleam in the eye of big business. Today the picture has changed considerably and the farmer with a small or medium-size operation is hard-pressed to show an equitable return for a year's labor. Consequently, a great many farmers are currently looking toward organics to provide a better market for their commodities.

A GIANT BUSINESS

Much of the farmer's current dilemma took root at the turn of the century, a time when everyone got caught up in America's industrial revolution. With the development of Henry Ford's first assembly line, the American discovered that mass production could drastically reduce costs and widen their profit margin. Whole new markets opened up while others, once considered outside big business' domain, were now being looked upon with rabid interest.

In a very short time, big business transformed farming into a booming national industry. Large corporate farms sprang up across the country. Mass production techniques helped to greatly reduce labor and other farming costs. Technology, fueled by business' unlimited capital, gave birth to a bumper crop of new inventions and scientific breakthroughs that almost completely institutionalized farming. Huge and sophisticated machines performed many time-consuming tasks so efficiently that human labor on the farm became relatively obsolete. New chemicals were developed that reduced or eliminated the chance of disease in seedlings. Growth stimulants insured higher yields per acre. Crop dusting by airplanes with powerful poison sprays like DDT eliminated entire insect populations. New herbicides effectively controlled weeds, and synthetic chemical fertilizers were pumped into crops, producing larger and more abundant harvests than anyone had ever imagined.

Each new breakthrough began another. Large corporate farms grew larger until farming itself became big business. America became the land of plenty. Due to an abundance of food, market prices were significantly lowered . . . while consumer prices rose. And for the first time in our nation's history, we were faced with a new kind of agricultural problem: food surpluses. Hundreds of thousands of tons of food rotted in huge silos and grain elevators annually, while hundreds of thousands of Americans still went hungry. To the amazement of many, the Federal government countered by subsidizing these corporate farmers for leaving fields unplanted.

The independent family farmer was the first to feel the effects of this rampant progress. Each year, many market prices fell to successive all-time lows. Many small farmers, unable to meet the competition and rising costs, simply sold their farms and went to work for the competition. Others fought back as best they could, utilizing every chemical and labor-saving technique they could. Many banded together in large cooperatives—a move that agribusiness barons openly opposed. The situation became so desperate that a few farmers abandoned crop rotation to concentrate on a single crop that proved consistently profitable. Still others soaked their fields with potent poison pesticides which annihilated all insect life, pests and beneficial bugs alike.

In less than 20 years, the nature of farming in America had entirely changed.

The family farmer was not the sole victim of this turmoil. Our nation's soil, once rich and naturally fertile, was rapidly being rendered void of all its minerals and moisture-retaining humus. Rainfall turned fields into huge mud bowls which the sun later baked rock-hard. Farmers found the soil becoming old before its time and larger doses of chemical fertilizers and synthetic minerals were necessary to sustain constant yields. Often the tired, depleted land refused to foster any life whatsoever.

As expected, the crops themselves also suffered. Though larger and better looking than those of the past, they contained but a fraction of the natural vitamins and nutrients. Instead, they became storehouses for toxic chemicals which could not be excreted from animal or human organisms. Widespread use of preservatives, ripening gases and artificial coloring was on the upswing.

Ironically, the consumer financed all of this. Crop production costs went down—as did market prices—but retail prices and corporate profits climbed. Unknowingly, the consumer paid higher and higher prices for food that was benefiting him and his family less and less.

A NEW FARMING—ORGANIC

The sudden popularity of the organic method today is evidence that people—farmers and consumers alike—want to reverse this unhealthy trend. Organic is offering farmers an opportunity to raise and profitably market nutritious food, while fulfilling their traditional, and possibly moral, obligation to conserve and improve the land they use.

Organic farmers are dedicated men, motivated by a concern that something is wrong, that we have allowed the convenience and techniques of our civilization to trespass too far—to the point of obscuring the real essence of living. While their methods may vary, organic farmers are firmly united in philosophy. They feel that quality of life, rather than material progress, should be our nation's most important product. It is high time, many say, that we harness and constructively channel technology before it destroys our environment.

Critics of the organic movement in agriculture frequently claim that this is faddism or merely a romantic step back to the outhouse days and a naive renewal of rugged pioneering. Such criticism completely misses the point and urgency of the issue. The physical frontiers in America are gone. Organic farmers are seeking to return to natural living, not to bend nature to their wills as the pioneers did, but to do a job yet undone: to work in partnership with nature. Perhaps Frank Ford, a Deaf Smith County, Texas, wheat farmer and organic veteran of 11 years, summed it up best when he said, "If you fight nature you're going to lose. You might do ok for twenty years . . . but in the end, you're going to lose."

In becoming acquainted with organic farmers, one thing tends to stand out. They are enjoying themselves; they like their farms and they like what they do. Most of them set aside a portion of their day, sometimes very early in the morning, to stroll among their orchards or vegetable crops. If they have animals, they usually have a favorite spot where they like to stand and watch them as they graze and move about. If one tree in a thousand is doing poorly, they worry about it. As a rule, they are well acquainted with the insects that inhabit their fields. Unless bird and insect damage becomes financially intolerable, most organic farmers are content to shrug their shoulders and say "live and let live."

But organic farmers are not the bucolic yokels that their critics and the media make them out to be. In California, for example, there is better than a 50 per cent chance that an organic farmer has a college degree or has attended college for at least one year. Estimates indicate that by the end of the decade the educational average of California organic farmers will include two or more years of college. Often, college degrees are in wholly unrelated areas and organic farmers, generally, enjoy a wide range of interests. It is not surprising that matters of health and ecology, along with increasing taxes and farm incomes, are of special concern to them. However, most organic farmers extend their interest to include an understanding of the problems of the cities. They are apt to view the traditional division between farm and city as invalid and unrealistic. They are knowledgeable activists—convinced that city dwellers must adopt many of the underlying ecological principles of the organic farm if they are to survive . . . and prepared to help cities recycle their wastes.

Until the late 1960's, the torch of the organic ideal was carried forth largely by older farmers who steadfastly resisted the rush to chemical agriculture. Even today it is not unusual to find old timers—60, 70, even 80 years old—who have farmed organically all of their lives as a matter of personal conviction, while marketing through conventional outlets at standard prices. But the age picture is shifting. Today, most of the commercial farmers contemplating the conversion to organic methods are in their late 30's and early 40's. And if current interest and public popularity continues—along with the exodus of our young people to the countryside—organic food production is very likely to provide the alternative lifestyle that much of our youth is seeking.

Indeed, organic farming is offering alternatives and solutions to many of our nation's current, pressing problems. Organic farmers feel they have been doing something concrete about solving the problems. Organic farmers feel they have been doing something concrete about solving the problems of pollution, waste disposal, soil conservation, ecology and the need for safer, more nutritious food. Moreover, they are doing these same things long before there was a general awareness that such problems existed. But there is only so much that a handful of men can do . . . and organic farmers themselves will be the first to admit that their future is uncertain. There are many problems that must be overcome before organic farming becomes a generally accepted practice.

ORGANICULTURE'S PROBLEMS

The major problem facing organic farmers is the organic phony. While most organic farmers feel that organics requires a commitment as a matter of personal conviction, they accept and include farmers who want to operate organically simply to supply a more profitable market.

They feel that it is a question of integrity, therefore when a farmer calls his product organic he has voluntarily assumed a certain public responsibility. Organic farming methods are expensive. Sometimes the cost is doubled, while the risks run much higher. Consumers, who are willing to offset the higher risk and increased production cost, pay more. This presents a temptation to many farmers and retailers, who might imply or label their produce as organic when in fact it is not, or is only partially so. Such fraudulent labeling and shortcuts sadden most organic farmers. Some are angered, but all want to join with consumers to protect the organic market. In this respect they feel that the best possible protection is an open industry and informed consumers.

Marketing is certainly a major problem. Generally speaking, the huge system of mass distribution is neither suitable nor available to organic farmers. For example, the uncontaminated quality of an orange is destroyed if the orange is processed and treated with chemical preservatives and possibly an artificial coloring. It is somewhat pointless for a farmer to carefully raise food without using harsh chemicals, only to market his commodity through a market which fumigates food as a standard practice. Almonds and most edible nuts, grains and legumes, are among those foods which are fumigated for cheap, easy storage. In order to protect organic foods from contamination, organic farmers and distributors are faced with the task of of building separate facilities. It is a staggering challenge.

Another problem which continues to plague organic farmers is neighbors who carelessly spray, or worse, dust their fields and orchards without regard to the toxic particles which blow over onto adjacent organic fields. In one irresponsible moment a neighbor's carelessness can coat an organic farm with poisonous residues and possibly destroy or hamper that farmer's organic verification. (Legitimate organic retailers and distributors will reject commodities when laboratory analysis indicates the presence of toxic pesticide residues.) Moreover, toxic blowovers kill useful insects, often destroying expensive bugs which were imported and released to protect the crop biologically from insect damage. Most organic farmers feel that conventional farmers should not be permitted to use harmful pesticides or herbicides, unless they can positively guarantee that no particles will blow over land which does not belong to them.

To top all this off, organic farmers must face opposition from the large corporate farmers as well as an attitude of ambivalence from the U.S. Department of Agriculture.

However, there are a few bright spots shining through all of this darkness. More and more farmers are considering, if not actually switching to organic methods. Frank Ford's Texas Panhandle county for example is rapidly approaching an organic commitment which might prove to be as high as 80 per cent. The public, too, is holding organic farmers in higher and higher esteem—no longer are they being written off as crackpots. Consumers are becoming better informed on such matters as ecology and nutrition and are consequently demanding better food.

Consumers have discovered that organiculture provides the safe, nutritious food that they have been asking for, and the organic market has dispelled the myth that they will not pay more for better. Organic farmers have discovered that consumers are, after all, their best friends, and that by providing more food—buying alternatives, they are increasing their opportunity to strengthen this friendship. Many well-established farmers receive letters regularly from food buyers, congratulating them upon the fine quality of the organic food they raise. Perhaps for the first time, farmers and consumers are united on a broad, unified objective. Today, at least in philosophy, they stand together in their combined desire to promote and protect the safe production of healthy food.

But the consumer is going to have to do more than talk about better food if he is to have it. The organic farmer is doing what he can, but if the movement is to spread—if our society is going to conserve our soil, clean up our environment and set a healthier table—the consumer must make his voice heard. And nothing, capitalism tells us, speaks louder than money. If the consumer demands that supermarkets carry pesticide-free produce, enzyme-free meats and preservative-free groceries . . . they will. Many supermarket chains already stock organic meat and produce for this reason. But they will never initiate this action without that consumer demand.

One thing is certain: no matter how the consumer acts and reacts in the supermarket, most organic farmers will continue to practice organics, if only out of personal conviction. For these are men who will not wait for legislation to permit them to enjoy a healthier, more fulfilling life. They are activists who always have and *always will* live the best kind of life possible under any circumstances, each reaping his own amount of personal victories.

Organic farmers aren't waiting. Perhaps the organic spirit is best exemplified by Harlan Lundberg, who recently joined the Peace Corps to teach organic rice growing to the Brazilians.

—James Punkre and Floyd Allen

The Backyard Gardener

Have you ever planted a seed and subsequently picked a crisp green vegetable, one that you could eat, skin and all, without fear of paraffin contamination or insecticide residues?

If you haven't, you haven't really lived! You haven't tasted true joy or true vegetable flavor.

No matter where you live, country, village, city, cottage or apartment house, you can know the pleasure of placing a seed in the moist earth and seeing it awaken and grow into something wonderful and nourishing to put into your salad. At the same time, you can help win a small but significant victory over the poisoning of our air, soil and food. How? Plant a sanity garden.

Remember the victory gardens of World War II, when we considered it our patriotic duty to utilize every back yard, vacant lot, meadow and park to raise food because of war shortages. That was a wartime emergency measure and almost to a man, we rallied to the call.

We are facing today an emergency of no less proportions—contamination of the food that is made available to us in the marketplace.

If you are so city bred that the idea of growing food for body as well as soul seems too esoteric to even begin to contemplate, then consider that a growing plant is much more than merely beautiful. A growing plant can vastly improve your own life.

Did you know that most vegetables start changing their delectable sugars to starches the minute they are picked? Have you ever tasted an ear of corn that traveled less than five minutes from field to pot? It's sweeter than sugar. Such corn is considered a green vegetable. Once the corn has aged a day or two, it becomes a starch vegetable; it has lost many of its vitamins.

When you grow your own, you not only enjoy the more choice varieties of the standard vegetables, you will have all the fun of poring over the seed catalogs for "exotic" vegetables that you rarely if ever can buy in your local grocery. You'll find wonderful additions to your meals in Japanese mustards, Chinese long beans, French leeks, Italian fennel, Mexican edible cactus. Did you ever find any of these at your supermarket? These are just a few of the many fine, vitamin-rich vegetables that will enhance your cooking inexpensively when you grow your own.

But, of course, the most important reason for home food growing is that you can raise them without resorting to chemical pesticides, fungicides, herbicides and synthetic fertilizers.

GARDENING AT HOME

The home gardener, by growing a large assortment of plants, can encourage the presence of many different insects which will control each other. The home gardener can hand pick and trap insects. He can concentrate on building up the health of his plants through soil conditioning. He can introduce biological controls such as ladybugs and praying mantises.

But, you might say, it's all right for someone with a backyard or a terrace. But I live in an apartment without a bit of outdoor space. I don't even have a sunny window.

You still don't have to hide your green thumb in your pocket. You can grow mushrooms. The spores of the commercially grown mushrooms can be bought from regular seed companies who will also provide you directions for growing them in a shallow box six or eight inches deep. You can grow mushrooms in a closet or under your sink. Mushrooms are quite exacting in their temperature requirements. They need about a 75 degree temperature to start and gradually lower temperature as they grow until they are harvested at around 55 degrees.

For the long part of the process you might find a closet or cabinet under the sink the right temperature. In the crucial sterilizing of the growing medium your home heating system or oven can be used. For the cool period you could try a dark corner of the basement or garage. If you grow the culture in a small drawer or other box lined with a plastic sheet to retain moisture, you should be able to transport it as necessary. It will take some experimenting and ingenuity on your part to find just the right conditions in your own home setting. But the results are certainly worth it.

In one square foot of growing medium you can produce at least two pounds of gorgeous mushrooms which are rich in essential amino acids and are a good source of protein, calcium and vitamin C. If you would like to develop a fascinating, rewarding hobby that will bring gourmet fare to your table, do try growing mushrooms.

TINY VEGETABLES FOR TINY AREAS

If you have nothing but a window to garden in, you can still grow some food for your table. If you have a window that gets light and a few hours of sun, there is an indoor tomato variety, TINY TIM, that will produce cherry tomatoes that are delightful with your salads. With this tomato you will have some success even with a nine-inch pot. A five-gallon can will give you far more spectacular results.

Chives and other herbs that add much flavor to your salads can also be grown in a window garden. It is rather simple to decrease the amount of sun received by any particular spot by the use of lattice work or by planting sensitive plants like lettuce in the shade of others during the hot season. But it is expensive and fairly complicated to attempt to increase the amount of light with artificial "grow-light" bulbs, reflectors or mirrors.

Here is a general rule to guide you: Leaf vegetables can withstand the most shade. Flowers and fruit generally demand the most sunlight, while root vegetables fall somewhere between the two extremes. Trial and error will teach you what garden varieties can grown under circumstances of apartment dwelling. If you have an outdoor window box, then why not plant a salad? Try loose leaf lettuce, one green such as BLACK SEEDED SIMPSON or GRAND RAPIDS and one red, RUBY. It is very rewarding to select plants from which you can snip off a few leaves at a time while the plant keeps growing, rather than harvest the whole plant at once, as with head lettuce, for instance.

Radishes are an easy to grow addition to a window-box salad. There are white icicle types as well as the familiar round red. The many exotic varieties of Japanese long radishes and long black and yellow types, take a slightly deeper container. Be sure to use the radish greens in your salads. They are a rich source of vitamins and minerals.

Try growing a few carrots in your window box and use the carrot greens. Also some cress—either pepper grass or upland cress—both of which taste rather like water cress as do nasturtium blossoms. Try shoving a few cloves of garlic (pointed end up) into the earth and cover with a quarter to a half inch of soil. After several leaves have formed, use the delicious mild tops for green garlic in your salad bowl. It provides a delightful gourmet touch. The TINY TIM cherry tomatoes would fit into such a planting scheme also, depending on how large your window box is.

If you live in an apartment and your green thumb itches to go a little deeper than a window box, then consider the idea of getting permission to use some outdoor space around the apartment house—the roof or interior courtyard. These areas are ideal for growing heat-loving plants like peppers, tomatoes and squashes. And once you have gifted the owners with some of the produce from your garden, they will encourage you heartily. If you have absolutely no recourse to any outdoor real estate, but do have a porch, a deck or the corner of a stair landing, you may have the perfect place to try a box or can of any of these vegetables.

As a matter of fact, for a small family, this kind of container gardening has many advantages. One zucchini plant in a five-gallon can will produce all you can keep up with. After all you don't want to eat it every night! Where the summers are cool, an unglazed ceramic pot may give just those extra degrees of heat necessary to produce certain vegetables you could not get to fruit otherwise. Remember that plants in small containers lose moisture rapidly. When you add lots of organic matter to the soil, this helps to hold in the water. So does a circle of burlap or other coarse grained material fitted around the plant's stem on top of the earth as a mulch.

Gardening in containers is also very practical if you are renting, since it does not interfere with the landlord's landscape design. But even if ground space is not your problem, the convenience and attractiveness of container gardening will intrigue you. In Berkley, California, for instance, tenants have covered cement driveways and patio areas with vegetable plants in wooden boxes or old drawers. Five-gallon metal cans make excellent planters, and they are discarded in great numbers by industrial plants, plastic manufacturers and paint and varnish consumers, such as cabinet shops. Some of these firms would probably be very happy to save you a few. Since every metal container is a potential polluter, there is no better way for the sanity gardener to perform a dual function than to utilize these metal cans until such time as they are reclaimed and recycled. To provide drainage these metal cans should have two holes punched in the sides at the bottom with a beer can opener. Wooden boxes, on the other hand, are rarely tight enough to make a drainage problem.

Container gardening does not have to be on a five-gallon scale. You can do a great deal to lessen the pollution problem if you use your own discarded cans for plants. Grow parsely, dill, mint, chives and even flowers in these tin cans.

To start your back-to-the-soil movement, choose a vegetable that is easy to grow and one that you enjoy eating. There are many kinds of vegetables that can be grown even during the winter in some temperate zone areas. But no matter where you live, you can create the necessary climate with containers indoors and outdoors, with plastic and glass enclosures or lattice shade.

Plant a sanity garden and you reap a source of food and satisfaction as well as a real victory over the poisons in the market place and in the earth and atmosphere.

You could also be sowing the seeds for a new way of life that you will thoroughly enjoy.

Part Two

Growing Your Own

1

The Organic Gardener

How to Start

An organic gardener believes that the humus part of the soil must be maintained at a high level if his garden is to be productive and pleasurable.

He believes that soil is a living, breathing organism, and because it is alive, it should be fertilized and cultivated in a manner as close as possible to nature's own methods.

An organic gardener strives to keep the soil covered, either with a mat of growing plants or with a mulch of organic material.

An organic gardener uses natural mineral and organic fertilizers to build his soil. The main fertilizers he uses are colloidal phosphate, phosphate rock, ground limestone, granite, feldspar dust (for potash), bone meal, dry blood, soybean meal, compost and the various dried manure products.

Soluble chemical fertilizers and poisonous insecticides are avoided by organic gardeners, because they feel that these artificial stimulants and "disinfectants" compromise their desire for perfectly healthy soil and produce.

Finally—and most important—an organic gardener wants healthy food. He feels that a soil fertilized naturally produces richer food, which will in turn give him and his family the vitamins and minerals they need in abundant supply.

It's easy to be an organic gardener. In fact, it's so easy it's a wonder all gardeners aren't organic. Once everyone has a chance to see organic methods demonstrated, there will be darn few "artificial" gardeners left.

The main reason organic gardening is easy to do and produces good results is the fact that it forces people to pay attention to their soil and build its fertility. Organic gardening is basically organic soil building. We all know that probably 90 per cent of all garden failures are caused by poor soil. So by improving the fertility of his soil, the organic gardener prevents the major cause of poor gardening results.

The first step in becoming an organic gardener is to think about the step you are taking. Consider in your mind that you are embarking on a new adventure—a voyage of discovery into the world of nature's wonders. You are going to create in your own garden an environment for plant life that is supremely fertile and natural in conception. You are going to grow plants that are superior in size and in nutritional quality to the average produce available in the market.

Most important, think about the fact that your organic garden will be a demonstration of the "cleanliness" and spirituality of nature's design for life on this planet. Your organic garden will prove to you that our lives and the way we grow our food are still best conducted along the patterns set down by nature.

DUMP THE CHEMICALS

Artificial chemical fertilizers not only have no part in the organic method, but they symbolize the basic objections to "unnatural" gardening and farming. True, chemical fertilizers supply food elements that plants use, but their method of doing so is unnatural. Feeding a plant chemical fertilizers is basically the same as feeding a person intravenously. You can get needed food elements into the organism, but you are not doing it the natural way.

The food elements in chemical fertilizers are almost all soluble, while in nature plants are accustomed to getting nutrients from many insoluble sources. This solubility of chemical fertilizers leads to trouble in the soil. It unbalances the soil's supply of nutrients.

Soluble food elements occur rarely in nature. So man in his factories adds various acids and other processing chemicals to insoluble minerals to make them into soluble chemical fertilizers. After years of continued use, these chemicals which weren't really needed in the first place, build up in the soil and can even change its structure and tilth.

So the first practical step you can take in becoming an organic gardener is to stop using artificial fertilizers. Throw them out, give them away, sell them—the important thing is to stop using them. A couple of seasons hence you will look back on "The Day You Threw Away the Fertilizers" with the feeling that on that day you accomplished something concrete.

NATURAL FERTILIZERS

The organic method of gardening is just what its name implies—organic. As an organic gardener you will gain a new familiarity with compost, manure, garbage, spoiled hay, straw, sawdust, peat moss, weeds and all other sources of humus for the soil. Just as chemical fertilizers symbolize man's vanity in setting up a chemical method of gardening, humus symbolizes the spirit of cooperation with nature that is the core of the organic method. Organic matter and pulverized rocks are the two substances which nature combined to form soil in the first place, and it's through these two substances that you as an organic gardener will work to maintain and improve soil naturally.

Pulverized rock powders assume a major role in organic gardening as a substitute for chemical fertilizers. (In reality, chemical fertilizers were man's first substitute for pulverized rocks that nature gave to the soil, so instead of substituting for chemical fertilizers we are just going back to the original product.) Major nutrients—calcium, phosphorous and potash—are supplied by these natural mineral fertilizers—along with a flock of very necessary trace elements.

Phosphate rock is a widely used natural rock fertilizer. It's mined in Florida and Tennessee and is an abundant source of phosphorous. Granite dust and greensand marl are two good natural sources of potash, an important major plant nutrient. Both these products also contain trace minerals, and phosphate rock carries quite a bit of calcium with it.

Key to Gardening Success: Compost

At the very base of the organic method lies compost. In its many forms and variations compost is the beautiful substance which gives fertility to soil, productivity to plants and health to man. It is the combination soil conditioner-fertilizer of the organic gardener and the hub of all his gardening activities. If you are a successful compost maker, chances are 100 to 1 that you are a successful organic gardener.

In the past two decades there has been a great amount of research in composting methods, resulting in the 14-day method, sheet composting, anaerobic methods and other variations. The foundation, however, is the original Indore method, developed by the father of the organic method, Sir Albert Howard. The Indore method is still the most widely used and is still practical and productive.

Sir Albert Howard found that when different organic materials were layered, decomposition took place more quickly and more completely. He started with a five or six-inch layer of green matter, then a two-inch layer of manure (blood meal, bone meal, sewage sludge or other nitrogen-rich material may be substituted), and a layer of rich earth, ground limestone and phosphate rock. This simple formula produced a rich, crumbly compost, high in nutrient value and valuable as a soil structure builder. In further research, Howard found that a heap five to ten feet wide, and five feet high, was ideal (the length is optional). He also found that decomposition was facilitated by aeration, so he placed pipes or thick stakes through the pile as it was being built, then pulled them out when the heap was five feet high. He then lightly pressed the entire outside surface to prevent blowing, formed a shallow basin on top to catch rainwater, covered the entire surface with a thin layer of earth and left the pile to decay.

COMPOSTING VARIATIONS

Organic gardeners have taken Howard's core of compost research and produced beautiful compost and beautiful gardens. Take the example of O. A. Severance of Watertown, New York, who transformed a completely unproductive piece of land into a lush garden spot, all through the use of compost. Severance makes compost in a pit, surrounded by a wall of loose fieldstone seven feet square on the inside and two feet high. The wall is laid on top of the ground and the soil inside is dug out a foot deep.

Into this pit go hen and stable manure, leaves, weeds, garbage, lawn clippings, sunflower stalks, some sod and ground limestone. The pile, layered according to Howard's Indore process, is level with the top of the stones when it is completed. Severance turns the pile in three weeks when he estimates the temperature has reached 150 degrees. Four weeks later he turns the pile again, to be sure all material has a chance to get into the center of the heap where decomposition is proceeding most rapidly. In a total of three months he takes out well over two tons of finished compost. In this way he can make two piles each season.

Gardeners often devise ways to improve the Indore method, at least in their own gardens. Lois Hebble of Decatur, Indiana, uses a strip composting method. In the middle of the growing season, she lays heaps of organic materials on top of vegetable rows from which she has just harvested early crops. The material is partially composted by the next spring, but is not broken down enough for small seeds. Into these rows she plants melons, squash or cucumbers.

"For each hill," says Mrs. Hebble, "I scoop out a small hole and fill this with a shovelfull or two of garden soil, then plant the seeds in this. Later in the summer, just before the vines start spreading out too much, I cover the strip with a good weed-smothering layer of old hay. By the following spring the soil under this strip has become mellow and homogenized enough to plant the smaller seeds. This method also keeps the garden crops in constant rotation."

Other gardeners use variations of the earthworm bed, sheet composting, mulching, pits, bins, shredding and numerous devices in trying to find the best method for them. You, too, can experiment with different methods to find *your* way of composting. But, remember, that the key to success is the Indore method. Learn it well and anything is possible.

HOW TO USE COMPOST

Now let's examine some of the better methods of garden compost application.

When to Apply: The principal factor in determining when to apply compost is its condition. If it is half finished or noticeably fibrous, it could well be applied in October or November. By spring it will have completed its decomposition in the soil itself and be ready to supply growth nutrients to the earliest plantings made. Otherwise, for general soil enrichment, the ideal time of application is a month or so before planting. The closer to planting time it is incorporated, the more it should be ground up or worked over thoroughly with a hoe to shred it. A number of garden cultivating tools and machines offer excellent time-and-labor-saving help.

If your compost is ready in the fall and is not intended to be used 'til the spring, it should be kept covered and stored in a protected place. If it is kept for long periods during the summer, the finished compost should be watered from time to time.

How to Apply: For general application, the soil should be stirred or turned thoroughly. Then the compost is added to the top four inches of soil. For vegetable gardening, it is best to pan the compost through a half inch sieve. Coarse material remaining may then be put into another compost heap.

In an orchard, time can be saved by making the compost right under the tree. It acts as a mulch. Start about three feet away from the trunk, applying the raw materials as if you were making compost. Instead of making the heap five feet high, make it only about two feet high. To hasten the formation of compost, a large quantity of earthworms can be placed in the material.

Where compost is desired to aid a growing crop, there are cautions necessary to avoid injuring plant roots growing near the surface. To avoid disturbing the roots of established plants, the compost should be mixed with topsoil and the mixture applied as a mulch. This is the best means of adding what is often termed a top dressing. It serves a double purpose in that while it is providing plant food which will gradually work itself down to the growing crop, it also affords an effective mulch to the soil, giving protection from extremes of temperature, hard rains, and so forth.

How Much to Apply: In gardening for best results, compost should be applied liberally, from one to three inches per year. Within a few years your garden will become the wonder and envy of your neighborhood. Of course, you can get by with as little as a half inch of compost, but in gardening with small plots, a heavy hand won't hurt. There is no danger of burning due to overuse, which is the case with the chemical fertilizers. You can apply compost either once or twice a year. The amount depends, of course, on the fertility of your soil and on what and how much has been grown in it. Incidentally, an average figure of weight for one cubic yard of compost (27 cubic feet) is 1,000 pounds. There would be variations depending on the materials used and the length of time composted.

In an orchard, compost should be applied under each tree. Start about two to three feet away from the trunk, and go to about a foot beyond the drip-line at the end of the branches. How thick shall it be applied? If you are going to use annual applications a half inch to an inch will do. First cultivate under the tree to work the grass mat into the soil; then work in the compost, keeping it in the upper two inches. It's a good practice to follow this with a mulch of old hay or other green matter. A layer of compost about three or four inches thick would be sufficient for three or four years.

Compost is the foundation of the organic gardening idea because it is the foundation of your garden. With an abundant supply of good compost, your garden will thrive. Compost is simple to make and simple to use. It's the key to your gardening success.

The Labor-Saver: Mulch

Mulching is a layer of material, preferably organic material, placed on the soil to conserve moisture, hold down weeds, and ultimately improve soil structure and fertility. As with composting, mulching is a basic practice in the organic method.

Experiments have shown these advantages:

1. A mulched plant is not subjected to the extremes of temperatures of an exposed plant. Unmulched roots can be damaged by the heaving of soil brought on by sudden thaws and sudden frosts. The mulch acts as an insulating blanket, keeping the soil warmer in winter and cooler in summer.

2. Certain materials used for a mulch contain rich minerals, and gradually, through the action of rain and time, the nutrients work into the soil to feed the roots of the plants. Some of the minerals soak into the ground during the first heavy rain. Mulch thus fertilizes the soil while it is on the soil surface as well as after it decays.

3. For the busy gardener mulching is a boon indeed. Many back-breaking hours of weeding and hoeing are practically eliminated. Weeds don't have a chance to get a foothold, and the few that might manage to poke through the mulch can be pulled out in a jiffy. And since the mulch keeps the soil loose, there is no need to cultivate.

4. A mulch prevents the hot sun and drying wind from penetrating to the soil, so its moisture does not evaporate quickly. A few good

soakings during the growing season will tide plants over a long, dry spell. A mulch also prevents erosion from wind and hard rains. Soil underneath a mulch is damp and cool to the touch. Mulched plants often endure a long, dry season with practically no watering at all.

5. At harvest time vegetables which sprawl on the ground, such as cucumbers, squash, strawberries and unstaked tomatoes, often become mildewed, moldy or rotten. A mulch prevents this damage by keeping the vegetables clean and dry. This is the season when most gardens begin to look unkempt. But the mulched garden always looks neat and trim, no matter what the season. Mud is less of a problem.

SOME CAUTIONS

There are some potential disadvantages of mulching.

1. Seedlings planted in very moist soil should not be mulched immediately. Keeping the soil at a high humidity—which a mulch does—encourages damping-off of young plants. Damping-off is a disease caused by a fungus inhabiting moist, poorly-ventilated soil. Allow seedlings to become established before mulching.

2. It is wise, too, to consider the danger of crown-rot in perennials. This disease is also caused by a fungus. If there have been especially heavy rains, postpone mulching until the soil is no longer water-logged. Do not allow mulches composed of peat moss, manure, compost, or ground corn cobs to touch the base of these plants. Leave a circle several inches in diameter. The idea here is to permit the soil to remain dry and open to the air around the immediate area of the plant.

3. Do not mulch a wet, low-lying soil, or at most, use only a dry, light type of material, such as salt hay or buckwheat hulls. Leaves are definitely to be avoided, as they may mat down and add to the sogginess.

The heavy mulching method, advocated by Ruth Stout, stands a better chance of success if the soil contains some humus (well-decayed organic matter) and is fairly high in nitrogen content.

Where the soil is poor and mostly clay in composition, it is best to test the soil and apply the needed major elements—nitrogen, phosphate and potash—according to test results. Then spread the mulch in thin layers without packing, to permit air and moisture to start breaking down the raw material. When the first layer of mulch shows signs of decay, sprinkle some cottonseed meal, blood meal or other nitrogen-rich material and apply another thin layer of mulch. By this method, any danger of the heavy mulch taking too much nitrogen from the soil is avoided.

With the few cautions noted, the gardener really can't do without mulching as a wonderful labor-saving helpmate.

MULCHING MATERIALS

When you set out to mulch a home garden of any considerable size, there are three factors to be considered: 1) how the material will affect the plants, 2) how the completed mulch will look, and 3) how easily and inexpensively the mulch may be obtained. Following is a list of commonly used mulch materials that have been found beneficial by many organic gardeners.

Grass Clippings: Fairly rich in nitrogen, grass clippings are useful as a green manure to be worked into the soil, for adding to compost heaps or for mulching. Clippings from most lawns contain over one pound of nitrogen and two pounds of potash for every hundred pounds of dry clippings.

Leaves: An abundant source of humus and mineral material, leaves are especially valuable for use around acid-loving plants. (Some leaves, as sugar maple, however, are alkaline.) They may be applied as a mulch or used for composting.

Sawdust: A very useful mulch material that should be used more widely. When plants are about two inches high, a one-inch layer can be applied. Prior to spreading the sawdust, many gardeners side dress with a nitrogen fertilizer as cottonseed meal, blood meal and tankage.

Seaweed and Kelp: High in potash (about five per cent) and trace elements. Many seaweed users apply it fresh from the sea; others prefer washing first to remove salt. It can be used as a mulch, worked directly into the soil or placed in the compost heap. Dehydrated forms are available commercially.

Wood Chips: Like sawdust and other wood wastes, wood chips are useful in the garden. They have a higher nutrient content than sawdust, and do a fine job of aerating the soil and increasing its moisture-holding ability.

Corn Stalks: Three or four inches deep, they provide a well-aerated winter mulch. Lay the stalks criss-cross with tops and butts alternating. Shredded, the stalks make a fine garden mulch.

Straw: This is clean, contains no weed seeds, is inexpensive, quick and easy to lay down, and it looks presentable. Once it has been applied it remains in place an entire season. In fall, dig it in, and by spring it will have become an indistinguishable part of the soil. It is estimated that one ton will give a one-inch mulch on an acre of land.

Corn Cobs: Ground into one-inch pieces, they have many uses. The sugar content will help to increase the microorganisms in the soil, and these will give a better soil granulation.

Pine Needles: Good for strawberries the year around. Keep in mind that they can be a fire hazard when dry. Use a two- to four-inch mulch and renew it every day.

Alfalfa Hay: Coarse and ragged in appearance, it is most easily handled when green and freshly cut. It has a high nitrogen percentage and will meet the needs of fruit trees. Rain-spoiled hay can always be used as a mulch material, so there need be no waste here.

Packing Materials: Trees and plants ordered from nurseries usually come packed in sphagnum moss or redwood shavings. Breakables shipped from out of town arrive packed in excelsior or shredded paper. Save these materials and use them as mulches, alone or mixed with other materials.

Weeds and Native Grasses: These make an excellent mulch around trees, where it is important to build a deeper covering than used in the garden and where this sort of mulch does not look out of place. They should be exposed to the air before applying to prevent rooting. They may be shredded to make a neat appearance and can be mixed with grass clippings.

Peat Moss: This is the partially decomposed remains of plants accumulated over centuries under relatively airless conditions. Though it doesn't contain any nutrients, peat moss serves to aerate the soil, to improve drainage and ultimately to help plants absorb nutrients from other materials. An inch or more can be spread and worked into vegetable gardens. It's extremely useful as a mulch.

Protecting Your Plants

Once you've mastered the art of composting, have your seeds and seedlings in the garden and a layer of mulch blanketing the earth, your thoughts will turn to protecting them.

The ideal way of protecting crops from diseases and injury is to develop resistant varieties. Much progress has already been made in this work, so when you're checking plant catalogs, be sure to look for such terms as "immune" or "slightly susceptible" in descriptions of plant resistance.

A big step in any control program is knowing who the villain is. With a little practice, you can learn to recognize at a glance the signs and symptoms of common pests.

The various chewing insects make their own patterns. Flea beetles make tiny round perforations; weevils produce rather typical angular openings; beetle larvae (grubs) "skeletonize" leaves, chewing everything but the epidermis and veins.

Sucking insects cause leaves to be yellowish, stippled white or gray. These insects, as well as their brownish eggs or excrement, can often be seen on the underside of foliage. Red spider can be spotted by yellowed leaves that are cobwebby or mealy underneath; whitish streaks mean thrips. When leaves are curled up, or cupped down, look out for aphids. Deformed leaves may be caused by cyclamen mite; blotches or tunnels by leaf miners; round or conical protrusions by aphids, midges or gall wasps.

The partial collapse and dying of a plant, termed *wilt*, may result from a number of causes—very often nematodes or grubs.

No one would think of going out of his way to visit someone who has a contagious disease. Yet this phenomenon occurs daily in gardens everywhere. The amusing hobby of keeping a "pet" diseased plant for anyone to handle should not be tolerated; it is very dangerous. Everyone who enters the garden is shown it and asked if he or she knows what the trouble is. While giving an opinion, the visitor does the natural thing—turns up the leaves to see the disease underneath, later examining plant after plant in similar manner, thereby infecting the entire garden.

There is a strong case for isolation and destruction of diseased and insect-ridden plants. Recent experiences show that it is not a good practice to use such plants as a mulch or in sheet composting. It's risky trying to use infected plants, except in the compost heap, and even then, you must be careful. When in doubt, it's better to destroy such material, and to make certain of not spreading the trouble.

Using resistant varieties of plants, nourishing them well and, when disease occurs, avoiding making the ailing plant a curiosity all contribute to the success of your garden. There are, of course, many other natural means of protecting your garden.

SAFE INSECTICIDES

When insect damage has been severe, organic gardeners have made use of certain non-toxic sprays ranging from miscible oil to pepper juice.

Used properly, for example, a three per cent miscible oil dormant spray is effective against a host of chewing and sucking insects. Aphids, red spider, thrips, mealybugs, whiteflies, pear psylla, all kinds of scale insects and mites fall before it. The eggs of codling moth, oriental fruit moth, various leaf rollers and cankerworms are destroyed.

A dormant spray is applied to orchard trees before any of the buds open. Some gardeners make it a practice to use it on all dormant trees, shrubs and evergreens every spring, but this is rarely necessary if the plants have been organically grown for a number of years. Fruit trees, however, have many enemies and dormant spraying should be a regular practice for them, along with a strict program of sanitation.

Ryania, another safe insecticide, is a powder made by grinding up the roots of the South American plant *Ryania Speciosa*. Although it is useful in controlling corn borers, cranberry fruitworm, codling moth, Oriental fruit moth, cotton boll worm and other insects, Ryania has little effect on warmblooded organisms.

The use of Ryania may not actually reduce the number of harmful insects present, but it will protect the crop by making the pests sick enough to lose their appetites. Some species are not killed outright by it. They are induced into a state of "flaccid paralysis."

Rotenone, sometimes called derris, is an insecticide derived from certain tropical plants, derris, cube barbasco, timbo and a few others. It is a contact and stomach poison, often mixed with pyrethrum, and is of very low toxicity to man and animals. Like pyrethrum, it can be obtained in the pure state only from pet shops and veterinarians. When purchased in commercial dusts and sprays, rotenone is often mixed with synthetic compounds that may be toxic in varying degrees. Devil's shoestring (Tephrosia virginiana) is the only native plant which contains rotenone. It is a common weed in the eastern and southern states, and its roots may be as much as five per cent rotenone. Rotenone can be safely used on all crops. It kills many types of insects and also certain external parasites of animals. However, it has little residual effect and the period of protection it offers is short.

We don't give an unqualified recommendation for Ryania and Rotenone or any other plant-derived insecticides. There are many organic gardeners who are proud of the balanced insect populations in their gardens and who don't need any other insect controls. Among these gardeners are those who use biological controls or practice companion planting.

PLANT A COMPANION GARDEN

Try a companion garden, where each plant is grown along with others that it "likes", away from those it "dislikes."

There is no explanation given for much of the information on companion plants. "Carrots and dill dislike each other" is all the usual treatment says. No one knows why tomatoes, asparagus and parsley are supposed to make a companionate threesome. But the value of some types of companionate planting can be explained.

Plants with deep root systems enlarge the feeding area of plants with shallow systems by plunging through compacted subsoil and loosening the ground. And beans can use corn to grow on.

When planting a companion garden, it's good to get the companions right in there together. One way is to plant zig-zag rows, with the zigs and zags of the beets and onions tucked into one another. Another method is to use the techniques of intercropping, and plant several companions in the same row. You'll find that your companionate garden breaks down into loosely defined "sections". The corn, squash, cucumbers and pumpkins might be in one section. The strawberries, spinach and beans might be in another. Paths are best between these sections, rather than between companions. Plant borders of wormwood, yarrow, and marigolds. Sprinkle these and the other insect-repelling herbs and flowers among the vegetables, checking the chart to make sure you're not near a foe instead of a friend.

Make up your own companionate garden by using the accompanying chart. Just remember that while your cucumbers like your peas, and your peas like your beans, and your beans like your potatoes, your potatoes just don't like cucumbers.

A List of Common Garden Vegetables, Their Companions and Their Antagonists

Vegetable	Likes	Dislikes
Asparagus	Tomatoes, parsley, basil	
Beans	Potatoes, carrots, cucumbers, cauliflower, cabbage, summer savory, most other vegetables and herbs	Onion, garlic, gladiolus
Pole Beans	Corn, summer savory	Onions, beets, kohlrabi, sunflower
Bush Beans	Potatoes, cucumbers, corn, strawberries, celery, summer savory	Onions
Beets	Onions, kohlrabi	Pole beans
Cabbage Family (Cabbage, cauliflower, kale, kohlrabi, broccoli, Brussels sprouts)	Aromatic plants, potatoes, celery, dill, camomile, sage, peppermint, rosemary, beets, onions	Strawberries, tomatoes, pole beans
Carrots	Peas, leaf lettuce, chives, onions, leek, rosemary, sage, tomatoes	Dill
Celery	Leek, tomatoes, bush beans, cauliflower, cabbage	
Chives	Carrots	Peas, beans
Corn	Potatoes, peas, beans, cucumbers, pumpkin, squash	
Cucumbers	Beans, corn, peas, radishes, sunflowers	Potatoes, aromatic herbs
Tomato	Chives, onion, parsley, asparagus, marigold, nasturtium, carrot	Kohlrabi, potato, fennel, cabbage
Eggplant	Beans	
Peas	Carrots, turnips, radishes, cucumbers, corn, beans, most vegetables and herbs	Onions, garlic, gladiolus, potato
Squash	Nasturtium, corn	

Vegetable	Likes	Dislikes
Onion (including garlic)	Beets, strawberries, tomato, lettuce, summer savory, camomile (sparsely)	Peas, beans
Leek	Onions, celery, carrots	
Lettuce	Carrots and radishes (lettuce, carrots and radishes make a strong team grown together), strawberries, cucumbers	
Radish	Peas, nasturtium, lettuce, cucumbers	
Parsley	Tomato, asparagus	
Potato	Beans, corn, cabbage, horseradish (should be planted at corners of patch), marigold, eggplant (as a lure for Colorado potato beetle)	Pumpkin, squash, cucumber, sunflower, tomato, raspberry
Pumpkin	Corn	Potato
Soybeans	Grows with anything, helps everything	
Strawberries	Bush bean, spinach, borage, lettuce (as a border)	Cabbage
Spinach	Strawberries	
Sunflower	Cucumbers	Potato
Turnip	Peas	

BIOLOGICAL CONTROLS

One of the best methods of protecting your garden plants from insect pests is with biological controls.

Biological insect control can be defined as "The practice of reducing the numbers of a pest by the use of natural agencies such as parasites, predators and diseases. The aim of biological control is to achieve the most practical means of pest control. The fundamental basis of such control is the fact that life in nature exists in a state of balance which is maintained by the competitive inter-action of various forces. However, man through his diverse activities frequently disturbs this natural balance, often with disastrous results to his own well-being."

To pit insect against insect is to identify and encourage the natural enemy of a pest in order to help keep it under control. Another promising development is the synthesizing of "juvenile hormones," substances similar to an insect's own natural hormones which regulate its growth. Applied in microscopic quantities at the right time, the hormones can prevent insect larvae from growing into adults and reproducing.

Still another exciting area of research is the use of microbes to fight insects. So far, some 280 insect viruses have been isolated. Unlike chemicals, but like natural enemies and hormones, viruses are highly specific. A strain of virus will kill just one type insect and will harm no other form of life.

The bug-eat-bug method of insect control is entirely reasonable. It encourages a healthy natural balance in the garden, orchard, or park. It avoids more contamination of our air and food with toxic sprays, and prevents further harm to wild life and pollution of the environment. And it actually costs far less.

So that you can understand how economical the method is and contrast it with the expense of spray equipment and poisons, we emphasize costs: ladybugs, $6.50 a gallon, from 100,000 to 125,000 per gallon. Average gardens need only a pint or two for protection from aphids, mites, scale insects, and so on. An adult ladybug eats 40 to 50 of them a day. Praying mantis cases, which hatch up to 400 insect- and pest-egg-eating young each, currently sell 8 for $3. Trichogramma wasps, 500 or more at a price of about $3. They come on a card because they are practically microscopic and are especially valuable in fruit orchards. By no means will the ladybug eliminate all insect problems in the garden, but aphids *are* its favorite food. Each ladybug consumes 40 to 50 aphids a day and will feed on other insects, eggs and larvae. The heavy-eating ladybug has several built-in protection factors. Water will not wash the beetle off the plant, and when other insects attack the ladybug, she exudes a smelly fluid detering the attacking insect.

Many people are now using ladybugs as a control in gardens, yards, greenhouses, parks, alfalfa fields, cotton and corn growing areas.

Praying mantises do their work, too. And they are "a lot friendlier than a can of DDT," says Edward S. Fisher, who raises the insects to control populations of other insects in his Billings, Montana yard. The mantises, which grow to two or three inches long, will eat any insect they can catch, including wasps. He started raising them several years

Where to Get
Biological Controls

LADYBUGS

Bio-Control Company
Route 2, Box 2397
Auburn, California 95603

L. E. Schnoor
Rough & Ready, California 95975

PRAYING MANTISES

Eastern Biological Con. Co.
Route 5, Box 379
Jackson, New Jersey 08527

Gothard, Inc.
P.O. Box 332
Canutillo, Texas 79835

Robert Robbins
424 N. Courtland
East Stroudsburg, Pennsylvania 18301

LACEWING (APHID LIONS) AND TRICHOGRAMMA WASPS

Vitova Insectary, Inc.
P.O. Box 475
Rialto, California 92376
Trik-O (Trade name for Trichogramma)

Gothard, Inc.
P.O. Box 370
Canutillo, Texas 78935

MILKY SPORE DISEASE

Doom
Fairfax Biological Laboratory
Clinton Corners, New York 12514

BACILLUS THURINGIENSIS DISEASE

Thuricide
International Minerals & Chemical Corp.
Crop Aid Products Dept.
5401 Old Orchard Rd.
Skokie, Illinois 60076

Biotol
Kobes Dist. Co.
Orange City, Iowa 51041

ago, purchasing eggs from a California firm every year. Fisher comments that 50 cents worth of mantises is enough to last all summer.

GETTING THE BIRDS TO HELP

One of the most successful and cheapest ways to control insects about gardens and farms is to get myriads of birds to do much of the work. Sixty or more helpful species of birds can be attracted to help with the eradication work in any agricultural area of the United States.

There are many ways of attracting these friends to your garden. In spring and summer provide suitable nesting areas and provide some suitable materials for making nests, so the birds will not have to carry materials far. While birds are very resourceful, a few strings, rags, hair, and feathers always help.

Most of the wonderful insect-eating birds prefer to build close to nature, but *more* of them will build near places where you want them to be if it is a *safe place* and has plenty of building material nearby.

Another rule that is a very important one is *provide water* for the birds, especially near nesting times, so the parents will not need to leave the eggs or the baby birds in search of water.

You also should provide water in places that are high enough for the safety of young birds when they are learning to fly, and for the older birds when they are weary from long flying.

After a house, materials and water, the fourth secret or rule for success in attracting birds is to provide feeding supplements, especially during the cold, hard winter. Good use can be made of dried seeds of melons and pumpkins which have been used earlier in the year. Dried baked goods are always good; rolled oats are good; crushed egg shells are sometimes greatly relished.

Companion planting of a different sort from that already mentioned will invite bird friends to your garden. Be sure to include sunflowers, cosmos, marigolds, asters or California poppies in your planting. These will encourage many weed-seed consumers to remain around your land.

However, a little care is in order if you've got fruits and berries growing. Your bird friends can be pests unless you plan for them. And companion planting is a good way.

Birds do *not* prefer the sweet, juicy fruits we humans enjoy. Instead, they like the bitter, sour, arid, or aromatic fruits we find distasteful.

Only when these fruits are unavailable do the birds steal from us.

The wild cherry or chokecherry, serviceberry, dogwood, thorn apple, holly, mountain ash, hackberry and mulberry are trees which not only produce colorful fruit but also beautiful blossoms in the spring. Among cherry trees, plant a mountain ash so the birds can enjoy its berries in preference to the sour cherries. Among apple trees, plant a dogwood or HOPA crabs. The contrast of the HOPA's deep pink blossoms to the pale blossoms of the DELICIOUS and MACINTOSH is breathtaking in the spring.

Berries from climbing plants are ornamental as well as appetizing to the birds. Wild grapes surrounding an arbor assure a peck-free domestic crop and bittersweet not only brightens any yard with its clusters of brilliant orange in the fall, but also provides delicacies for birds. Bittersweet can climb protectively on the fence near your everbearing strawberries. The Virginia creeper—seen throughout the United States—is another colorful ornamental vine whose small clusters of berries are savored by the birds, while the vine provides housing for their numerous species.

All these methods are simple, inexpensive and effective in protecting your fruits and vegetables from pests and diseases. But it's important to remember that the job of protecting your plants will be easier if your soil is charged with organic matter through composting and mulching. These are the keystones to organic gardening success.

2

Marketing Your Excess Produce

The Specialty Market

In one sense, of course, every organic vegetable garden more than pays for itself, since the money spent on it is returned several times over in the value of the superior food it produces, to say nothing of the pleasure of all the activities connected with it. In many localities, however, it is possible to make the garden pay for itself in cash, as well as in other ways. Where this can be done, all the usual advantages of gardening can be enjoyed free of charge. In other words, you can actually get paid to do what you would be happy to pay to do. All you need are a few close neighbors and some excess produce. Your neighbors presumably buy vegetables and there is no reason why they should not buy some from you, particularly since yours have a freshness and quality they cannot obtain elsewhere.

Now, there appear to be two main ways of making the home garden pay for itself. You'll have to choose which is best for you.

Briefly, the first type consists of doing the minimum of work and concentrating on a single specialty crop of high value. The second type includes methods of production and sale that involve a good deal of time and effort. They are best suited to gardeners who have retired from other work and who find the extra activity more enjoyable than not. Let's consider these alternatives in more detail.

The gardener who is regularly employed in a business or profession and who can harvest crops only in the evenings and on weekends can make his garden pay for itself by growing a specialty crop. The only real difficulty is in choosing the right crop to grow, and success depends almost entirely on your choice. Let us see what sort of product it should be.

1. It should be one that everyone particularly likes, so it can be sold without special effort. Your own favorite vegetable may not have such general appeal.

2. It should be easy to grow, with the minimum expenditure of time and labor. Crops that need thinning, weeding or much other attention are unsatisfactory.

3. It should be equally easy to harvest. Crops like peas and beans will not do at all. Strawberries, raspberries or blueberries are not much better.

4. It should have high value for the space it occupies. Radishes, cucumbers, squashes, carrots, beets and the like do not qualify.

5. The whole crop should be ready for sale over a short period. Since your time is limited, you want a specialty that can be marketed in a few evenings or over a weekend.

6. The quality of the product should depend primarily on its freshness, so your potential customers will recognize that nothing equally good can be bought elsewhere.

7. Your specialty should be a crop that is not grown by every neighbor with a dozen square feet of land at his disposal. In some areas, for instance, nearly everyone grows his own tomatoes and, though few may grow anything else, tomatoes would be the worst possible specialty.

As you consider these criteria for a specialty crop, you may find it hard to think of anything that meets all of them adequately. If so, you are not alone. But there is one crop that is ideally suited to the purpose and that is sweet corn. Fresh sweet corn is a delicacy that nearly everybody appreciates and one that comparatively few home gardeners grow.

Using some of the year-round system of mulching, in combination with close planting and manure or other organic fertilizer, an enormous crop of corn can be grown in a very small space. Virtually nothing has to be done to the crop between planting and harvesting, and the harvesting itself is extremely quick and easy. At prices of 75 to 95 cents a dozen, $10 worth of sweet corn can be gathered and sold in an hour or two. In an area as small as 12 feet by 25 feet you can easily grow more than 30 dozen ears of corn, which should sell for at least $20. This is actually a low figure. A good gardener should expect to do better.

A few suggestions on production and sale.

1. If you live in an area that is not liable to late frosts in the spring, you will do best to concentrate your efforts on a single crop of corn and to aim at having it ready to sell before any is available in the stores. In this way you will have a local monopoly at a time when demand is greatest, and you will be regarded as a public benefactor in selling it at premium prices.

2. If you cannot beat the market with your corn, it is well to grow two crops rather than one. Your early corn will thus be ready when your customers have had just enough of the store product to see how much better yours is and you can inform all of them that you will have even finer corn for them a few weeks later.

3. A few telephone calls should locate all the customers you can handle. If possible, get them to come after their corn in person and let them watch you harvest it. Customers who get their corn from you just before dinner, and cook it immediately, are going to come back for more. It will probably be the best they have ever eaten.

4. Husk all the corn as you harvest it, removing the silk cleanly, and snapping off any tips that are not filled out. This small trick takes very little time, and it enables you to see that every buyer gets perfect ears ready to cook. Explain to your customers that corn retains its flavor best if husked at once. This is not only good psychology, it also happens to be true.

5. Ask your customers what stage of maturity they prefer and try to give them what they like best. Since you inspect all the ears, this is easy enough to do and your buyers get corn that is virtually custom made.

6. Add an extra ear to each dozen without calling attention to the fact. Add two, if some of the ears are a trifle small. Customers who think your prices are high will change their minds when they discover this. Oddly enough, the extra corn is more appealing than a lower price would be.

7. Impress on everyone the importance of getting your corn to the table without delay. A customer who cannot do this should be told to get it into the refrigerator as soon as possible. Quality is what he

is paying for, and he will appreciate your care in seeing that he gets it.

The Diversified Market

A gardener with time on his hands can use some of it to advantage by simply growing more of all his favorite crops and keeping his neighbors supplied with a variety of vegetables through the season. He will have early peas for them in the spring and Brussels sprouts after the autumn frosts. In between, he will have such delicacies as baby carrots and beets, leaf lettuce, scallions, early cabbage and vine-ripened melons. He will have at least one or two items to offer each day of a quality that cannot be matched by any store anywhere. How much money he makes naturally depends on the scale of the operation; it may be anywhere from $20 to $100 or more. Whatever the size of the enterprise, it should easily pay the whole money cost of the garden that helps to support it.

Although every gardener must develop his own program in the light of local conditions, experience suggests that a number of general principles are likely to be applicable everywhere.

1. It is better to supply all the vegetables required by a few neighbors than to supply only part of those needed by a large number. If you are able to count on a steady, if modest, demand for your products, you can arrange your plantings on an appropriate plan, instead of growing crops haphazardly and then trying to find buyers for them. By dealing steadily with the same customers, you learn their preferences and can satisfy them better as time goes on. You can also keep your customers informed concerning crops shortly to be ready and they can tell you their needs for the near future.

2. Remember that the most noticeable superiority of your vegetables over those available elsewhere is their freshness and prime condition, and be sure that your customers get the full benefit of this. Explain the importance of getting peas and sweet corn served within minutes of harvesting and arrange in advance for delivery of such perishable items just before mealtime. Encourage buying for immediate needs and discourage buying ahead for storage. Pass along hints on preparation and serving that will preserve the full flavor of your vegetables.

3. Keep your garden looking neat and attractive and invite your customers to make some of their own selections on the spot. If they form the habit of calling in person for their vegetables, you can discuss the garden with them and let them watch you at "work." When you are pulling a bunch of carrots for a customer, and he sees you casually discarding one or two with slight imperfections, he appreciates what he is getting better than he otherwise could.

4. Be sure that everything you sell looks as good as it really is. Since nearly all vegetables in the stores look much better than they are, this means that yours must present a specially attractive appearance. Every gardener knows that a slightly crooked carrot or a cracked cabbage is exactly as good to eat as any other, and it is tempting to convey this intelligence to a customer along with the item in question. It is better, however, to save such things for your own use. When you must supply something short of the handsomest specimens, make the price a little lower than usual. Be firm, but unostentatious about this and it will leave fewer doubts about your standards than would any amount of conversation.

5. Do not be afraid to charge fair prices for your products. They are much superior to any available in chain stores or supermarkets, and they are likewise better than anything offered by roadside stands. It is the rare quality, rather than the cheapness of your vegetables that you should stress and that your customers are going to recognize. If any of your neighbors is unable to see how much better your products are than those he can buy elsewhere, you do not want him for a customer at all.

A good way to determine your prices is to check occasionally with the stores at which your customers trade and charge the nearest price above this figure that is evenly divisible by five. In other words, if snap beans are 27 cents a pound at the local stores, you charge 30 cents; if they are 33 cents, you charge 35, and so on. This makes bookkeeping easy, saves trouble in making change, and keeps your prices in line with market conditions.

6. Keep accurate records of cash expense and receipts. An excellent device for doing this is a low-priced five-year diary in which you enter purchases and sales each day, together with any other data you wish. A useful technique is to keep totals up to date as you go, circling these figures, or distinguishing them from the rest in

some other simple way. A five-year diary provides just the right amount of space for daily records, and has the special advantage of enabling you to compare the current year's operations with those of preceding years from day to day.

7. Do not undertake this method of making your garden pay for itself unless you are sure that you have ample time for it. If you are to supply one or more families with vegetables every day, you must be on hand to take orders and make deliveries whenever your customers choose to do business. To be sure, you can, by prearrangement with them, take a day or two off from time to time. But unless you mean to be at home as a rule for other reasons, you should not try to keep your neighbors steadily supplied with vegetables. Another way of making your garden pay will work better for you.

Although gardeners with limited time at their disposal are unlikely to be drawn into selling much besides their specialty crops, those who have plenty of time may be tempted to add the corn specialty to their other methods of making the garden pay. Since this effort can easily lead to trouble, it may be well to insert a word of warning here.

The difficulty in trying to combine the alternative ways of making your garden pay is that you must keep your markets separated, which is very hard to do. As soon as your numerous corn customers discover that you are supplying not only corn but all kinds of other vegetables to a few families steadily, they are going to want more than corn from you. If you refuse to sell them other vegetables, you are likely to lose valuable good will. On the other hand, if you try to sell what you can spare, these new customers are not going to be satisfied. At best, they will feel that they are getting what is left over after others have had their pick and this will be perfectly true. At least, it had better be true. If you became sufficiently demoralized, you might try to please your new customers at the expense of the rest and make a mess of the whole thing.

Choose the one alternative that fits your own situation, and make the most of it. If you do, you will find that making your garden pay its way financially is easy. You will also find that your garden is paying better than ever in enjoyment, quite apart from the money you make.

—*Richard V. Clemence*

3

Preserving Your Excess Produce

Storing Your Food Crops

The gardener who doesn't find himself with more vegetables than his family can consume is a rarity. We've already suggested how you can turn your excess produce into dollars through a small marketing program. But for all gardeners, it's also good economics to preserve the excess—without preservatives or additives, of course—so the fruits of your garden labors can be enjoyed throughout the year, rather than just during the harvest season.

For you organic gardeners, storing the surplus is especially advantageous because your vegetables are likely to be better keepers than those grown with chemical fertilizers and because they will be of far better quality and flavor than those bought in the supermarket. On all counts, therefore, you should give serious thought to the problem of winter storage.

There are four basic ways to successfully preserve foods—hold them in storage, or dry, can or freeze them. Elements of these processes overlap. You may find that just one suits your needs, or you may end up using all of them.

Vegetables—and all produce—can be roughly divided into three groups:

1. *The quickly perishable* such as green peas, green limas, corn and asparagus and green vegetables such as spinach, chard and lettuce.

2. *The slowly perishable,* in which we include broccoli, cauliflower, late cabbage and onions.

3. *The good keepers,* consisting of potatoes, turnips, beets, carrots and similar root crops, together with pumpkins, late squash and celery.

The three groups are not very sharply divided. Under proper conditions, late cabbage and onions will keep for a long time, but with them there is a greater danger of spoilage than with most root crops. Cauliflower and broccoli seldom remain in good condition for more than two or three weeks, so they almost belong in the quickly perishable group.

Given the proper facilities, the carrying of the good keepers through the winter is a simpler process than either canning or freezing, yet there are probably 10 households that freeze or can for each one that stores root crops without processing. It's common enough to store potatoes but few back yard gardeners seem to provide themselves with a winter supply of turnips, rutabagas, beets, carrots, onions and celery and even fewer trouble to put away pumpkins, squash, late cabbage or sweet potatoes.

Two obstacles seem to account for this: in the first place there is a good deal of uncertainty regarding the conditions needed; in the second, there is a feeling that such conditions are difficult to provide. Let's remove the uncertainty and learn the simple methods of providing the necessary conditions.

VEGETABLES

Chard, beets, carrots, turnips and *rutabagas* should be harvested in late November, after 30-degree nights. Root crops of this type can be stored by removing the tops—do not wash them—and placing in an area just above freezing, with 95 per cent humidity. They can be packed in cans, boxes or bins, surrounded by straw, or they can be placed in moist sand or in any of several outdoor storage pits or root cellars.

Cabbage and *Chinese cabbage* should be prepared for storage by removing loose outer leaves. If produce is to be wrapped, roots and stem should be removed; otherwise leave these in place. Wrapped cabbages should be stored at a just-above freezing temperature in a cool, damp area in boxes or bins. When stems and roots are left on, any of the outdoor storage ideas which call for damp soil or sand are effective.

Celery is best maintained by pulling the crop. Leave the tops dry—do not wash. The roots should be placed in slightly moist sand or soil, and the plant maintained at 32 to 34 degrees F. To avoid odor contamination, do not store with cabbage or turnips.

Parsnips, salsify, Jerusalem artichokes and often *carrots* can be left in the ground throughout the winter. To make digging easier, cover the rows with about one foot of leaves or straw before the ground has frozen.

Kohlrabi can be stored, after removal of leaves and roots, at 32 to 34 degrees with 95 per cent humidity. Root cellars and basement storage rooms are ideal locations.

Beans, soybeans and *peas* should be shelled and dried. To eliminate fumigation, which is the way commercial growers kill weevils, simply heat the crop in an oven for 30 minutes to an hour at a sustained temperature of 135 degrees. Spread the vegetable in pans for this treatment, and do not let the temperature drop or rise significantly, After drying thoroughly, place in jars or bags for storage. The temperature of the storage area is not important, but it must be dry.

Storage Containers

In most storage areas, there is a need for small containers. Here are several suggestions:

Wooden boxes—used for apples and other fruits originally, they make ideal small storage units to be placed in root cellars or larger areas. Interior packing can be leaves (dry and crisp), hay, straw, string-sphagnum moss or crumpled burlap. When stacking boxes, place furring strips between them, the floor and other tiers to permit full air circulation.

Metal tins—Adaptable for nut storage. Also can be used open-topped in place of barrels and boxes. Be certain that rusting is a minimal factor by using galvanized metals, or patch-painting raw metal areas.

Crates (orange) or mesh bags—excellent for onion storage. Remember to keep above freezing. Should onions ever freeze, allow them to thaw naturally before handling.

Bins—Used primarily in larger storage units, these can be constructed some four inches off the floor. Good for potato and other root crops.

Pails, baskets—similar treatment as boxes. Layer packing materials and produce alternately, finishing with two inches or more of packing at the top. Used in pit storage as well as larger units.

Water-tight barrels—pack similarly to the above. Use outdoors or indoors as described in storage area illustration.

Onions must be cured. Leave the vegetable on the ground after pulling for at least two to three days, then place in crates in an open shed for several weeks to complete curing. Remove the tops and store in bins or stringbags at temperatures ranging from 33 to 45 degrees with 60 to 75 per cent humidity. Attics often prove to be good storage areas.

Pumpkins and *squash* must also be cured. Leave them in the field for two weeks after picking. Leave a partial stem on the fruit, and take exceptional care to prevent bruising, storing only the best undamaged produce. After curing, place them gently on shelves, separated from each other, in a 50 to 60 degree dry place. They should last for five to six months.

Potatoes must be stored in the dark. For several months after harvest they can be held in almost any storage location, as this is their normal resting cycle. After this period, temperatures between 34 and 41 degrees are necessary to prevent sprouting. The lower temperatures tend to turn starch to sugar and sweeten the vegetable. Only experience with the crop will enable you to determine proper storage in your area. During the storage period, moisture should remain high. Never store with apples.

Sweet Potatoes should be free from injury and need to be cured before final storage. One writer suggests the wooden floor of a barn driveway which can be opened at both ends, as an ideal curing site. Lots of air circulation and high temperature over a period of ten days to three weeks is necessary to eliminate excess water, change some starch to sugar and cause "corking over" of cuts in the skin. After curing, sweet potatoes should be placed in a warm, 50-to-60 degree room which is well ventilated with moderate—up to 75 per cent—humidity.

FRUITS

Many major fruits do not take storage for extended periods of time. Of the ones that do (principally apples and pears), the varieties vary in keeping quality. The WINESAP and YELLOW NEWTON are among the best apples, frequently lasting from five to eight months satisfactorily. Next in keeping quality are the STAYMAN WINESAP, NORTHERN SPY, YORK IMPERIAL, ARKANSAS BLACK TWIG, BALDWIN, BEN DAVIS and ROME BEAUTY. Normal storage figures range from four to six months in this grouping. Among those apples which can be stored for shorter periods (two to five months) are the following: JONATHAN, MC INTOSH, CORTLAND and DELICIOUS (red or golden). Other factors must be considered: locality (i.e. MC INTOSH apples grown in New England store better than those grown in the Middle Atlantic States), seasonal conditions, maturity when picked and length of time between picking and storing.

Good keeping qualities are increased with careful handling to prevent bruising. Storage at between 30 degrees to 32 degrees and 85 to 90 per cent humidity is preferred for most varieties. YELLOW NEWTON, RHODE ISLAND GREENING and MC INTOSH are better when stored at 36 degrees to 38 degrees. Wrapping with oiled paper or in shredded oiled paper helps prevent scald, acknowledged to be the most serious disorder.

While many of the storage ideas mentioned in the vegetable section are suitable for fruit storage, fruit should never be stored with potatoes, turnips or cabbage. The gases released from apples in respiration can sprout potatoes, while cabbage and turnips can transmit their odor to apples and pears. Free air circulation in fruit storage areas is essential to remove volatile gaseous substances released by the produce.

Pears can be held for periods of from two to seven months depending on variety. WINTER NELIS, ANJOU and EASTER BEURRE are the most hardy, with BOSC, KIEFFER, BARTLETT, COMICE and HARDY in the lower range. Pears should be removed from the tree when their dark green coloring begins to lighten and the lecticels have corked over. Ideal storage is around 32 degrees with humidity in the 90 to 95 per cent range.

GRAINS

Growing organic grain is a satisfying operation, but improper storage can lose all the advantages inherent in the process. The old-time farmer used to cut and bind grain in sheaves, where it stood and cured gradually in the fields before being threshed. Today's mechanized methods save time, but have certain disadvantages. When grain is harvested by combine, it is cut, hulled and poured into 100 pound bags, but it is still "green" and must be treated with care to prevent mold. It may seem dry, but it will continue to give off moisture for over a month. Furthermore, wild garlic, ragweed and other seeds will be included in each bag. The grain must be cleared with a fan seed cleaner, or winnowed outdoors by throwing it up in a breeze or dropping it past a fan to blow away chaff. Once cleaned, bags should be placed on end on slats in a dry place (not on a dirt or concrete floor), and separated by several inches to allow air circulation. The presence of a good cat will prevent mouse damage—otherwise use a metal, screened enclosure. After a few days, invert the bags and disturb the grain to permit air to reach all kernels. Invert again each week for about a month after which time the grain should be cured. The most logical method for storage after curing is a metal drum in a dry place. We have indications that 40 degree temperature with humidity no higher than 50 per cent has proven effective for bulk storage. Small quantities can be stored in glass jars. Some people use their freezers which will keep grain indefinitely.

If grain becomes moldy from inadvertent exposure to moisture, it may not be a complete loss. Just wash in plain lukewarm water several times and dry over a hot-air furnace grate or similar source of warmth. You can tell from the smell whether it is still musty or not.

SEEDS

Many garden vegetable seeds can be stored for longer periods of time than might be suspected. We have known instances of squash or pumpkin seeds which sprouted after being shelved for as long as three or four years. Certain grains buried with the Egyptian pharaohs thousands of years ago have been planted and have grown. In general, low seed-moisture is the critical factor. It is important to maintain fairly cool temperatures and low humidity if seed is to be successfully held for long periods of time. Certain seeds, furthermore, adjust poorly to any attempt at storage . . . principally onion and shelled peanut, celery and sweet corn.

NUTS

The difference between prime flavor and bitterness depends largely upon how promptly outer hulls are removed. It is advisable to hull all varieties within a week after gathering. Black walnuts pose problems in that hulls are tough, porous and contain an acrid staining agent. An old-fashioned corn sheller is useful, but some growers spread the nuts on a hard road and drive over them until they are mashed. In either case, walnuts still in their inner shell should be washed before curing. After hulling all nuts should be dried gradually by exposure to moving air. A clean, cool, darkened well-ventilated location is best. Place nuts in wire trays (no more than two layers deep) for periods of two to six weeks until cured. After curing, nuts still in their shells may be stored in attics (for up to a year) but cool underground cellars may be preferable. Store them in large cellophane bags with ventilation holes punched in them, inserted in tin cans lined with paper and tightly closed except for a small hole below the lid. Store at 34 to 40 degrees and inspect regularly for mold or mildew. It is believed that moderately low temperatures keep the oil in the kernel from turning rancid.

Once a nut has been cracked and the kernel removed, the ordinary kitchen refrigerator is as good a depository as any. Kernels should be placed in tight jars or plastic bags and maintained at a temperature of 40 degrees or less. A deep freeze unit is also satisfactory.

—Charles Beck

Storage Areas For Your Food Crops

The old folks weren't so dumb when they devised "the old root cellar." The root cellar is probably one of the finest ways to preserve food, although construction costs may deter many people from bothering to build one.

But there are other ways proper storage environments can be achieved at less cost. We are tackling that aspect here, providing information on how many kinds of food should be stored, plus ideas and suggestions on how to build various enclosures. Some units are impossible to describe adequately in words. These are available from Rodale Press in the form of plans and specifications, complete with a material list and cost approximation. Hopefully, from our ideas and suggestions, you will be motivated to use your imagination, improvise, innovate and create inexpensive storage facilities of your own.

Charles Boxer of the Bucks County Natural Food Center in Richlandtown, Pennsylvania, just recently completed a new natural foods outlet that includes a storage facility. In the north corner of the basement a 13-by-18-foot concrete block room has been built. The cores of the blocks have been filled with loose granular insulation, while the ceiling contains full-thickness insulation rolls between the wood joists. The natural ground floor is covered with about four inches of crushed stone, allowing moisture in the earth beneath to penetrate upward.

Temperature and ventilation are controlled manually by a regular basement window installed on the outside concrete block north wall of the room. Incidentally, Boxer previously used his unheated crawl space under his old store for storage. He says that "although it wasn't the best, it did serve the purpose for awhile."

John Keck of the Organic Gardening Experimental Farm near Allentown, Pennsylvania, has taken an old truck body, supported the roof with pipe columns and light beams and sodded it down under earth. A small stairway down to the truck door acts as an entry.

Ventilation is provided through the roof in two places. Cost of materials including the truck was less than $150. Complete details are available.

Keck felt that if he had had a steeper bank in which to imbed the truck, coverage would have proven more satisfactory. The more earth coverage, the better the storage unit.

Another original, inexpensive method of off-season food storage is the outside cellar steps of your cellar entrance. Install an inside door to keep out basement heat, and if you want to create an even larger storage area, build inward into the basement, but take care to insulate the extra wall space. Temperatures in the stairwell will rise as you go up the steps, and a little experimenting will help you determine the best levels for the different crops you are storing. If the air is too dry, set pans of water at the warmest level for extra humidity.

In a pinch, window area wells can be utilized by covering the well. If basement windows open inward or are the sliding type, access can be convenient and simple during the cold winter months. If you are building, basement food storage rooms, greenhouses and exterior stairways can be combined as a unique additional feature to a contemplated new home.

AN ATTACHED STORAGE ROOM

In Myerstown, Pennsylvania, Enos Hess, with the help of his county farm agent, has constructed an extensive and unique storage facility in the form of a modern "old-fashioned root cellar." He has constructed a large garage-type building attached to the house in which he stores packaged foods. At the outside wall of the structure, and near the garage door, a door opens onto a stairway and conveyor belt which leads downward for about twelve feet.

Behind the door at the base of the steps is a 12-by-18 foot room with 12-inch-thick concrete block walls and a 10-inch thick reinforced concrete ceiling, covered by four solid feet of earth. The cellar is built over a natural spring which is covered by a four-inch-thick concrete slab. Hydrostatic pressure forces the cool water up though the slab, wetting the surface of the concrete floor. Wood slats lie over the concrete, and any excess water is pumped out of the cellar automatically.

Air circulation is most effective. Intake air entering through a 12-inch-round concrete overhead flue is directed out at the floor through an adjustable grill. The air is cooled as it passes over the water and flows through the room.

Asked why he installed a concrete floor when the water condition was as indicated, Hess explained there could be a muddy condition if he hadn't used concrete. He is so well-satisfied that when he builds an adjacent 12-by-30-foot room, he won't change this proven method one bit.

The flat ceiling created one problem he had not anticipated which will be solved in his new room. Condensation on the ceiling causes dripping all over the room. A tent-life installation of plastic sheeting slopping to either side of the room catches the water and directs it to the walls, and thence to the floor.

Hess has very successfully stored potatoes, beets and carrots in open boxes and celery and cabbage in plastic bags well into spring of the following year. After experimenting with ground limestone at the rate of 10 tons an acre on one acre of his land he found that, although slower in maturing, his produce had better storing qualities than ever before. All of his land has now been so treated. His large carrots, stored since October, cracked beautifully in half in mid-April. He also found that among his best storing onions were onion sets of the European STUTT-GART variety.

Have you ever thought of using railroad ties to construct your storage cellar? Or have you ever thought of using corrugated metal or concrete pipe culverts such as those used by highway departments? If these pipes, seven feet or better in diameter, are placed lengthwise or parallel into a bank, and covered over with adequate soil, access and through ventilation are available at both ends. Another idea is to place these culverts under the bank of a bank barn against the back outer wall of the barn. Here again, access and ventilation would be available from both ends.

Manufacturers of prefabricated walk-in coolers have indicated definite interest in this market. One company manufactures prefabricated walk-in cases of insulating styrofoam sandwiched between sheets of galvanized steel. Ceiling and wall construction is uniform throughout and a door of similar construction is included. As an example, a four-by-six room would cost about $1,000 shipped to you knocked down. Assembly instructions permit easy erection, and any saw will cut through the sandwich panel, thus giving access to an outside basement window. Additional information is available.

Another idea along the same lines is to use the prefabricated package manufactured by sauna bath companies. Here insulating styrofoam is sandwiched with plywood skins. A knockdown five-by-seven-foot room can be had for as little as $500 FOB.

Of course you don't have to build your rooms with prefabricated units. Walls can be constructed of concrete block, with insulation batts and plywood walls being still another method. In both cases the ceiling must also be sufficiently insulated. Detailed plans are available.

If you have a rodent problem, be extremely careful when using styrofoam rigid insulation board. "Styrofoam is a magnet for mice," says A. P. Thomson of Golden Acres Orchard, Front Royal, Virginia. Fiberglass, rigid foamglass or urethane boards seem to be effective substitutes and just as good insulators.

LARGE-SCALE STORAGE

Thomson has a beautifully balanced organic orchard consisting of 1,300 apple trees, GOLDEN DELICIOUS for the most part. Approximately one-tenth of the harvest fills his mail-order list. Another tenth is picked up in refrigerated trucks by Shiloh Farms of Sulphur Springs, Arkansas. The remainder of the harvest is stored against eventual conversion into apple juice and whole-apple cider vinegar which he patiently "lets age" in vats for a full year before bottling and selling.

The 40-by-40, 12-foot high storage room is situated in an outside, above-ground building. It's prefabricated steel and has insulated inner walls and ceilings made up of two units of three layers each of aluminum-sheathed fiberglass insulation. The concrete ground floor slab encases six inches of styrofoam. A list of similar, prefabricated steel build-ings situated across the country is available. Fungus growth developing on stored apples has been virtually eliminated by rinsing the apples with a seaweed concentrate solution prior to storing. The mixture, two ounces of kelp concentrate for every 100 gallons of water, is recom-mended for all types of produce.

Urban dwellers are now asking for natural foods year-round. Cogni-zant of this demand, the food supplier must consequently prepare for proper storage to supply fresh produce at any time. Some believe that natural food outlets should provide storage and refrigeration for up to 90 per cent of their consumer line.

The Kennedys of Falls Church, Virginia, have enormous storage facilities, both refrigerated and dry, in all three of their natural food outlets. All bread, produce and bulk flour are kept cold. Having saved a four-by-six foot walk-in cooler when they expanded, they are now using it for storing flour exclusively.

The refrigerator layout for the produce in the store has worked out beautifully. Employees walk into the cooler and refill shelves emptied by the customers. The consumer has full visual access through glass doors, and when the choice is made he opens the door, takes the prod-uct out and closes the door, allowing only minimal heat entry. Cool temperature recovery is swift and the produce remains fresh and appe-tizing.

Paul Keene's Walnut Acres in Penns Creek, Pennsylvania, produces canned and dry goods almost exclusively, but there is fresh produce in season and meat is also available. All the various grains are stored in a bin-divided 10,000-bushel-capacity storage room above the milling chamber, and when a particular grain is needed, it is poured through a funnel into the milling area where it is ground and bagged.

Cool air circulation in the refrigerated storage room is rather inter-esting. Not only is cold air forced down from the ceiling, but piping, which drops down between the wooden bin walls to the floor, blows cold air upward to assure complete cooling of all grain.

Insects and rodents are nonexistent. Keene was really worried one time when he spotted some grain moths flying about in the refrigerator as grain was coming in from the weeding out process. But the moths settled on the refrigerator wall, only to fall to the floor, dead. The

40-degree-plus temperature did it. Daily cleaning and vacuuming of the milling area eliminates insects there.

If insects and rodents are a problem, the following recent developments may be of some value. One is the use of ultrasonic devices. The other involves introduction of carbon dioxide. When forced into the upper portion of a storage area, the heavier CO_2 filters down through the space and smothers all life. Your local county agent should be able to supply further information.

Walnut Acres also has two large walk-in refrigerators for storing all of their root crops harvested on the farm. Portions are allocated for in-store selling, while the remainder is canned on the premises. Peanuts, stored in a portion of the cooled grain storage area, are roasted and ground into peanut butter daily.

STORAGE FOR THE HOMESTEAD

Rodale Press as an experiment, had a building designed by a professional architect and constructed on the experimental farm. The walls are a double thickness of concrete block with rigid insulation between, and the cores filled with loose insulation. The fully insulated hip roof overhangs the walls by about four feet on all sides, thus protecting them from the glaring midday sun.

A visit to Grace and Tim Lefever of Sonnewald Farm near Spring Grove, Pennsylvania, will substantiate your thinking about the advantages of storing fruits and vegetables.

Grain is simply and efficiently ground and stored. A secondhand supermarket coffee grinder is used for all grinding. "Hand grinding flour and grains is totally unreasonable," claims Tim Lefever, so grain is stored in reused large metal cans and is milled and bagged at time of sale or for use in the home. The storing area is the unheated shop and store outlet area.

Do you know of a supermarket going out of business, or remodeling and getting rid of their "useless junk"? With a little help, some effort, time and determination, you can have a six-cubic-foot cold storage unit sitting in your house for as little as $25! An insulated commercial ice-maker box was procured for that amount from a supermarket by the Lefevers.

At home, with the box in place in the unheated shops area, a new floor was constructed, and five-inch-deep styrofoam was placed between wood supports which were cut to a uniform slope to the center drain. The understructure was covered with plywood and finally faced off with a sheet metal floor. Although apples, beets, carrots, green beans, onions, potatoes, and turnips have been successfully stored over the past winter without the box being closed, a door will eventually be added.

The other pit is accessible from the inside of an outbuilding situated about 40 yards from the rear of the house, while a considerably smaller six-foot-square pit allowing additional storage of food is useable during less severe winter days.

These two pits have a natural earth floor in which all root crops are placed. The areas provided storage space for five bushels of beets, 15 bushels each of carrots and potatoes, three bushels of turnips, and about 30 bushels of apples. Artichokes were also stored after being harvested in the spring.

As you may have gathered by now, there is much to gain when you devise some method of storing and preserving your fruits and vegetables wholesomely.

—James Harter

Drying Vegetables and Fruits

General instructions for drying vegetables are to wash, trim and prepare as for serving in slices or strips approximately 1/8 inch thick or in cubes about 3/8 inch on each side. All except onions and herbs, which are used primarily for seasoning, should be blanched or precooked. Blanching may be done either with steam or with hot water.

Blanching with steam saves more nutritive value than does blanching with hot water and in commercial practice has given the best-quality product. A heavy kettle with a close-fitting lid is needed. The vegetable to be blanched is arranged *loosely* in cheesecloth or in a wire basket on a rack above one or two inches of rapidly boiling water. The lid is put on the kettle and a *constant active head of steam* is maintained during the entire blanching period. If food is packed tightly or if the active head of steam is not maintained, uneven or inadequate blanching will result. This causes serious flavor and color losses, as well as vitamin destruction.

Blanching with boiling water requires a large kettle containing a gallon of boiling water for each pound of vegetable to be blanched at one time. (Two gallons for each pound of leafy vegetable.) The vegetable is put loosely into cheesecloth or into a wire basket and immersed in the *boiling* water for the required length of time. If the cloth or basket is gently lifted up and down in the water, blanching probably is more even. Water blanching takes approximately two-thirds as long as does steam blanching.

Although steam blanching conserves quality and food value, some persons contend that water blanching is more practical in the home, as there is less danger of its being uneven or inadequate.

Commercially dried fruits contain large amounts of sulfur which is used to process the fruits before they are dried as a preventive for discoloration. Sulfured fruits should always be avoided, even though the unsulfured product is tougher, because it must be dried to a lower water content to improve its keeping qualities.

Where the atmosphere is arid in the fall, drying may be accomplished outdoors in the sun. Where heavy dews and frequent rains are the rule at harvest time, drying must be done in the oven, in a specially constructed drier or in a dry attic.

Fruit should be perfect for drying. Blemished or bruised fruits will not keep as well and may turn a whole tray of drying fruit bad. Wash and drain the perfect fruit and remove all inedible portions. The smaller the pieces to be dried, the briefer will be the drying time. Slice or quarter apples, peaches, pears or other large fruits. Place the pieces on clean trays or racks which have ventilated bottoms made of wire mesh or narrow wooden slats. The layer of fruit should be no more than one piece deep.

If drying is to be done outdoors, place the trays on raised racks above ground in a comparatively dust-free location. Turn the fruit often and cover the racks at night to prevent dew from settling on the fruit. Be sure to exclude animals of all kinds from the drying yard.

Drying by artificial heat is to be preferred if the heat can be closely regulated. Quick drying is better than slow, but the heat must not be sufficient to cook the fruit.

Drying is finished when the fruit feels dry on the outside but slightly soft inside. It should not be brittle, nor should it be possible to squeeze out any juice.

Drying Chart

Product	Drying time	Tempera- ture
Apples	4–6 hours	110°–150°
Apricots (let stand 20 minutes in boiling water)	4–6 hours	110°–150°
Cherries	2–4 hours	110°–150°
Peaches	4–6 hours	110°–150°
Plums (treat same as apricot)	4–6 hours	110°–150°
Rhubarb	6–8 hours	110°–130°

After the drying is finished, store the fruit in glass or cardboard containers. For four successive days stir the contents thoroughly each day to bring the drier particles in contact with some that are more moist. In this way the moisture content will be evenly distributed. If, at the end of the four days, the fruit seems too moist, return it to the drier for further treatment. When well dried and conditioned, the fruit should be stored in a cool place. It is better to examine it occasionally, to discover molds if they appear. The danger of molds is prevented if the dried product can be stored at freezing temperatures or below.

Canning Vegetables

Many of the principles concerning the quality of vegetables apply to canning as well as freezing. You should always choose young, tender vegetables, sorting them for size and maturity so they'll cook evenly. Always can vegetables quickly, while they are still fresh, preferably on the day you harvest them. This is especially important for vegetables, since a delay of even a few hours means change in flavor and the growth of many resistant bacteria.

TYPES OF CANNERS

There are three basic types of canners:

Steam-Pressure Canner. For safe use of the steam-pressure canner, clean the safety valve and petcock openings by drawing a string or narrow strip of cloth through them. A dial pressure gauge should be checked each year before the canning season. See your dealer or manu-facturer about checking it. A weighted gauge needs only to be thor-oughly cleaned.

Wash the canner kettle well before using it. Wipe the cover with a damp, clean cloth—don't put it in water.

When using the canner, follow the manufacturer's directions. At the end of processing time, be sure to let the pressure return to zero before opening the canner.

Pressure Saucepan. A pressure saucepan having an accurate indica-tor or gauge for controlling pressure at 10 pounds (240° F.) may be used for processing vegetables in pint jars or No. 2 cans.

Water-Bath Canner. Any large vessel will do for a boiling-water bath canner if it meets these requirements: It should be deep enough to have at least one inch of water over the top of the jars and an inch or two of extra space for boiling. It should have a snug-fitting cover. And there should be a rack to keep the jars from touching the bottom.

If your steam-pressure canner is deep enough, you can use it as a wa-ter bath. Set the cover in place without fastening it. Be sure to have the petcock wide open, so that steam escapes and no pressure is built up.

CONTAINERS

There are two basic types of containers that can be used: glass jars and metal cans.

Glass Jars. For processing foods in a boiling water bath or a steam-pressure cooker, use only jars made especially for canning, be sure all jars are in good condition, clean, and hot before packing food in them.

There are four types of closure for glass jars. Be sure to follow the sealing directions that come with each type closure. *Mason Top:* If porcelain lining is cracked, broken, loose, or if there is even a slight dent at the seal edge, discard the cover. Opening these jars by thrusting a knife blade into the rubber and prying ruins many good covers. Each time you use a jar, use a new rubber ring of the right size. The *Three-piece Cap* fits a deep-thread jar with or without a shoulder. The metal band holds cap in place during processing and cooling. Remove it when the contents of the jar is cold, usually after 24 hours. Use a new rubber ring each time. *Two-piece Cap:* Use the metal lid only once. The metal band is needed only during processing and cooling. Do not screw it further after taking the jar from the canner. Remove the band after the contents of the jar is cold, usually after 24 hours. *Glass Top with Wire Clamp:* Wire clamps must be tight enough to click when the longer one is snapped into place on the cover. Unless cracked or nicked, the glass cover may be used again and again, but a new rubber ring is needed each time. *Tin Cans:* Use only perfect cans and lids and gaskets. Wash the cans in clean water and drain them upside down. Do not wash the lids, as washing may damage the gasket. If the lids are dusty or dirty, wipe them with a damp cloth just before putting them on the cans.

Tin cans need a sealer. Be sure the sealer you use is properly adjusted. To test the sealer, put a little water in a can, seal it, then submerge the can in boiling water for a few minutes. If air bubbles rise from the can, the seal is not tight and you will need to adjust the sealer, following manufacturer's directions.

EXHAUSTING TIN CANS

The temperature of food in tin cans must be 170 degrees Fahrenheit or higher when the cans are sealed. Heating food drives out air and helps prevent loss of color and flavor. Hot sealing also keeps cans from bulging and seams from breaking. To get the right sealing temperature, pack food while it is hot or heat it in the open can (exhausting).

To exhaust tin cans, place the open, filled cans in a large kettle with boiling water about two inches below the tops of the cans. Cover the kettle, bring the water back to boiling and boil until the food reaches 170 degrees Fahrenheit (about 10 minutes). To be sure the food is heated enough, test the temperature with a thermometer, placing the bulb in the center of the can.

Remove the cans from water one at a time. Replace any liquid spilled from them by filling them with boiling packing liquid or water. Place clean lid on filled can. Seal at once and process.

Cans don't have to be exhausted if the temperature of food is 170 degrees or higher when the cans are filled. If you don't exhaust, work out the air bubbles after filling the cans. Add more boiling liquid if needed to fill the cans to top. Seal at once and process.

PROCESSING IN A BOILING-WATER BATH

High acid foods like fruit, tomatoes and pickled vegetables may be safely processed in a boiling-water bath.

General directions. Place filled glass jars or tin cans in a canner. If you've used a cold pack in glass jars, the water in the canner should be hot but not boiling. For hot pack in glass jars or for tin cans, have the water boiling. If necessary, after you have put the jars or cans in the canner, add enough boiling water to bring the water an inch or two over tops of containers.

Cover the canner and start timing the processing as soon as the water returns to a rolling boil. Process as long as necessary.

Out of the Canner. Unless the jars have self-sealing closures, complete the seals on *glass jars* as soon as you take them out of the canner. Set the jars on a rack, top side up and far enough apart so that air can circulate around them. Don't set hot jars on a cold surface or in a draft as sudden cooling may break the jar. Do not cover jars while they are cooling.

Cool *tin cans* quickly in cold water, using as many changes of water as necessary. Remove tin cans from the cooling water while they are slightly warm so they will dry in the air. If you must stack the cans, stagger them so that air can circulate around them.

PROCESSING IN A STEAM-PRESSURE CANNER

It is not safe to use a boiling-water bath for any vegetables other than pickled ones or tomatoes. The temperature of boiling water is not high enough to destroy spoilage organisms in low-acid foods in a reasonable length of time. By using a steam-pressure canner in good condition, however, you can obtain a temperature of 240 degrees Fahrenheit at 10 pounds of pressure—which is high enough to kill the organisms if the foods are processed for the required length of time.

Salting vegetables is not necessary. The small amount of salt used in canning does not prevent spoilage. To can unsalted vegetables use the same processing times recommended for salted vegetables.

In using the pressure canner, be sure to follow the manufacturer's directions. Some general pointers are given below:

General Directions. Put two or three inches of hot water in the bottom of the cooker. Set filled glass jars on the rack so the steam can circulate around each one. Tin cans can be staggered without a rack between layers. Fasten the cover securely so no steam escapes except at the open petcock or weighted gauge, and let the pressure rise to 10 pounds.

Start timing the processing as soon as 10 pounds of pressure is reached and process for the required time. Keep the pressure as uniform as possible by regulating the heat under the canner. At the end of the processing time, slide the canner away from heat.

Out of the canner. If you've used *glass jars,* let the canner stand until the pressure returns to zero. Wait a minute or two, then slowly open the petcock or remove the weighted gauge. Unfasten the cover and tilt the far side up so the steam escapes away from you. As you take the jars from the canner, complete the seals if jars are not the self-sealing type. Set the jars upright on a rack, placing them far enough apart so the air can circulate around all of them. Don't slow down the cooling by covering jars.

For *tin cans,* release the steam in the canner at end of the processing time by slowly opening the petcock or taking off the weighted gauge. When no more steam escapes, remove the canner cover. Cool the tin cans in cold water, changing it often enough to cool them quickly. Take the cans out of the cooling water while still slightly warm so they will air-dry. If you must stack the cans, stagger them so the air can get around them.

Canning Fruits

Small fruits, overripe fruits and defective fruits may be used to make jams and jellies, or they may be used in a much more healthful way in fruit purees or juices. Jams, jellies and other sweet preserves contain such large quantities of sweeteners (whether honey or sugar) that any nutritive value of the fruit is overshadowed by the concentrated sweets which supply nothing but calories.

The same fruits which might be used for jams and jellies can be more profitably stored for the family's winter use in the form of fruit juices and purees.

Nowadays, a wide selection of modern equipment—including some astonishingly quick and efficient blenders, liquefiers, juicers and mechanical presses—makes on-the-spot juice extraction of any fruits or vegetables supersimple. But if you don't own a mechanical juicer, you can use home improved equipment and methods to "put up" any fruit juices; you don't have to use automatic appliances of this type. You *will* need to follow a careful procedure to prepare juice to be stored—which differs from squeezing or readying any that is used right away, of course.

PREPARING FRUIT JUICES

Nutritionist Adelle Davis, in her popular book *Let's Cook It Right,* provides one of the best ways to prepare fruit juices for preserving. Her directions are uncomplicated and the method is one that seeks to retain as much vitamin value as possible. On this point, she explains: "In extracting juices to be canned, such as tomato or grape juice, far less loss of vitamin C occurs if the raw fruits are first quickly cooked and the enzymes (responsible for vitamin loss) destroyed before the juice is extracted."

Miss Davis adds that any fruit for juicing is to be cooked *only* until tender. "After the enzymes are destroyed, the shorter the cooking time, the less the nutritive loss." Sour fruits, she points out, such as plums, green apples and rhubarb, sustain little loss of vitamin C because the acids they contain inhibit enzyme action.

The following "recipe" can be used in making juice or sauces (or both) from these fruits: apricots, apples, plums, berries (all kinds), grapes, cherries, peaches, pears, nectarines and red or yellow tomatoes.

Use ripe fruit; it may be smaller or riper than suitable for other canning. Do not peel, core or cut apples or tomatoes except to remove damaged spots; do not remove stems from strawberries or stones from small apricots or cherries. Add only enough water at the beginning of cooking to prevent sticking.

Set the fruit in a large utensil (stainless steel, pyrex or enamelware) over high heat. Use a large knife and cut through the fruits, bringing the knife from one side to the other, as if cutting a pan of fudge. Mash them slightly to squeeze out juice.

Cover the pot; keep the heat high and cook until the fruit is tender, stirring occasionally to ensure even heating. Then press the fruit through a cone-shaped colander. Collect the thin juice in one utensil and the thick puree in another.

Now bring the juice to a rolling boil. Set a clean jar in a pan of warm water (to prevent breaking) and pour the boiling juice into it filling to within ⅛ inch of the top; wipe the edge of the glass, adjust the rubber and lid and seal.

Invert the jar to sterilize the lid. Let it stand in a place free from draft, not moving it until cool. If a screw top is used, remove the ring after 24 hours.

Use the puree for making fruit sauces; or bring it to a rolling boil, stirring frequently; pour it into clean jars and seal.

If clear berry, plum or grape juice is desired, strain it through a cloth after passing it through the colander. And if you have rose hips available, add them at the beginning of the cooking, to enhance both the flavor and the vitamin value.

Once you've readied any fruit juices for canning, you can freeze them if you prefer—and if your storage space permits. Prepare for canning (as just outlined), then chill thoroughly, pack into suitable containers, freeze and store.

PRESERVING NUTRIENTS

To keep vitamin and mineral content as high as possible in the finished product, remember a few always-true pointers on retaining food values:

1. Pick fruits when they're fully ripe. Nutritive levels are lower in immature tree or vine produce.

2. Use them promptly. If fruit is to be processed for canning or freezing, get to the project with as little delay as possible; refrigerate harvested fruit right after picking—until eaten or prepared.

3. Wash the fruit quickly, just before use. Don't soak it or let it stand in water. (A quick rinsing is usually ample for spray-free organic fruit.)

4. Avoid any cutting, peeling or chopping ahead of time—or at all if unnecessary for preparation. The less surface area of fruit or vegetable that is exposed to air (oxidation) the smaller the vitamin loss.

5. Cook rapidly when required for canning. Apply high heat for fastest processing. Don't overcook. Use a *minimum* of water. Avoid aluminum or copper-inner-surfaced utensils.

6. Store carefully. Keep from exposure to heat or light. If the fruit is for frozen storage, freeze it quickly.

And as for fruit juices themselves, keep another hint or two in mind: All fruits contain three *natural* sugars (glucose, fructose, sucrose) and rarely need sweetening. Get your family to like foods and beverages as nature flavors them. Add honey when actually needed—never white sugar or synthetic sweeteners.

CANNING WHOLE FRUIT

If a large supply of perfect fruit is available, some of it may be canned whole by the cold-pack method. The rules given above apply here, too. Follow them to preserve vitamins and nutrients in the fruits to be canned. Wash the fruit briefly, prepare and process it promptly to get the best nutritive value from it.

Fruits may be canned in one of two ways—by cooking before or after they are packed in the containers. If they are cooked by the open-kettle method, more vitamins are lost through oxidation, though the product may contain little or no water, since the juicier fruits may be cooked in their own juices. Cold-pack canning requires that the raw fruits packed in the jars be covered with a syrup made of water and sugar or honey. For your health's sake, use honey and use it *sparingly*, rather than refined sugar.

General recommendations include cooking gently in the heaviest syrup and stopping just before the fruit is tender. Then put it into the hot sterilized jars, filling them to the top and screwing on the lid until almost tight. The jars are then placed on a rack in the kettle, covered with water to at least an inch over their tops and processed in a rolling boil for 10 to 15 minutes before being removed and sealed tightly.

Freezing Fruits

Fruits lend themselves to freezing better, in most cases, than do vegetables, because fruits do not need to be blanched or cooked before they are frozen. It is true that certain changes take place in the texture of frozen fruits which are similar to the changes in cooked fruits. A few fruits, notably pears, watermelons, papayas, mangoes and avocados cannot be frozen very satisfactorily—some not at all. But wherever it is possible to freeze them, fruits can be made to retain more nutritive value and flavor when frozen than by any other method of preservation. And the process usually takes only about half as much labor as canning.

Studies published by Ohio State University show that frozen foods retain their food value the same as fresh foods. Vitamin A is practically all retained in fruits and vegetables during processing and freezing. Vitamins B and C and riboflavin are water soluble and tend to suffer some loss during the blanching and cooling of vegetables before freezing and in the leakage or drip after defrosting. Vitamin C of cooked frozen or fresh foods is about the same. Vitamin C of fruits is well retained since fruits are not blanched, but vegetables lose variable amounts.

FREEZING CHANGES FOOD

There are changes brought about by the freezing of foods. It is known, for example, that a uniform distribution of the ice crystals in the fruit aids in the retention of the texture. Texture change is largely due to the separation of water from the fruit tissues in the form of ice. Once separated, little of the water can be reabsorbed.

The cellular breakdown or softening—the loss in crispness—is similar to the effect of cooking. Some fruits, such as papaya, are more subject to softening than are other fruits. Some varieties of a given fruit may be more subject to this effect than others.

One of the best ways around the problem is to serve frozen fruits before they're completely thawed and while some ice crystals remain.

Spoilage of foods, in general, is caused largely by enzyme activity, by the growth and activity of microörganisms and by decomposition of certain of the constituents through reactions with each other, with the oxygen of the air or with container walls.

Microbial spoilage: In sound fruits, microörganisms are present only on the surface. As already noted, fruits ripened on the tree or vine should be prepared and frozen immediately. If they must be held, refrigerate them. The rate of growth of all microörganisms decreases as the temperature is lowered. Reducing the temperature to 40 degrees F. as quickly as possible will markedly retard the growth and activity of microörganisms and reduce the danger of fermentation and spoilage of the fruit during storage and thawing.

Precooling the fruit is important for obtaining the best results. This may be done by refrigeration or, in the case of freshly picked berries and small fruits, by washing them in water containing ice.

Microörganisms are retarded in growth and activity during freezer-storage and many are destroyed. They are not all destroyed, however, and those remaining may increase in number and activity during thawing and during holding of the fruit after thawing. In frozen fruit, the softening of the plant tissue permits a more rapid rate of spoilage after thawing than in the corresponding fresh fruit.

The type of spoilage naturally occurring in frozen fruits is fermentation. The changes are similar to those occurring in the making of fermented beverages, and the products aren't likely to be harmful.

Enzymatic activity: Changes in color, taste, aroma and ascorbic acid (vitamin C) content of fruits during freezing and thawing are caused mainly by oxidative enzymes. The discoloration of fruits, the loss of characteristic flavor and the development of off-flavor are caused largely by oxidative enzymes. No browning will occur in fruit tissues until practically all the ascorbic acid has been oxidized.

Low temperature retards, but does not entirely prevent, the activity of enzymes. To obtain high-quality products:

1. Select varieties which do not readily change in color, flavor and texture.

2. Freeze mature fruit. Immature fruit is usually higher in the constituents involved in darkening. Some contain compounds which become bitter during freezer storage and thawing.

3. Handle fruit and fruit products quickly during preparation for freezing, packaging and partial thawing and serving to minimize exposure to air. Cut directly into the syrup any fruit that is likely to discolor.

Non-enzymatic activity: Even though the enzymes may have been inactivated, self-oxidation may occur. This is difficult to control, but it can be minimized by excluding oxygen and by adding sugar or syrup. Off-flavors and off-colors may be caused by self-oxidation.

Sometimes a white fondant-like material, which after thawing appears as white patches, forms on the surface of frozen fruits during storage. This is due to the crystallization of sucrose.

METHODS OF FREEZING

Fruits are usually frozen in one of two ways: dry or floated in a sweet syrup. The usual directions recommend freezing fruit by mixing it with dry sugar or by floating it in a sugar and water syrup. Nutritionists interested in natural foods recommend the substitution of honey for sugar in freezing fruits. In general, recipes for freezing with sugar may be converted to honey recipes by substituting honey in an amount one-fourth to one-half that of sugar called for. This means that two to eight tablespoons of honey are mixed with one pint of fruit when the sugar recipe calls for one-half to one cup of sugar. A honey syrup suita-

Fruit Freezing Chart

Product	Varieties to freeze	Preparation	Packing
Apples	Yellow Transparent Early Cooper Lodi Duchess Wealthy Golden Delicious Jonathan McIntosh Spitzenburg Winesap Yellow Newton Rome Beauty Northern Spy Cortland Gravenstein	Slices: Peel, core and slice. Sauce: Grind whole apples, including skins, in blender. Juice: Wash fruit, crush, press out juice.	Pack dry or mix with 2 to 4 tablespoonfuls of honey mixed with 2 tablespoonfuls lemon juice. Add honey and lemon juice to taste. Add lemon juice to taste.
Apricots	Moorpark Tilton Royal Blenheim Chinese Riland	Blanch and peel or leave skins on. Cut in half and remove pits. Add a few pits to each container for flavor.	Trickle over honey thinned with warm water. Or pack in honey syrup.
Blackberries	Eldorado Lucretia Ebony King Wild berries Brainerd Evergreen Himalaya	If organically grown, pick out leaves and debris but do not wash.	Pack dry or trickle small amount of honey into bag. Seal and turn end for end until mixed.
Blueberries	Herbert Coville Dixi Atlantic Pioneer Cabot Concord Jersey June Rancocas Katherine Rubel Wild berries	If organically grown, do not wash. Pick out stems and leaves. If wild, scald for one minute to prevent toughening of skins.	Pack dry or with small amount of honey added.
Cantaloupe	Honey Rock Hale's Best Hearts of Gold	Cut flesh in slices, cubes or balls. Texture best when served partially frozen.	Add honey and lemon if desired. For salads, add whole seedless grapes.

Fruit Freezing Chart

Product	Varieties to freeze	Preparation	Packing
Carambola		Wash and slice. The tough rind is not softened by freezing, so it is best used as a garnish.	Pack in honey syrup.
Cherries sour	Montmorency Morello Early Richmond Late Duke	Wash, chill, stem and pit.	Add a small amount of pure honey. Mix and pack.
Cherries sweet	Bing Lambert Black Tartarian Deacon Black Republican Royal Ann Schmidt	Wash, chill, stem and pit.	Add lemon juice or honey. Light varieties need more lemon than dark varieties.
Bush cherries	Keyapaha Oaho Teepee Wampum	Sort, wash, pit or pack whole.	Add honey to taste.
Coconut	Any variety	Drain out milk, remove hull and skin, grate or grind in meat chopper.	Pack dry. Will keep well for one year.
Cranberries	Early Black Howes McFarlin	Sort, wash and drain. Raw relish: Grind 1 orange with 1 lb. berries. Add 1 cup crushed pineapple.	Pack dry. Add honey to taste.
Figs	Celeste Brown Turkey Magnolia Lemon Ischia California varieties	Whole or slices: Wash, sort, cut off stems, peel, leave whole or slice. Crushed: Wash and coarsely grind figs.	Cover with thin syrup. Add honey if desired.
Gooseberries	Red Lake Champion Houghton Glendale Pixwell	Sort, remove stems and blossom ends. Wash.	Pack dry or in honey syrup.
Grapefruit	Marsh Seedless Ruby Any seedless variety	Sections: Peel by cutting through white membrane. Remove sections from membrane. Juice: Squeeze juice, trying to avoid mixing in oil from rind.	Pack dry or add honey to taste. Pack and freeze quickly.

Fruit Freezing Chart

Product	Varieties to freeze	Preparation	Packing
Grapes	Concord Lutie Lucille Any good eating varieties	Whole: Wash and stem. Leave seedless whole, cut in half and remove seeds from others. Juice: Crush and heat to 140° in top of double boiler. Extract juice.	Pack dry or in thin syrup. Thaw and strain before serving.
Guavas		Purée: Remove seedy portion and strain to remove seeds. Shells: Pare and halve. Slice if desired.	Sweeten with honey. Cover with thin syrup.
Lychees		Leave about ¼ inch stem on fruit. Wash.	Pack dry.
Mulberries		Stem. Wash if necessary.	Pack dry or in honey syrup.
Oranges	Any good juice varieties	Squeeze juice. Work quickly, but avoid mixing oil from rind with juice.	Pack and freeze quickly.
Passion Fruit		Wash fruit. Cut in half. Remove pulp and seeds with spoon. Extract juice through a cheesecloth.	Add honey to taste.
Peaches	Halehaven Elberta J. H. Hale Rio Oso Gem Champion Redhaven Sunhigh Triogem Golden Jubilee Georgia Belle Afterglow Eclipse Erly-Red-Fre Raritan Rose Gold Medal	Use only peaches ripe enough so that skins may be pulled off without blanching. Wash, skin, pit, freeze in halves or slices. Prepare only fruit enough for one package at a time, to avoid discoloration.	Add honey mixed with a small amount of lemon juice, if desired.

Fruit Freezing Chart

Product	Varieties to freeze	Preparation	Packing
Persimmons	Japanese Native varieties	Sort, wash, slice and freeze or press through a purée sieve.	Add 2 tablespoonfuls of lemon juice per pint. Sweeten to taste with honey.
Pineapple	Smooth Cayenne	Use only fruit ripened on plant. Pare, trim, core and slice or cut in wedges.	Pack in own juice in thin syrup.
		Juice: Cut pared fruit into 8 or more pieces. Squeeze in a poi cloth or flour sack.	Freeze without adding sweetening.
Plums and Prunes	Methley Italian President Agen Sugar Imperial Epineuse Abundance Damson Toka Wantea Oka Stanley Reine Claude	If freestone, wash, pit, halve or quarter. If clingstone, crush slightly, heat just to boiling, cool and press through purée sieve.	Add 2 tablespoonfuls lemon juice per pint. Sweeten with honey or add honey syrup.
Raspberries red	Washington Indian Summer Cuthbert Latham Newburgh Lloyd George Chief Taylor Herbert	Clean and remove stems.	Pack dry or fill bags and trickle in 2 tablespoonfuls of honey per bag. Seal and turn end for end to mix.
black	Cumberland Bristol Dundee Munger		
purple	Columbian Ruddy Sodus		

Fruit Freezing Chart

Product	Varieties to freeze	Preparation	Packing
Rhubarb	Victoria Wine MacDonald Ruby Canada Red Valentine	Wash. Cut in 1-inch pieces.	Pack dry.
Soursop		Peel and cut lengthwise through the center. Remove and discard seeds. Force through purée sieve.	Sweeten to taste with honey.
Strawberries	Evermore Dunlap Gem Brightmore Dorsett Catskill Fairfax Improved Oregon Marshall Narcissa Redheart Rockhill Blakemore Pocahontas Howard 17 Robinson Sparkle Temple Klondyke	Wash, hull, slice, cut in half or freeze whole.	Sweeten to taste with honey or use honey syrup.
Surinam cherries		Prepare and freeze quickly. Wash and sort. Remove stems, blossom ends and pits.	Pack in honey syrup.

ble for use with most fruits may be made by mixing three parts of honey with five parts of warm water and chilling before using. If desired, two tablespoons of lemon juice may added as an antioxidant.

One precaution must be taken into consideration in the use of honey for freezing fruits. Only the mild-flavored, high-quality honeys are suitable for this purpose. In some areas this is the spring or early summer honey which is locust or clover honey. The honey harvested in the late summer or in the early fall usually has a more pronounced flavor which will overpower the delicate fruit flavors. It is important to find a reliable source of good, mild-flavored honey, but you'll be pleasantly rewarded for any trouble you take to obtain the proper honey.

Any container may be used to quick freeze fruit that will exclude air and prevent contamination and loss of moisture. Ice cream containers, waxed inside, are ideal. If tins cans with friction lids or glass jars are used, leave at least an inch of space at the top to allow room for normal expansion of the food. Fruits which are to be packaged dry should be placed in moisture-proof cellophane bags, sealed with a hot iron at a point as close to the contents as possible so that there's a minimum of air in the package. Waxed containers could be used, too. It's advisable to overwrap cellophane packages with stockinette to prevent the plastic material from either breaking or tearing.

Instructions for freezing specific fruits are given in the accompanying table. We have substituted honey for sugar in our recommendations for processing. Since the sweetening quality of different honeys differs, you should use your own taste to guide you in the final decision about quantities to be used.

Freezing Vegetables

To keep the largest possible amounts of vitamin C in the vegetables you freeze and to keep them tasty and appetizing, it pays to blanch carefully before freezing. Whether you want to store your own organic surplus for a healthful supply next winter or if you'd like to be sure of putting up enough naturally grown produce bought throughout this season, here are some tips on freezing:

1. Line up everything needed for blanching and freezing *first*. Nothing counts more than speed in holding on to freshness, taste and nutritive value. Plan a family freezing operation. Have all hands on deck to help arrange equipment and containers in advance for a smooth production.

2. Pick young tender vegetables for freezer storage; freezing won't improve poor-quality produce. As a rule, it is better to choose slightly immature produce over any that is fully ripe. Avoid bruised,

damaged or overripe vegetables. Harvest in the early morning. Try to include some of the tastiest early-season crops; don't wait only for later ones.

3. Blanch with care and without delay. Vegetables should be thoroughly cleaned, edible parts cut into pieces if desired, then heated to stop or slow down enzyme action. For scalding, use at least a gallon of water to each pound of vegetable, preheated to the boiling point in a covered kettle or utensil (preferably stainless steel, glass or earthenware). Steaming is better for some vegetables, as it helps retain more nutritive value. Suspend a wire-mesh holder or cheesecloth bag above one inch of boiling water in an 8-quart pot to steam vegetables. The same arrangement, to hold one pound at a time, is handy for plunging vegetables into boiling water. Start timing as soon as basket or bag is immersed or set in place for steaming. (See *chart* for scalding or steaming times required for different vegetables.)

4. Cool quickly to stop cooking at the right point. Plunge blanched vegetables into cold water (below 60 degrees)—ice water or cold running water will do best—changing the water often. Then drain well, using absorbent toweling.

5. Package at once in suitable containers. Glass jars require 1 to 1½ inches headspace; paper containers usually require ½ inch headspace, except for vegetables like asparagus and broccoli that pack loosely and need no extra room. Work out air pockets gently and seal tightly.

6. Label all frozen food packages, indicating vegetable, date of freezing, variety, and so on. Serve in logical order—remember food value and appeal are gradually lowered by long storage. Maximum freezer periods for most vegetables is eight to 12 months. Except for spinach and corn on the cob, cook without thawing. Avoid overcooking.

THE BEST FREEZE BEST

The most important of these elements in obtaining a frozen pack of high quality is the condition of the fresh product at the time of processing. Freezing is primarily a process aimed at preserving the fresh characteristics as long as possible. Properly done, it is an excellent method of preservation since it maintains very satisfactorily the initial color, texture and flavor of the fresh product as it comes from the garden. At the same time the original nutritive value is largely retained. Remember, however, that quick freezing cannot improve the quality of the fresh product, so you should consider only the finest fresh vegetables for freezing. The variety, the stage of maturity at the time of harvest and the nature of handling between harvesting and processing are the chief variables responsible for the condition of the fresh product.

The home gardener has the great advantage of being free to pick and process his vegetables when their quality is at its best. He can harvest them at the proper stage of maturity and as short a time as possible before use.

You usually find the finest flavor when vegetables are still young: peas and corn while they taste sweet and not starchy; snap beans while the pods are tender and fleshy, before the beans inside get plump; summer squash while the skins are still tender. Carrots and beets, too, have a particularly delicious flavor when they are young.

It is not always economical for the commercial grower to harvest a crop at the same early stage of development a home gardener can. Thus the surest way to obtain fresh produce of high quality for freezing is to grow it yourself and pick it yourself or at least obtain it garden fresh direct from a grower.

A crop of vegetables which doesn't mature all at once requires repeated pickings to ensure a uniform, high quality. This may mean processing a few packages at a time. By planning your garden to allow for succession plantings you can extend the harvesting season and provide a continued supply of fresh produce at a desirable stage of maturity. A poorly planned garden often results in an oversupply of certain vegetables. Then not all of the crop can be used at the prime stage of development. As maturity advances, vegetables increase in size and fiber content. Changes in color and nutritive value take place. In peas, corn and other crops, sugar content, after reaching a maximum, may decrease while starch increases, giving the particular produce a characteristic starchy flavor. Overmature leafy vegetables are tough because they contain too much fiber.

Unfortunately, too often the overmature portion of the crop is used for canning or freezing. This is poor policy. As a general rule for most satisfactory results, vegetables for freezing should be harvested when slightly younger than desired for eating fresh.

In canning, the prolonged cooking process sometimes improves texture and flavor of fully matured vegetables. The same results cannot be expected when overmature vegetables are frozen.

CAREFUL HANDLING PAYS

The next important influence on the condition of a vegetable at the time of processing is its handling between the picking and the freezing. Vegetables should be prepared for freezing and put into the freezer immediately after harvest.

A few examples may serve to explain why speed is so essential and why delay interferes with the quality of the final product. Physiological and chemical changes continue after harvesting. The rate of these changes depends on the temperature of the product. In the case of corn and peas, for example, at high temperatures the sugar contained in these crops changes rapidly to starch. At a temperature of 85 degrees Fahrenheit sweet corn loses half its sugar in 24 hours. Asparagus, too, undergoes marked changes in chemical composition after it is cut. The chief changes are a loss in sugar and an increase in fiber; they are most pronounced during the first 24 hours and at high temperature. Losses in sugar and increases in starch and fiber obviously affect the quality of the product. Furthermore, the vitamin content may be seriously reduced when processing is not done immediately after harvesting. A delay of 24 hours may cause a loss of 50 per cent of the vitamin C content and smaller losses of other vitamins.

If you cannot avoid a delay in processing, cool vegetables immediately after harvesting. Do not keep them at room temperature or, even worse, expose them to the sun. The quickest way of cooling them is to immerse them in ice water. After draining, keep them at low temperatures preferably between 32 and 40 degrees Fahrenheit. Covering the produce with cracked ice is another means of cooling and thus of slowing down the loss of quality. These aids, however, do not replace the need for prompt processing.

A crop of superior quality improperly handled will give disappointing results. On the other hand, an inferior raw product can result only in an inferior frozen product even though the handling is carried out with the greatest of care. In other words, you cannot expect to get anything better out of the freezer than you put in.

Generally speaking, vegetables best adapted for freezing are those that are usually cooked before serving. These include asparagus, snap beans and lima beans, beets and beet greens, cauliflower, broccoli, Brussels sprouts, peas, carrots, kohlrabi, rhubarb, squash, sweet corn, spinach and other vegetable greens. Freezing procedures for them are discussed in the following chart. Vegetables that are usually eaten raw, such as celery, cabbage, cucumbers, lettuce, onions, radishes, and tomatoes, are least suited for freezing.

Blanching Time Chart

	Minutes	
Vegetables	*Water*	*Steam*
Asparagus	2–3	4
Beans, green snap	2–3	3
Beans, wax	2–3	3
Beans, lima	2	3
Beets (until tender)	25–50	—
Broccoli (split stalks)	3	5
Brussels sprouts	3–4	5
Carrots (small, whole)	4–5	5
Carrots (diced or sliced)	2	4
Cauliflower	3	4
Corn on the cob	7–11	—
Corn (cut after blanching and cooling)	4	—
Kale	2	—
Peas, green	$1\frac{1}{2}$	$1\frac{1}{2}$
Spinach	2	—
Squash, summer	3	4
Squash, winter	20	—

Vegetable Freezing Chart

Vegetable	How to select	How to prepare	Scalding time in boiling water
Asparagus	Use young, rapidly grown stalks. Freeze same day harvested. Discard short stubby white stalks. Cut stalks 5- to 10-inch lengths in garden.	Wash in several waters. Sort for size. Eliminate tough portion of stalk. Cut into ¾- to 1-inch lengths or to fit container.	Small stalks, 2 min. Medium stalks, 3 min. Large stalks, 4 min. Cool.
Beans— Lima	Pick when ready for table use and pods slightly rounded and bright green. Discard overmature and discolored pods or use in dry form.	Wash. Scald 4 minutes before shelling; cool in cold water; drain. Shell with pea sheller or by hand. Rinse shelled beans in cold water.	Scald in pods 4 min. No additional scalding necessary. Cool.
Beans— Shelled Green	Pick when pods are well filled but beans are still green and tender.	Shell beans. Wash.	1 minute. Cool.
Beans— Snap	Pick when pods desired length but before seeds mature. Pods must be tender. Discard moldy or imperfect pods.	Wash in cold water. Rinse and drain. Snip ends and cut into desired lengths or leave whole.	3 to 4 min. depending on maturity. Cool.
Beans— Vegetable Soybeans	Pick when pods fairly well rounded, but while still bright green. Yellowish pods indicate overmaturity. Two or three days too long in garden result in overmaturity.	Wash. Scald 5 minutes before shelling; cool in cold water; drain. Shell with pea sheller or by hand. Rinse shelled beans in cold water.	Scald in pod 5 min. No additional scalding necessary. Cool.
Beets	Harvest while tender and mild flavored. Beets are preferred canned.	Wash. Leave on ½ inch of tops. Cook whole until tender. Skin and cut as desired.	No further heating necessary. Cool.
Broccoli and Brussels Sprouts	Select well-formed heads free from insect infestation. Buds showing yellow flowers are too mature.	Wash, peel and trim. Split broccoli lengthwise into pieces not more than 1½ inches across. Remove outer leaves from Brussels sprouts.	Broccoli, 5 min. Brussels sprouts, 3–5 min. depending on size.
Carrots	Harvest while tender and of mild flavor. Root cellar storage is preferred to freezing.	Top, wash and peel. Small tender carrots may be frozen whole. Others, cut into ¼-inch cubes or slices or Frenched.	2 min. for small cubes; 3 min. for slightly larger pieces. 5 min. for whole. Cool.
Cauliflower	Select well formed heads free from blemishes.	Wash. Break into flowerets. Peel and split stems. Soak in salt water 30 minutes.	3 min. May add acid to scalding water to keep white.
Corn— Sweet	Select tender, ripe ears in full milk stage. Do not use in dough stage. Discard smutted and badly worm-infested ears. Hard cutting ears indicate old corn.	Husk, de-silk, wash, sort and trim. After scalding cut off kernels. For corn on cob, cut off tips of ears and square up basal ends.	For cut corn, 4 min. Corn on cob— small ears, 7 min., medium ears, 9 min., large ears, 11 min.
Eggplant	Select firm, heavy fruit of uniform dark purple	Wash, peel, cut into ⅛ to ½-inch slices or cubes.	4 minutes. Cool.

Vegetable	How to select	How to prepare	Scalding time in boiling water
	color. Harvest while seeds are tender.	Dip in solution of 1 T. lemon juice to 1 qt. water. Dip again in lemon juice solution after heating and cooling.	
Kohlrabi	Harvest while tender and of mild flavor. Avoid overmature products.	Wash and trim off trunk. Slice or dice in ½-inch pieces or smaller.	1 to 2 min. depending on size of cubes or slices. Cool.
Mushrooms	Select firm, tender mushrooms, small to medium size.	Wash, cut off lower part of stems. Cut large mushrooms into pieces. Add 1⅓ t. ascorbic acid to 1 gallon scalding water.	Small whole—2 min. Large whole —4 min. Slices— 2 min.
Okra	Select young tender pods.	Wash, cut off stems so as not to rupture seed colls. Freeze whole or slice crosswise after scalding.	Small pods—2 min. Large pods—3 min. Cool.
Peas	Pick when ready for table use as seeds become plump and pods roundish. Pack same day harvested. Sugar and quality are lost rapidly at room temperature.	Wash peas, before and after shelling. Discard immature and tough peas.	1½ min. Cool.
Peppers— Sweet and Pimentos	Select deep green or red color, glossy skin, thick flesh, and tender.	Wash, halve, remove seed. Slice or dice as preferred.	Scalding not necessary but makes packing easier. Sliced—2 min. Halves—3 min. Cool.
Pumpkin and Winter Squash Summer Squash	Harvest when fully colored, firm and when shell becomes hard. Use only fully matured pumpkin and squash, ripened on healthy vines. Select summer squash before rind becomes hard.	Wash, pare, cut into small pieces. Cook completely. Do not add seasoning. Cool in air or float pan in cold water to cool. Slice summer squash ½ inch thick.	Cook before packing. Scald summer squash 4 min. Zucchinis 2 to 3 min. Cool.
Spinach and Other Greens	Harvest while tender, before plants become extremely large. Cut before seed stalks appear. Harvest entire spinach plant. Use only tender center leaves from old kale and mustard plants. Select turnip leaves from young plants.	Wash through several changes of water. Trim off leaves from center stalk. Trim off large midribs and leaf stems. Discard insect-eaten or injured leaves.	2 min. Stir to prevent leaves matting together. Cool.
Sweet Potatoes	Use only high quality, smooth, firm sweet potoes.	Wash. Cook in water until soft. Cool, remove skins. Pack whole, sliced or mashed. To each 3 cups pulp mix 2 T. lemon or orange juice or dip whole or sliced sweet potatoes in ½ cup lemon juice to 1 qt. water.	

Part Three

Buying From Others

1

The Food

Basic Natural Foods

Organic foods are becoming more popular than ever and are appearing in more stores all the time. People are beginning to think twice about the quality of the food they eat. If you're confused by the words "organic" and "natural," it's about time you learned just what they mean.

As pointed out earlier, health food is the vaguest term, while organically grown food is the most restrictive. The following list doesn't contain all the good, whole foods that should be a part of your diet, but these are probably the most important ones—ones that shouldn't be overlooked or misunderstood. Many of them—rice, grains, flours, soybeans, for example—are available from organic growers, but others—raw sugar and carob, for example—may be difficult, if not impossible, to find from organic growers. The key for the shopper is to understand what organically grown means and to ferret out those foods that are so grown whenever and wherever possible. Failing that, the shopper should seek out the foods that are as close to their natural forms as it is possible to find.

Food yeast—brewer's or primary-grown are also called nutritional yeast. These microscopic yeast plants grow on food substances. They are then washed and dried in such a way as to preserve all the rich nutrients. The plants are no longer alive and cannot be used in baking. They are especially high in protein and B vitamins and may be added as a food supplement to many foods. Food yeasts are sold in powdered form.

Brown rice—is a less refined, more nutritious rice than the white, polished type. In its processing the bran and germ, which contain the vitamins, minerals and much of the protein, are not removed as they are in the polishing of white rice. It is an excellent source of B vitamins. It may be used in the place of white rice and has a nutty, wholesome flavor.

Carob—is the fruit of the carob tree, finely ground to take the place of cocoa and chocolate in most recipes. It contains substantial amounts of A and B vitamins, trace minerals and is especially high in natural sugar. It may also be found in a syrup form.

Honey—is the sweet nectar extracted from combs by centrifugal force or strained from crushed honeycombs. It is high in natural sugars. Its vitamin and mineral content varies according to the type of honey and locality from which it comes. Darker honeys are richer in minerals than the lighter ones. Because of its high nutritional value, it is an excellent substitute for sugar. Some honeys are boiled and clarified to remove the slight cloudiness that may be present, resulting in a crystal clear product which is less nourishing than the unprocessed kind.

Organic eggs—are produced by chickens who are fed organic feeds without the addition of chemicals for growth, ovary stimulation or routine disease prevention. Hens are allowed to run free in a natural environment and peck food from the ground.

Organic meats—are products of stock raised on land which is managed organically. Both feed and environment are free from pesticide and herbicide residues, DES, antibiotics, growth hormones and irradiation. All animals must have free range and natural grazing is encouraged. Food supplements are all natural products. Animals must be periodically examined for vitamin and mineral deficiency. Beef is raised with the view of minimizing, not maximizing, the fat content; this fat content should be 30 per cent less than that of commercial beef of the same quality.

Raw milk—is milk that has not been pasteurized or homogenized. Raw milk is more nutritious than commercial milk because it has the vitamins that are normally lost in the pasteurization process. It should be obtained from reputable dairies, preferably ones that have certified cows.

Raw sugar—brown, unrefined sugar, the first crystallization of cane syrup. It is 96–98 per cent pure sucrose. Due to unsanitary shipping conditions and contamination, the retail sale of true raw sugar was made illegal in this country in the late 1940's. Turbinado sugar, the most common type found in health food stores, is made of raw sugar of the highest purity which is given an additional washing. It is drier and brighter and contains slightly more sucrose than the raw product.

Soybeans—differ from most legumes in chemical composition, but resemble peanuts, as they are rich in both fats and proteins. They contain, on the average, 35 per cent protein, surpassing every other known vegetable in that respect. They are endowed with large amounts of calcium, iron, and other minerals as well as B and E vitamins. In the Orient, soybeans largely take the place of dairy products and meat. In addition to the bean itself (which may be sprouted, baked, ground into meal), there are many other soy products: soy oil, soy sauce, soy flour, soy milk and milk products.

Soy flour—a highly nutritious food, rich in complete proteins, vitamins, and minerals. It cannot be used alone for baking bread as wheat flour, because it lacks the gluten involved in the process of raising wheat bread. It can be added to any recipe in which flour is used and will successfully replace up to 10-20 per cent of wheat flour in recipes.

Sunflower seeds—one of the seed foods richest in nutritional value. They contain a higher proportion of first-class protein than any other seed in use. Many cuts of meat rank below sunflower seed meal in protein. In addition, they are rich in B vitamins and unsaturated fatty acids. Because of their protected seed case, the seeds store well and lose few of their vitamins in prolonged storage. Seeds may be eaten raw, they may be roasted, chopped and used in place of nuts in recipes. They may be ground into meal.

Unbleached flour—does not contain certain chemicals found in bleached white flour. In the bleaching process chlorine, dioxide, alum, ammonia, gypsum (plaster of Paris) and other chemicals are used. Bleaching enables the miller to use inferior flours, and vitamins are removed by this process. Unbleached flour is similar, however, in every other way to bleached white flour and may be used as a substitute.

Wheat germ—that part of the wheat which is responsible for sprouting and making the new plant. It is removed from bleached and unbleached white flours. Very high in B vitamins and minerals, it may be added to enrich foods. It has a nut-like flavor, and because it spoils easily, it must be refrigerated.

Whole wheat flour—is flour in which the wheat germ and bran are still present. They have not been removed in the milling process and cause the flour to be brown and nutty flavored. The bran, or outer coat, and the germ, the heart and life of the seed, contain valuable B and E vitamins that are removed from white flour.

Yogurt—is milk which has been fermented with a mixture of bacteria and yeasts to convert the lactose to lactic acid. It contains all the food values of milk and is especially important because the lactic acid aids in indigestion by supplementing the action of the hydrochloric acid in the stomach.

BE INQUISITIVE

Health foods, natural foods, organic foods—the terms are confusing. Even people in the business get them mixed up. To make sure you're getting what you want, ask the store manager about his foods and read that fine print on food labels. Be inquisitive and demanding. Know what you want and ask the right questions. Keep store managers on their toes. Here are some questions to ask store managers about the food you buy. If you've followed us this far, you know the answers.

1. What do you mean by organically grown food?
2. Who grew your produce? Where's the farm?
3. How is the soil fertilized? What materials are used? How are insect pests and weeds controlled?
4. If the foods are meat or poultry, have any antibiotics, hormones, or feeds containing chemical ingredients been used in raising them? Have any chemicals been used in processing or packaging?
5. If eggs, have the hens been raised on free-run range—that is, with access to outdoor soil, plants and worms? Have they been kept with roosters so the eggs are fertile?
6. If fish or seafood, where's it from? Is it regarded as an unpolluted waterway, lake, bay or oceanic territory?
7. Are the fruits or vegetables free from waxes? Gas applications? Have they been exposed to contaminants or poisons in shipping? How fresh are they?
8. How long have any packaged, canned or frozen foods been stored or on the shop's shelf? Are they dated in any way to safeguard consumers?

9. Have grains, cereal products, nuts and root crops been stored without fumigants or other undesirable pest control materials?

10. Are all processed, packaged, canned or frozen products free from additives, dyes, synthetic flavorings, sweeteners, preservatives, spoilage retarders, non-food fillers and stabilizers, as well as refined sugars or other unhealthful ingredients?

—Carol Stoner

Natural Cereal Grains

Is grain the foundation of civilization? Maybe. It was not until man had learned to cultivate the cereals as a rapidly maturing, high-yielding foodstuff—one that could be successfully stored and counted on to supply food from one harvest to the next—that tribal wanderings in search of food came to an end

Actually, ancient womankind is credited with this early agriculture, and fittingly the divine overseer of the crop is the Goddess of Grain, Ceres, from whom the name "cereal" is derived.

It might surprise you to hear that over half the land cultivated for agriculture is used for grain production—which in turn provides almost half of the world's dietary protein. Today, with the exception of our own country, some form of cereal grain furnishes the world population with its largest source of energy and nutrition. The simple reason is that cereal grains supply an abundance of carbohydrate and vegetable protein most economically.

All cereal grains are seeds. The grain plant is a member of the grass family and has characteristic blade-like leaves and seeds that grow like fruit from the stalks. These seeds are harvested as cereal grains, but could just as well be sown to produce the next crop. When left in the whole state each seed is composed of three elements: the germ, the endosperm, and the bran. The germ is the heart of the seed, the embryo, which sprouts and grows when the seed is planted. This part is richest in protein and thiamin, the vitamin needed to regulate carbohydrate metabolism, good appetite, growth and normal functioning of the nervous system. Iron, riboflavin, niacin, carbohydrate and fat are also present in the germ.

The endosperm is the food reserve for the growing plant, composed mainly of carbohydrate (to supply energy) and protein. This is the part of the grain that remains in highly-refined cereals and flour.

The bran is made of several layers which compose a protective coat around the seed. The outer portion is rich in bulk-forming carbohydrate, which acts as a natural regulator in the body; the B-complex vitamins (thiamin, riboflavin, niacin); and iron, utilized to build red blood cells. The inner layers of the bran boast protein and phosphorus, used by the body to build bone and nerve tissue.

The seed, then, is not only a vital center of growth for the germinating plant, but is also capable of contributing seven of man's dietary essentials: calories, protein, iron, phosphorus, thiamin, riboflavin and niacin. These seeds, or cereal grains, when combined with vegetable or milk products, provide all the elements necessary for life, growth and health.

STOCKING UP WITH GRAINS

It is easy to see why the cereal grains are a primary source of nourishment for millions of people. With so much to offer, they certainly should be a highly regarded staple in your own kitchen. So, on your next trip to the market begin stocking your cupboard with a selection of these:

Rice: In the hot, wet lands known as Monsoon Asia, extending from India to Japan, about 90 per cent of the world's rice is grown. The grain is eaten daily by the majority of the Asian people. Because money and technology are limited in these nations, most rural Asians do the reaping, threshing and milling by hand. In this process they remove *only* the husk, leaving the grain intact as a product known as "natural brown rice." In addition to the seven essential nutrients we've credited to the cereal grains, brown rice contributes calcium to the diet. When milling is carried further, as done by Western technology, the outer layers of bran—the richest source of vitamins and minerals—are ground away, producing white rice. Follow the example of the rural Monsoon Asians who rely on rice for sustenance—use only the natural brown variety in your kitchen.

Millet: In northern China, as well as much of Africa and India, it is not rice but millet which is the staple grain. The millet consumed in these areas is usually steamed to form a porridge or coarsely ground into flour for puddings and flat cakes. Millet seeds vary greatly in size, shape and color, but those commonly available in this country are tiny, shiny white or cream-colored ovals. The cooked grain is tender, yet chewy, and it's ideal for puddings.

Barley: A popular food in North Africa and parts of Europe, barley has been uncovered among the ruins of the oldest known habitats of man. The crop is very hardy and growing even within the Arctic circle. Most of us are familiar with barley in the form of "pearl barley" popularized in Scotch broth and soups. The bran has been removed and the grain polished to create the "pearled" variety. Where barley is considered a mainstay in the diet, however, "naked barley" is used. In this type, the grain is left loosely surrounded by the husks in the threshing. Barley, like rice, contributes a significant amount of calcium to the diet, along with the seven essentials attributed to all the grains.

Buckwheat: Often called groats or kasha, buckwheat is not actually a member of the grass family, but it is cultivated and consumed in much the same way as the cereal grains. Although one of the less important crops in America, it is one of the most popular foods in Russia. You are probably acquainted with buckwheat in the form of flour to make buckwheat pancakes, but the unmilled grain is the main constituent of the kasha used to nourish millions in Eurasia.

Always keep in mind when buying cereal grains that once the grain is milled, the seed is no longer intact, or whole, and the essential nutrients we spoke about begin to deteriorate. A look at the following table, derived from "Composition of Foods," Agriculture Handbook No. 8, U.S. Department of Agriculture, shows what happens to the nutritive value of buckwheat as it is transformed from groats, the whole grain cereal, into light, highly milled flour:

Table 1

1 pound	protein	phosphorous	iron	thiamin	niacin
Buckwheat groats	53.1 g.	1279 mg.	14.1	2.71 mg.	20.0 mg.
Light flour	29.0 g.	399 mg.	4.5	.35 mg.	1.8 mg.

Since rice is so widely consumed in America, the government has set up standards for replacing some of the nutrients robbed during the milling, but as the next table from the same source indicates, this replacement is hardly adequate for protein, phosphorus, niacin, calcium and potassium, while it increases thiamin and iron to above-normal levels.

You can purchase all of these nutritious grains in the health food

Table 2

1 pound	protein	phosphorous	iron	thiamin	niacin	calcium	potassium
Brown rice	34.0 g.	1002 mg.	7.3	1.52 mg.	21.4 mg.	145 mg.	971 mg.
White rice	30.4 g.	426 mg.	3.0	.02 mg.	7.2 mg.	109 mg.	417 mg.
Enriched rice	30.4 g.	426 mg.	13.0	2.0 mg.	16.6 mg.	109 mg.	417 mg.

store. Many supermarkets carry them as well. As with all foods, those grains organically grown, without any chemical treatment of the soil, will provide the most nutrition with the least chemical residue in your diet. The grains sold in health food outlets may or may not be organic, so be sure to ask. If you purchase them in your supermarket you probably forfeit this extra benefit, since only a few have started to stock organic foods.

Having a good selection of cereal grains on your kitchen shelf is your assurance of a meal always being on hand. The grains all store well, so you can maintain a well-stocked kitchen. Buy the freshest grain available and keep it in a tightly covered container in a cool, dry place. Since the germ and fat are still intact in the whole grains they can become rancid, but held in this manner buckwheat, barley, millet and rice will keep for about a year. Because insects thrive on the healthy grain, the tightly closed container will protect your supply against infestation as well.

Store cooked grain in a covered container in the refrigerator. They can be kept for 4 to 6 days.

COOKING CEREAL GRAINS

When cereal grains are cooked, they absorb liquid and swell; uncooked rice and buckwheat triple in volume, while millet and barley expand to four times their original volume. Plan on serving ½ cup cooked grain per person for breakfast or as an accompaniment to the meal and one cup cooked grain for main-dish servings.

The same basic cooking method can be applied to all the cereal grains:

1. Rinse raw grain in cold water and drain well. This will help remove both surface contamination and excess starch and start the swelling process.

2. Bring to a boil an amount of cooking liquid equal to twice the volume of the uncooked buckwheat or rice and three times the volume of the uncooked millet or barley. Meat or vegetable stock, juice, milk or water may be used. The more flavorful the cooking liquid, the more flavorful the cooked grain will be.

3. Add the boiling liquid to the grain in a pot just large enough to accommodate the increase in volume after cooking. Stir once.

4. Allow the liquid to return to a boil, then turn heat as low as possible, and cover and cook the grains slowly until all liquid is absorbed. This will take anywhere from 30 to 45 minutes. Millet and buckwheat cook rather quickly, while rice and barley may require additional time.

To determine if the grain is cooked, use the bite test: well-cooked grain will be chewy, but not tough or hard. If not quite done, add a little more water, cover and continue cooking.

If you'd like a creamier product for porridge or pudding, don't heat the cooking liquid initially, but combine it first with the uncooked grain, then bring the mixture to a boil. Cover and continue as above.

The addition of salt slows the cooking so it is best to wait until the grain is tender, then season. Allow ¼ to ½ teaspoon per cup of cooking liquid used.

Too much stirring makes the grain gummy, so stir only once as suggested.

Cooked grain can be held in a covered pot off the heat until needed. This will keep it hot and allow further drying.

Cooked grain has a delicious nutty flavor, but for an even nuttier taste, try the sauteing technique: Place the rinsed grain in a pot and stir over low heat until dry. Then add enough oil to just coat each kernel, about 1 to 2 tablespoons per cup and continue to cook, stirring until dry and golden. For added savor, sauté a chopped onion along with the grain. When the grain takes color (and the onion is limp) add the boiling liquid and continue as above.

There's a place for cereal grain dishes in every course of the meal from soup to dessert. Grain prepared according to the basic cooking instructions can be served as an accompaniment to meat or fish or used as a base for vegetables or stew. The cooked grain can be seasoned with honey, dried fruit, herbs or cheese for a breakfast or dinner porridge.

Cook the grains in a pot of soup for a rich chowder. Knead left-over grains into dough for a very special bread.

Cereal grains open the door to creativity in your kitchen.

—Nikki Goldbeck

Wheat Germ—For Natural Enrichment

We *can* greatly increase the nutritional values of food with only a very slight effort. And one of the best ways that this can be done is with wheat germ.

Wheat germ is found in the darkish-colored speck about the size and shape of a pinhead found near the end of each kernel of wheat. This speck is the heart or the seed of the wheat which, if planted, will send forth a sprout to grow into a new plant. At one time, before the invention of steel rollers, the wheat germ was included in flour and, at that time, bread was much closer to being the so-called staff of life. With the use of steel rollers, which were introduced in our country at the turn of the century, the wheat germ is not pulverized as it was when stone was used. The germ now goes through the rollers intact and is later sifted out of the flour. The parts sifted out are where most of the nutritional values of the wheat live.

Scientists are continually finding new values in the kernel which contains the wheat germ and the bran.

SOME NEW VALUES

Some very new research studies indicate it is this portion of the wheat which provides something akin to an antibiotic effect and can prevent salmonella infections in laboratory mice. There is an ingredient in this hull portion of grains that can actually lower cholesterol levels.

The newly discovered "resistance" factor, called pacifarins, was found in the outer fraction of the wheat kernel and in certain natural foods (corn, rye and rice) in addition to wheat by Dr. Howard Schneider of the Institute for Biomedical Research of the American Medical Association. His experiments are described in *Science,* November 1967.

When Dr. Schneider and his colleagues fed two mouse colonies two different diets and then infected both with salmonella, one group had a notably higher survival rate. Ninety out of 100 lived. In the other group, 90 out of 100 died. The group with the high fatalities were fed a precisely assembled semi-synthetic diet, containing all the known required amino acids (protein), carbohydrates, vitamins, and minerals. The other colony, the one in which 90 out of 100 lived, was fed a natural diet only (whole wheat was important in the natural diet).

The cholesterol-lowering function of the whole grain was cited by Dr. Hans Fisher of Rutgers University during Texas A & M University's 24th Annual Nutritional Conference. "Wheat, barley, and oats all contain this cholesterol-absorbing activity," Fisher said, adding that "further results show that it is the hull portion of the cereal that is beneficial." (*The Poultryman,* October 25, 1969).

When white bread is "enriched," the baking industry and many nutritionists writing for the popular press tell us, nutrients are restored, giving it the value of whole wheat.

We, of course, know that this is not so. There are at least 23 nutrients present in the wheat germ of which only three or four are restored to the white flour.

What these "nutritionists" do not realize is what Dr. Schneider's experiments so pointedly bring out. There are always elements in the whole food, eaten just as it was grown, that remain unknown to the food scientist; elements which our bodies, through thousands of years of adjustment, have learned to utilize and flourish on. Even those elements which are known and believed to be synthesizable in a laboratory cannot possibly be duplicated perfectly. No one in a laboratory has been able to duplicate perfectly the mysterious quality of life. If you plant a wheat seed, it will grow. Has anybody in a laboratory been able to create a seed that would grow? It is the height of folly to make something which is lifeless, and then claim that even though it does not have life and never did and never will, it is the same as the living substance.

Farmers, with their innate wisdom, knew this long before the scientists got around to acknowledging it. It was the farmers, for instance, who recognized vitamin E as a fertility factor in animal breeding. They didn't call it vitamin E. They called it freshly ground wheat, and they fed it to their stallions. They fed it to their sows before farrowing to promote large litters of vigorous pigs. Poultrymen insisted that fresh wheat in the diet was essential to high egg production. Wheat germ oil was reported in the scientific literature as aiding the conception of cows. Breeders of hogs, horses, sheep, foxes and minks reported their observations of the value of wheat germ oil in aiding reproduction, in an article "Hormones From the Wheat Fields" by Samuel R. Guard, published more than 20 years ago in *Breeder's Gazette* (May, 1950.)

A NUTRITIONAL ANALYSIS

You get high-grade protein in wheat germ, too, as much as 25.2 grams in every cup.[36] That's more protein than you get in four ounces of turkey or in two eggs, more than you get in a four-ounce lamb chop, and more than you get in a three-ounce porterhouse steak or a four-ounce hamburger.

Besides the protein, you get many important enzymes, every known B vitamin—and perhaps a few that have not yet been discovered—and practically all of the minerals that are required.

Though the wheat embryo containing the germ is only a small fleck of the berry, it is, in essence, a highly concentrated form of many life-giving elements.

Assay Report on Wheat Germ
Prepared by Wisconsin Alumni Research Foundation, Madison, Wisc.

Food Elements	Amounts per oz.	Food Elements	Amounts per oz.
Vitamin A	30.4 units A as B-carotene	Alpha-Lipoic Acid	2.07 mg.
Vitamin E	7.6 mg. a-tocopherol	of sample are equivalent	
		to 1 mg. of acetate	
Vitamin C	3.6 mg.		
Niacin	1.47 mg.		
Riboflavin	.19 mg.	Calcium	7.69 mg.
Thiamine	.49 mg.	Phosphorus	340 mg.
Inositol	311 mg.	Magnesium	88.7 mg.
Folic Acid	0.103 mg.	Sodium	0.67 mg.
Folinic Acid	6.4 y	Potassium	270 mg.
Biotin	0.82 y	Iron	2.50 mg.
Vitamin B_6	0.25 mg.	Copper	0.30 mg.
Vitamin B_{12}	2.9 mcg.	Manganese	4.82 mg.
Choline	156 mg.	Cobalt	0.0007 mg.
Pantothenic Acid	0.33 mg.	Molybdenum	0.016 mg.
Para aminobenzoic Acid	10.6 mcg.	Zinc	4.79 mg.

[36] Burton, B. T. *Heinz Handbook of Nutrition*, 2nd Ed. New York: McGraw-Hill Book Co., 1965, p. 430.

USE WITH INGENUITY

You would be making an important contribution to your family's health and happiness if you used your ingenuity to devise ways in which you could get more wheat germ into their dietary. Introduce it to your children when they are still in the high chair. It has a wonderful nut-like flavor that little ones and big ones enjoy if their taste buds haven't been jaded by too much sugar, salt and overprocessed foods. Add wheat germ to everything you put in the oven—cookies, cakes, pies, casserole dishes. Use wheat germ and crushed nuts to make a delicious crust for fresh fruit pies. Use a generous dollop of wheat germ in your meatloaf and hamburgers. Many people enjoy wheat germ as a coating on fish, cutlets and liver. Try a generous sprinkling of wheat germ on fresh fruit. Yogurt, fruit and wheat germ make a delightfully refreshing dessert or snack. Use wheat germ tossed in garlic butter on your Greek salad in place of the usual crouton. Sprinkle it on soup like a garnish. Add it to your oatmeal, cream of wheat or corn meal (¼ cup in recipes serving six). Try cutting bananas crosswise in four pieces; then dip them in yogurt and roll them in wheat germ. Blend equal parts of wheat germ, soy flour, carob flour, peanut butter, honey and seasame seeds, then roll in wheat germ to make a most delicious confection which the children will love and you will love giving them.

Use your own imagination and toss some wheat germ in your dishes. It's a good way to greatly increase the nutritional values of the foods you serve and eat.

Corn—A Vital Food

The people of this nation are surrounded by a jungle of synthetic, artificially colored, flavored and preserved supermarket foods of doubtful nutritional value and purity. What can save them? What food can help make eating fun again? Why corn can.

Our present use of sweet corn, fresh off the cob from our gardens or canned and frozen from the store, is just a small part of what corn is doing and can do if we use some creative ingenuity. Let's look first at the corn food we are already using. One of the most important is corn oil, very rich in those valuable unsaturated fats. Corn oil tastes good too—always a valuable attribute in a health food. Then there is the important role that corn plays in feeding the animals that supply us with meat, eggs and other animal protein products. Without corn, we would hardly be a nation of beef-eaters.

Our ancestors, to whom corn was a vital food, did not make it into oil or feed it extensively to cattle. They ate most of the corn themselves, thereby saving the 90 per cent of food energy that is expended by the normal life processes of warm-blooded animals and not harvested in the form of meat. A pound of corn eaten by a person will keep body and soul together 10 times as long as if that pound of corn is fed to animals and harvested eventually as one-tenth of a pound of meat. Cornmeal, cooked as mush or made into biscuits or spoonbread, was the inexpensive, tasty fuel that powered whole generations of American nation-builders.

TOO CHEAP

Why is cornmeal no longer a staple food today in many homes? We should not overlook the factor of cost. Cornmeal is so cheap that people living in a money-oriented society began to feel that it was "not as good" as more expensive food, like white bread and fancy cakes. What self-respecting parent in this day and age would ask the family to sit down to a meal costing only a few cents? We have been conditioned to think that a dinner of polenta—which is Italian for cornmeal mush on a platter with a few pieces of meat and some gravy in the center—is not soul food for affluent Americans. Delightful to eat, yes, but too cheap to really satisfy the ego. The same logic applies to the general abandonment of such tasty foods as hoe cakes, corn gems, fried mush and cornmeal dumplings. They would be out of place on the menu of an expensive restaurant, so they are also out of place on the tables of affluent families.

An equally important reason why ground corn is no longer widely eaten is the lack of good corn from which to make first-class meal. And it's closely related to the reluctance of food processors to put out a good product. Before I explain why store-bought meal tends to be inferior, I will tell you what has happened to corn to make raw material for meal scarce.

The first white men to grow the plant were confronted with an early version of what we now call Indian corn, decorative and often very suitable for meal, but yielding only moderately.

IMPROVING THE STOCK

In the last century, plant breeders went to work on the corn plant and improved it in two separate and distinct ways. They produced sweet corn for good corn-on-the-cob eating and for general table use as a canned or dried vegetable. And moving in another direction, plant breeders selected high-yielding types of field corn for greater production of maize for cattle feed and silage. The field corn ears are big and numerous, but they aren't good-tasting for meal use or as nutritional as the older, "inferior" types of corn they replaced.

I have yet to find a current seed catalog that offers seed for corn to produce meal, as I remember was available perhaps 10 or 20 years ago. One seedsman advised the planting of STOWELL'S EVERGREEN open-pollinated sweet corn for meal, or COUNTRY GENTLEMAN as a second choice. A fortunate few gardeners and farmers have in their possession the seed of tasty white corn that has been passed down in their families from fathers and grandfathers who knew and valued a good pot of mush or batch of journey cakes.

To my way of thinking, the best corn for meal is white, because white corn has a more sophisticated flavor that blends with a variety of other foods. Yellow corn is richer in the precursors of vitamin A, and therefore has greater nutritional value. But the flavor of yellow corn seems to appeal less to people who are really heavy eaters of cornmeal foods. Too, in my experience yellow corn more often has the horny endosperm which makes for gritty meal that must either be ground very fine or cooked a long time. Many white corns have a floury endosperm that allows coarse grinding and brief cooking.

Now, let's address ourselves to that question—why is good meal seldom available in the supermarkets? First, there is the question of shelf life. Whole corn ground into meal and stored in a warm place may "leak" some of its natural oils and stain the bags in which it is packaged. It may also attract bugs, because natural, whole cornmeal is a living, vital food that appeals to insects and other critters. The scientific approach to those problems is to degerminate the meal, removing the source of the staining oil and the taste that appeals to the bugs. In the process, however, the millers also castrate the meal nutritionally and esthetically, making it taste like some gritty, inferior product with which one hesitates even to bread chicken. The thought of eating it in cakes without a liberal mixture of wheat flour and/or sugar is seldom even recommended by the packers.

Inferior meal will frequently be labelled "enriched"—which is a backlash from the condition that existed in the South years ago when people ate almost nothing but cornmeal and as a result got pellagra. That is caused by a deficiency of niacin, one of the B vitamins. Remember, I didn't say that corn was the perfect food. Nothing is perfect. The valuable protein, minerals, complex carbohydrates and other vitamins in corn make it an extremely valuable food, and if eaten with a balanced diet of other vegetables and some meat, there isn't the slightest chance of getting pellagra. More often than not, food enrichment is a government/scientific/industrial smokescreen to hide the more important fact that for some reason (usually related to profits) people are not being encouraged to eat natural, unprocessed foods.

A GOOD CORNMEAL

If you are not one of those lucky people with a large garden and a legacy of first-class seed stock from your grandparents, don't despair. There are still a few places around selling good meal, at very reasonable prices. Finding a good source and then continuing to use it is extremely important, because a really good meal can be used easily in a wide variety of foods, and will always satisfy your taste buds. Every cornmeal recipe, especially those calling for a large proportion of meal among the ingredients, will work out for you every time without fail. But when you use a degerminated or other low-quality meal, you will never open for yourself the door to true cornmeal eating pleasure.

One of the code words to look for is "bolted." A bolted meal is usually not degerminated, but has had some of the larger particles filtered out through a bolting screen. A bolted meal is half way between processed junk and real natural cornmeal ambrosia. Sometimes, in certain applications, a bolted meal will do until better meal comes along.

Another phrase to watch for is "water ground." Personally I don't think it makes much, if any, difference if meal is ground by water power or by electricity—except for the ecological implications. But, and this is a big but, millers who go to the trouble of keeping an old mill going under water power usually have the strength of character to use a good variety of corn to make their meal. And they probably don't go in for degerminating and enrichment either. Searching for water-ground meal—often sold in speciality food stores and sometimes even in supermarkets—is a good way to start looking for a good cornmeal source.

Health food stores sometimes sell the very finest of all cornmeals, and sometimes offer products that are less than the best. Buy the smallest size of each brand and give them the taste test before making up your mind.

CORN AND PEANUTS

One thing the old-timers didn't learn was that cornmeal and raw peanut flour go together as beautifully as ham and eggs, to name but one of many outstanding food combinations. Perhaps they liked plain cornmeal so much that they didn't feel the need to do much experimenting. More likely, raw peanuts seemed to them to be an odd and tasteless food.

The fact is, though, that ground-up raw peanuts can amplify the already-good taste of superior meal, in a wide variety of recipes. Raw peanuts add not only flavor when they are baked, but also contribute a softness and higher oil content to biscuit recipes, which appeals to the current public taste for foods that are easier to chew.

You can buy raw peanut flour in some natural food stores and by mail from at least one supplier whom I'll not name, because he already has trouble meeting the demand. Perhaps the simplest thing to do is to negotiate a supply of whole raw peanuts from your local nut house, and then grind them yourself in one of those blender-like small grinders, selling for about $10. A tip when grinding: too few peanuts in each batch will result in an uneven grind. And don't let the grinder run for more than seven or eight seconds or you will start the peanuts on the way to being peanut butter.

Experiment with adding raw peanut flour, preferably organically grown if you can get it, to every one of your corn bread recipes.

Speed of preparation is one virtue of cornmeal cookery that has appealed to everyone from the time of the Pilgrims down to the present. Cornmeal mush used to be called hasty pudding, because the harried housewife could cook up a batch in minutes when company appeared unexpectedly. Convenience foods have been around a long time and can be natural, too.

Corn is an amazing plant, and I have just scratched the surface of corn lore. The main point is that our urge to do things bigger and better and richer has caused most of us to forget about cornmeal, a food that

is both very inexpensive and extremely useful. Get on the old corn
bandwagon yourself and find out how easy it is to improve your diet.

—*Robert Rodale*

The Fascination of Seeds

There are uncountable millions of non-gardeners who look at seeds and
see not plants but a square meal. The simple fact is that seeds are by
far the most popular food in the world. More than half of all human food
is made from seeds. Rice, wheat and corn are the most popular seed
foods, but there are also places in the world where soybeans, millet, rye,
barley and other grains and beans are staple items of diet. And don't
forget the sunflower seed, which is one of the most important sources
of vegetable oil in world markets.

Plants tend to concentrate their best and most nutritious qualities
in their seeds. The seed has to last through the unfavorable climatic
conditions of winter, be buffeted by wind and rains, freezing and thawing, and still live the next spring to provide not only the chromosomes
to the next generation but a substantial part of the sprout's nutrition
as well. Seeds are packed with protein, oils, minerals and a fair amount
of vitamins too. They have the power to increase their vitamin content
dramatically as they sprout, which makes bean sprouts, for example, an
important item of food in many places.

Seeds, the Department of Agriculture Yearbook for 1961, contains
the interesting observation that people in the advanced industrial
countries—particularly in Western Europe and the United States—
don't eat nearly as much seed food as people in the less privileged
countries. While primitive people eat far more than half their food in
the form of seed, we fill up more on meat, potatoes, sugar and dairy
products. As a result, only about one-third of our diet is seed food.

It is also interesting that gardeners, who respect seeds for their
almost mystical quality of creating life, don't do much harvesting of
seeds. Corn and beans are probably the biggest seed harvests of the
gardener. We tend to concentrate instead on the fleshy part of plants,
the roots, tubers, fruit and leaves. That is good, because those parts of
plants concentrate many virtues. They have liberal amounts of vitamins, minerals, oils and the best quality of carbohydrates. Not only that,
but they taste good, which is most important.

THE SEED AS SPROUT

Bean sprouts are an important item of food in many parts of the world, particularly in the Orient, and they are becoming more popular here every year. You can find canned bean sprouts in any supermarket, and housewives are becoming accustomed to putting them into a variety of dishes.

We should make much more use of sprouts than we do now, though, because they are a most delightful way to increase the amount of seeds we eat and to add new taste thrills to our diets. Sprouts have two qualities which are not always found together. They are a health food with a gourmet taste. Not long ago I was able to purchase a small container of alfalfa seed sprouts in a health food store, and we used them in a salad made up of roughly equal parts of lettuce, tomato and alfalfa sprouts. A simple vinegar-and-oil dressing was used. The taste was excellent. I'm sure the patrons of the most expensive gourmet restaurants would go wild over such a salad if they ever had a chance to try it. Remembering the taste of that salad, I have been a sprouter ever since. Now I do the sprouting myself in our kitchen.

Many different kinds of seeds can be sprouted and eaten in salads, stews, cereals, sandwiches or as raw snacks, including alfalfa, barley, buckwheat, fava, mung, lima, pinto and soybeans, corn, cress, clovers, caraway, celery, dill flax, fenugreek, garbanzos, kale, lettuce, lentils, millet, parsley, purslane, pumpkin, peanuts, onions, oats, radish, red beets, safflower, sunflower and wheat.

Of course, it isn't necessary to use such a great variety of seeds to get a lot of fun, health and taste thrills from sprouts. Alfalfa is fine for a delicate taste in salads, and soybeans are the classic for Oriental sprouts. But the mung bean is probably the best of all and maybe the most popular around the world as a sprout.

SPROUTING TECHNIQUE

The basic sprouting technique is simplicity itself. Start with clean seeds that have not been treated with fungicides. Health food stores sometimes handle seeds for sprouting, or you can buy lentils or small beans in your local supermarket and use them. Many garden seeds sold by stores or mail-order companies are not treated, but some are. Be sure they are not chemically treated if you are going to eat them as sprouts.

Soak the seeds overnight in lukewarm water. Then keep them for three to five days in a place where they are moist, but not submerged in water. A number of small devices have been made for seed-sprouting in the home but it's easy to improvise one. Many people do their sprouting in mason jars that are covered with cheesecloth or wire mesh. Others use clean flowerpots, with the drain hole covered with wire mesh. The basic idea is to keep the seeds dark and moist. They should be sprinkled two or three times a day and kept where the temperature is about 70 degrees. It is also necessary for the sprouting seeds to have a certain amount of air, so they won't mold.

Sprouts need little preparation before use. I prefer to flush away the green husks of the mung beans, but that's all that's needed.

One of the best virtues of sprouting as a way to prepare seeds for eating is that it preserves their completeness. Wrapped up in the hard, dry coat of a seed is the universality of life itself. Most of the popular seed foods have a proper balance of minerals, carbohydrate and protein and are rich in vitamins and oils. When primitive people eat seeds, they tend to leave the nutritional balance undisturbed, because they don't have the means to process them too much. But when advanced, industrialized people eat seeds, they usually get only part of the original nutrition.

The outer coat of rice and wheat is stripped away in our factories, taking much of the mineral and protein value. The germ of the seed, rich in vitamin E, is also taken, so the food prepared from the grain won't spoil in storage. Nutritionists are finding that people in the advanced countries eat diets that are too low in the very thing that are stripped from the seeds when they are milled and processed. Our diets tend to be too low in calcium, magnesium and unsaturated oils—all things that are present in the unused part of the seed. By sprouting, you can introduce into your diet the whole seed, with all its goodness. And it is good in taste as well as health.

—Robert Rodale

Beans—A Neglected Food

Beans are a neglected food, scorned by most as too cheap and unglamorous, yet a food that is assuming increased importance to health.

It has been found, for instance, by Dr. P. T. Kuo, a leading investigator of blood serum and heart disease, that complex carbohydrates like beans are of great value to heart health, in distinction to the simple carbohydrates like sugar and refined flour which are deadly. It has been found by Professor Ancel Keys that while complex carbohydrates like bread and potatoes have no effect on serum cholesterol, beans in the diet will cause cholesterol levels to drop.

Furthermore, many people find the higher cost of organic food a definite problem in their efforts to stay organic. Beans, which are very cheap and make a good filling meat substitute, can go a long way toward solving this problem.

What's surprising is the number of people today who go for the poor-quality foods, when there are so many good foods available. It's surprising that people don't hunt these good foods out and work with them.

COOK THEM YOURSELF

Beans are a good example. You can buy a can of baked beans ready to warm and eat. But they are second-rate, because the taste is standardized. You always know what a canned bean is going to taste like. It's edible, and in fact not really bad. But there's no mystery. Now if you will go to the dried bean section of your store, pick up a pound of marrow or pea beans and follow the recipe on the back for making baked beans, you will have something worth eating. You can experiment, varying the ingredients each time you prepare them. Your house will be filled with the aroma of baking beans for several hours. I find it fun. And there is no doubt that you end up with a healthful food.

If by some chance you don't know how to cook beans, just look on the back of the package they're sold in. The best recipes can be found that way. The bean companies want you to succeed, so they give you time-tested directions for use. And bean recipes *are* time-tested.

The Chinese in their culinary wisdom prepared gravies, soy sauce, cheese and meatless "meat" dishes from beans years before the rest of the world considered doing such a thing. In India and Indonesia a variety of beans and lentils have been used to garnish or complement rice dishes, and French chefs, second to none, braise beans with lamb, bake them into *cassoulet,* marinate them for salad and press them through a sieve to make a delicate puree. The great French chef Escoffier said of beans that "when they are cooked with care, no other vegetable can surpass them in perfection of flavor."

How does one eat them, then, to savor the quality great cooks have found, but Americans have never known? Since there are 10,000 bean varieties in the world and possibly half that many ways to prepare them, the person who claims he doesn't like them doesn't know his beans.

People hesitate to cook beans from scratch because the procedure seems to require an inordinate length of time. But it doesn't have to. Some varieties such as aduki and garbanza require less than two hours total preparation time, including soaking and simmering. Other varieties average about three hours in all, though kidney and black beans take longer. Hours in the pot can work to your advantage, however, if you wish to go off and leave them awhile. Beans might be considered a convenience food because they need not be cut up or browned, and except for a peek and a stir now and then, no more than five or ten minutes is spent in actual preparation of a dish. Anyone who has stood for the better part of an hour patiently browning meatballs or sautéeing vegetables can appreciate this feature. And you can always cook up a large batch and freeze or can the surplus for future use.

PLAN OF ATTACK

First, you must buy the bean. Organically grown, unsprayed food is, of course, always best, but even commercially grown beans have a thick pod to protect them against pesticides. Groceries which serve non-English speaking peoples are likely places to find a variety of beans, since every country but ours seems to have recognized their value. Your local supermarket may well surprise you, too, especially if you live in a Spanish-speaking neighborhood. Vitarroz packs a wide variety, so does Red Bow, and the latter is worth looking up because they claim to use no preservatives. Cost, as you already know, is cheap: a quarter's worth will feed four ravenous people.

Now having bought the bean, you sort out the wizened ones and possible stones, rinse well and put to soak.

About soaking: To preserve vitamins, you will not want to cook any food longer than necessary. Dried food must be rehydrated by soaking, and if the soaking process, which unlike cooking destroys no vitamins, takes place beforehand, the softened bean will, of course, take that much less time to cook. This is accomplished by dropping the beans into boiling water—we use broth. The ratio of liquid to beans should be three to one unless you are making soup, then the ratio should be four to one. Drop the beans into water slowly so the boiling is not interrupted, boil for two minutes and let sit for an hour or more. Boiling ruptures the hard shell of the bean so the bean swells and cooks in a shorter time. If you prefer a cold water soak, six hours will be sufficient. During overnight soaks the beans should be refrigerated, otherwise they may ferment.

COOKED BEANS THE BEST

At this point you may wonder if, in the interest of nutrition, you would be better off eating beans raw, since other vegetables ideally should be eaten raw. Not beans. Researchers in the Department of Home Economics at the University of Chicago have tested soybeans, navy beans, limas, Chinese and Georgia velvet beans, lentils, kidney and pinto beans and learned that the amino acids crystine and methionine, both of which are important to growth, are not available until the bean has been heated. However, don't rush to the opposite extreme and overcook, because pressure cooking at temperatures above 120°C has a deleterious effect on not only the amino acids mentioned above, but lysine as well.

Which brings us to the next point: cooking. Even baked beans may be simmered first to the point where they are almost tender, then finished off in the oven. A heavy pot is best for this. Cast iron enamelware is good, but unglazed pottery is good also, or heavy-bottomed stainless steel, the most practical cookware for the large-scale serving we do in Rodale Press's Fitness House kitchen. We do not, of course, throw away the water in which beans were soaked, but reserve it for simmering.

Cooking time depends on many variables such as age of the bean, what foods are cooked with it and nature of the cooking water. Acids, (tomato, for instance), molasses, fats and salts all harden the skin and make for longer cooking time. Hard water leaves a deposit of mineral salts with similar results. Some varieties take longer than others; old beans have a tough hide and hence a longer cooking time. The procedure we follow is to cook the beans—young ones if possible—in distilled water (you could use rainwater if you are lucky enough to own a cistern) and to add fats, tomato and salt only when the beans are well on their way to becoming tender—about an hour before they are done. Some authorities recommend that you add soda to the water to hasten the cooking process. Don't do it—it destroys the thiamin.

Once simmered close to completion, the final creation is a matter of personal taste. Beans in one form or another could be served every day for months without your having to repeat yourself, the possibilities are so numerous. Many foods marry well with beans: tomato, garlic, onion, molasses, honey, bacon and pork, savory, mustard, soy sauce, thyme are all good companions. Also corn, green beans, peppers and celery on occasion. White beans, soy beans and limas take well to white sauces and mayonnaise; white beans, soy beans and chick peas (garbanzas) make splendid salads. Use crunchy vegetables with them for contrast. Kidney beans go nicely with snap beans in salad, or you can mix several kinds of beans, slice in some tomato and garnish with egg. Garbanzas have a pleasantly nutty flavor, and they are a good bean for people who think they don't like beans—children, for instance.

If after all this persuasion you still feel beans are not for you, there are more unbeanish ways. They can be soaked, frozen overnight, roasted in a slow oven, oiled and salted. Soy beans and lentils are good this way. Then there is bean flour, good in your wheatless baked goods, and finally bean sprouts, which have all the vitamins and minerals of their unsprouted counterparts plus C and F. We often sneak them into salads. They are also good with scrambled eggs (really!), sautéed with rice or mixed vegetables or added to sandwich spread. We have found that sprouts 1 to 1¼ in. are best. They will contain chlorophyl if you expose them to sunlight for a few hours. Refrigerate or eat. Enjoy.

—Sally Freeman

Fats and Oils

"Fat" is the general term applied to both fats and oils. The criterion for distinguishing a fat from an oil is its physical form at room temperature. A fat is solid at room temperature and contains more of the saturated fatty acids than oil; whereas at the same temperature, an oil is liquid and contains more unsaturated fatty acids in its structure.

Fats have been highly prized in man's culinary history. From early times they have denoted prosperity and hospitality—as, for example, when the fatted calf was prepared for celebrating, or the widow shared her oil with the prophet.

NUTRITIONAL ROLE OF FATS

Fat—the body's prime fuel reserve—is the most concentrated energy source that the diet can provide. Gram for gram, it furnished more than twice the energy of proteins or carbohydrates (9 calories per gram compared to 4 calories per gram from proteins and carbohydrates). Fat, too, is the only source of energy which the body can store in quantity. Stored fat is readily mobilized and quickly available when needed as a fuel.

Fat per se lends palatability to the meal, and a certain amount of it is necessary to please most people and to make the diet acceptable. Bread with butter, besides containing more calories, is tastier than dry bread; mayonnaise adds to the dietetic pleasure of green salads. Many of the substances responsible for the flavor and aroma of foods are fat-soluble and associated with fat in the diet.

Fat slows the emptying time of the stomach and decreases intestinal motility. This deceleration of the digestive process delays the onset of hunger. Thus, fat-containing meals have a high satiety value—that is, they "stick to the ribs" longer. A balanced fat intake is essential to ensure the dietary supply of fat-soluble vitamins and essential fatty acids.

Fat-Soluble Vitamins and Their Functions are:

Vitamin A—Helps to form and maintain healthy eyes, skin, hair, teeth, gums and various glands. It is also involved in fat metabolism.

Vitamin D—For strong teeth and bones. Helps the body utilize calcium and phosphorus properly.

Vitamin E—Helps form normal red blood cells, muscles and other tissues. Protects fat in the body tissues from abnormal breakdown.

Vitamin K—For normal blood-clotting.

Not all fatty acids are synthesized in human and animal tissues. Those acids not synthesized—called essential fatty acids—must be supplied in the diet. Early speculation that these essential fatty acids form an important part of the actual structure of certain cells has been confirmed by recent investigations. Infants experimentally deprived of the essential fatty acids develop skin lesions which respond specifically to the administration of linoleic and/or arachidonic acid.

The essential fatty acids are found in natural vegetable oils, in the fat of mammalian organ tissues, in poultry fat and in fish oils.

FAT IN THE DIET

The contemporary emphasis on a possible relationship between dietary fat and atherosclerosis should not obscure the fact that fat is a necessary component of living tissue and essential in human nutrition. We suggest that the recommendations of a national commission of medical experts be considered. The commission's recommendations are as follows:

The current American diet which draws about 40 per cent of its calories from fat should be cut down to 30 to 35 per cent. The saturated fat level (animal and hydrogenated fats) currently at 16 to 20 per cent should be cut in half. Saturated fats tend to raise the cholesterol level in the blood serum. On the other hand, some studies indicate that the substitution of polyunsaturated fats (corn, peanut, soybean, wheat germ and sunflower seed oils) for saturated fats serves to lower serum cholesterol levels. The intake of polyunsaturated fat, which currently averages 7 per cent of caloric intake, should be increased to 10 per cent. The remaining dietary fats should come from mono-unsaturated fats like olive oil.

Honey—Food For A Queen

Since the earliest days of recorded history, men have been using honey as a food, a preservative, a medicine. A cave stone-painting from the neolithic age shows that about 15,000 years ago men gathered honey-combs for food, even as we do today. In the Egyptian pyramids, some 3,000-year-old honey has been found—dry and dark, but still pure honey. In Greek and Roman civilizations honey was used for preserving and embalming as well as for the choicest food. It served as a sacrifice to the gods and contributed an important part to the folk ceremonies of all nations.

In some countries the bee was regarded as sacred. No so many years ago, in most countries the beehive was considered such an important part of the household that special ceremonies were held there on holidays. And should a tragedy or some great blessing befall the family, someone was dispatched immediately to notify the bees!

In 1747 the use of beet sugar for sweetening was introduced by Markgraf. With humanity's usual broad assumption that anything new is necessarily better, we took to using sugar rather than honey for baking and cooking. The full story of the results in terms of health may never be known.

The average American eats well over one pound of sugar every three days! Our average consumption of honey is about 1½ pounds per person per year. An average bee colony may produce as much as 400 pounds of honey a year for its own use, the surplus of 50 pounds or so being what the beekeeper has for sale or for personal use.

If you want some fascinating reading, get yourself a book on bees and read the incredible story of the lives of these little creatures whose society is organized perfectly and ruthlessly for work and production, with no time for loafing or pleasure. Bees process the nectar and pollen of flowers to make honey. This complex and not-fully-understood procedure involves gathering the nectar and pollen on sunny days, packing it into the bee's pollen basket and honey stomach, then transferring it to the symmetrical wax cells of the hive. Somewhere along the line the flower nectar is changed by enzymes into the sweet, fragrant, nourishing honey that we know, which never spoils, molds or ferments.

PRODUCTION AND PROCESSING

We are told that bees visit about 10,000 different kinds of flowers, acting, of course, as pollinators to these flowers in the process of gathering the pollen (protein) and nectar (carbohydrate) for their food. One pound of honey requires about 37,000 trips of the honeybees and one bee colony may travel 17 million miles back and forth in a single year to provide honey for the population of the hive! In addition, of course, each colony collects 40 to 100 pounds of pollen each year.

We don't often get honey in combs these days. Most honey has been removed from the tiny geometric cells of the comb in which the bees placed it. To extract it, the tops of these cells are sliced off and the open comb is placed in a centrifuge which whirls the honey out in liquid form. This is called "extracted" honey. When the comb is crushed and the honey strained from it, this is called "strained" honey.

We have heard marvelous stories of the curative powers of honey. Through the ages, it has been used as a medicine. Pythagoras advocated a honey diet, declaring that honey brings health and long life. Charles Butler in his *History of the Bees,* written in 1623, says, "Hooni cleareth all the obstructions of the body, looseneth the belly, purgeth the foulness of the body and provoketh urine. It cutteth up and casteth out phlegmatic matter and thereby sharpens the stomach of them which by reason have little appetite. It purgeth those things which hurt the clearness of the eyes and nourisheth very much; it storeth up and preserveth natural heat and prolongeth old age." It has been used to treat inflammation, kidney diseases, disorders of the respiratory and digestive tract, bad complexions, liver trouble, infectious diseases, poor circulation and as an ointment for wounds.

NUTRITIONAL CONTENT

What is the food value of honey that has led people for so many thousands of years to believe in it as food and medicine? In modern times the first answer to such a question must be given in terms of vitamins. White sugar contains no vitamins. Does honey? Indeed it does. H. A. Schuette of the Department of Chemistry of the University of Wisconsin, is one of the outstanding investigators of vitamins in honey. In an article in the *Journal of Nutrition* for September, 1943, he, George Kitzes and C. A. Elvehjem describe the determination of B vitamins in honey. Each of the samples varied in its vitamin B content, according to the locality from which it came and the kind of flower the honey was made from. These researchers turned up some interesting aspects of vitamins in honey. They found that some of the B vitamins might be destroyed in storage over a period of years. They found that the vitamin content of pollen is much higher than that of honey, suggesting that perhaps the vitamins in honey are contained in the small pollen grains found in it. They also remind us that clarifying honey reduces the vitamin contents by 35 to 50 per cent of the original values. Clarifying is a process which removes the slight cloudiness that may be present, resulting in a honey crystal-clear and brilliant but less nourishing than the unclarified product.

The vitamin C content of honey varies, too, both with the kind of honey and the locality from which it comes. Some researchers have found as much as 311.2 milligrams and as little as 0 milligrams of vitamin C in 100 grams of honey. An orange weighing 100 grams contains from 25 to 50 milligrams of vitamin C. Naturally, one cannot eat 100 grams of honey as casually as he might eat an orange because of its concentrated sweetness.

Honey contains minerals, too. Here, interestingly enough, the mineral content depends largely on the color of the honey, those dark honeys, like buckwheat, being richer in minerals than the lighter ones. It is an intriguing aspect of our study of foods to note that nature likes color and lavishes her richest abundance of health-giving nourishment on foods in which color is most intense. Keep this in mind when you're shopping for food. If you're buying honey for its mineral content, choose the dark honeys, even though you may not at first care for their stronger flavor. Shopkeepers should stock a good selection of whole-some, untreated or unclarified honeys for today's health- and taste-conscious consumer.

Fertile Eggs—Source of Life

Crack an ordinary egg into a bowl. Next to it open a fertile, organically produced egg. Now make a few comparisons. The sterile version dis-plays a pale-yellow, often wobbly-looking yolk and a loose, watery or "runny" white. By contrast, the organic egg has a dark, full colored yolk and a firm white. More often than not, it also has a brown instead of white shell, usually a thicker, more protective one.

But the difference doesn't stop there. A fertile egg is alive. It holds a "life factor" akin to that found in seed foods. Besides, it tastes dozens of times better. Yet fertile eggs are overlooked; many city folks who've had nothing but flat, sterile eggs don't even know true "egg flavor."

Why? Because today's laying hen is raised in a false environ-ment. She spends her mature life in a wire cage about twice her own size, stacked in tiers high off the ground. Her diet is limited to processed pellets, deficient in trace nutrients and proteins, but laced with one or more of the modern "wonder drugs" and synthetic vitamins. Stimulants and lights keep her awake all night—but she gets tired of eating. Then arsenic is fed her to produce an appetite!

The hen thus becomes a mechanized commercial egg-producer—a literal "animal machine." Oh, she's efficient all right—but soon ex-pended. Productive life expectancy is about one-third less than when fowl of both sexes are allowed to run on the ground and peck their food. But the absence of the rooster in the hen yard promises up to 30 per cent more production from the same amount of feed, and sterile eggs will keep longer in shipment and storage. So economics and greed once more rule the roost.

The dark yolks and strong whites of the fertile type are no accident.

They result from natural feeds, fresh greens and insect life eaten by chickens in a free-range environment.

Okay, so they're much better eggs. And nearly all of us realize that eggs make up an important part of the well-rounded diet. Besides being a protein-rich breakfast favorite, they play a major role in every sort of baked foods, breads, noodle, spaghetti and macaroni products, desserts and even some beverages.

Cheese—The Slice Of Life

The origin of cheese-making is lost in antiquity. Legend has it that an Arabian merchant, in preparing for a long journey, poured some milk into his canteen, which was made from a dried sheep's stomach. He traveled through the heat of day, then paused in the evening to partake of the food he had brought with him. To his amazement, only a thin, watery liquid came from the canteen. On cutting open the canteen, he found a mass of white curd. Thus was produced the world's first cheese. Actually, the ancient Asiatic traveler had witnessed a simple natural phenomenon—the rennin in the dried sheep's stomach had produced curds and whey from the milk placed in the canteen.

The Pilgrims brought cheese with them when they came to America. Until 1850 the art of cheese-making was largely carried on in the home. In 1851 Jesse Williams started the first cheese factory in Rome, New York. By 1870 hundreds of cheese factories had sprung up throughout that state. The industry rapidly moved westward, and now cheese-making is carried on throughout the U.S., with Wisconsin being the most important producer.

MAKING NATURAL CHEESE

Cheese is made by coagulating milk and then separating the curd or solid part from the whey. Truly natural cheese is made from certified raw milk produced from animals on farms not using chemical fertilizers or pesticides.

Many of the popular varieties of natural cheese, although originating in Europe, are now produced in the United States and are available in your health food store.

Flavors range from bland cottage cheese to tangy blue (bleu) or pungent Limburger. Textures vary too—from the smooth creaminess of cream cheese to the firm elasticity of Swiss cheese. Flavor and body and texture of cheeses are closely related to degree of ripening or aging. Some natural cheeses are used unripened.

Soft unripened varieties, such as cottage, cream, Neufchâtel and ricotta cheese, contain a relatively high amount of moisture and do not undergo any curing or ripening. Examples of firm, unripened cheeses are Gjetost and Mysost.

In the soft, ripened cheeses, curing progresses from the outside or rind of the cheese toward the center. Particular molds or cultures of bacteria, which grow on the surface of the cheese, aid in developing the characteristic flavor and texture during the process of curing. Curing continues as long as the temperature is favorable. These cheeses include such varieties as Brie, Camembert and Limburger. They usually contain more moisture than semi-soft, ripened varieties.

Semi-soft, ripened cheeses cure from the interior as well as from the surface. This ripening process begins soon after the cheese is formed, with the aid of a characteristic bacterial or mold culture or both. Curing continues as long as the temperature is favorable. Examples of these cheeses are Bel Paese, Brick, Muenster and Port du Salut. They contain more moisture than the firm, ripened varieties.

Firm, ripened cheeses—which include the popular Cheddar, Colby, Edam, Gouda, Provolone and Swiss—mature with the aid of a bacterial culture throughout the entire cheese. Ripening continues as long as the temperature is favorable. The rate and degree of curing is also closely related to moisture content; therefore these cheeses, being lower in moisture than the softer varieties, usually require a longer curing time.

Very hard ripened cheeses are also cured with the help of a bacterial culture and enzymes. The rate of curing, however, is much slower because of the very low moisture and high salt content. In this category are Parmesan, Romano and Sap Sago.

Blue-vein, mold-ripened cheese curing is accomplished by the aid of bacteria, but more particularly by the use of a mold culture that grows throughout the interior of the cheese to produce the familiar appearance and characteristic flavor. The well-known blue-veined cheeses include Blue (or bleu), Gorgonzola, Stilton and Roquefort.

CHEESE AND NUTRITION

Cheese is one of the most concentrated foods—a pound containing the protein and fat of approximately a gallon of milk. Cheese containing milk fat is also an excellent source of vitamin A. Iron protein compounds of milk are retained in cheese and well utilized by the body.

Here is what we find in *one ounce* of a variety of cheeses:

Per Ounce	Cheddar	Cottage (*From skim milk*)	Roquefort	Swiss
Water %	36	79	40	39
Calories	115	25	105	105
Protein Gm.	7	5	6	7
Fat Gm.	9	trace	9	8
Carbohydrate Gm.	1	1	trace	1
Calcium Mg.	221	26	122	271
Iron Mg.	.3	.1	.2	.3
Thiamine Mg.	.01	.01	.01	.01
Riboflavin Mg.	.15	.08	.17	.06
Vitamin A I.U.	380	trace	350	320

With more than 400 varieties of natural cheese, there are bound to be several for every taste. For many people, their adventuresome spirit takes over when they see an attractive cheese display, and they buy unfamilar varieties for the pure enjoyment of getting acquainted with new cheese flavors and textures. Try the mild cheeses first and then the stronger-flavored ones. Alert yourself to the shapes, textures, aromas and tastes of cheese—and the nutritional concentration, too.

Peanut Butter—The Nutritious Snack

The tremendous rise in the consumption of snacks over the past five years has been of great concern to those of us interested in sound nutrition. Potato chips, corn chips, cookies and crackers apparently satisfy a psychological craving but contribute little to our physiological requirements. Food store owners have a snack that fills both needs— peanut butter.

Peanut butter was invented around 1890 by a St. Louis physician seeking a high protein food for his patients. He ground up some roasted peanuts with a little salt in a food grinder. Soon patients and friends were asking for this prescription.

First produced commercially about 1907, peanut butter rapidly attained wide popularity. However, the commercial product available today—a far cry from the original—contains peanuts (90-92 per cent), which have been roasted at high temperatures for extended periods, destroying a large portion of the vitamin content; hardened or hy-drogenated vegetable oil (3-4 per cent), increasing the intake of satu-rated fats and contributing to higher cholesterol blood levels; plus sugar and salt.

The producers of peanut butter supplying health food stores offer a carefully processed product containing 98-100 per cent peanuts, de-pending on the amount of salt added, and a flavor and texture unavaila-ble in the usual commercial product.

Properly made peanut butter is a valuable protein source, being higher in protein than beefsteak. It has twice the fat, a good source of the essential polyunsaturated fatty acids, seven times the calcium, three times the phosphorus, twice the vitamin B, and four times the niacin as an equal amount of beefsteak. It also has amino acids like meat, and when reduced to a fine butter is a most valuable food for all the family, including small children and elderly people. Just for the record here's how 100 grams of each compare:

	Peanut Butter	Beefsteak
Water %	1.7	54
Calories	576	297
Protein Gm.	26.1	23.0
Fat Gm.	47.8	22.0
Ash Gm.	3.4	1.1
Calcium Mg.	74	10
Phos. Mg.	393	175
Iron Mg.	1.9	2.9
Vit. B_1 Mg.	.12	.06
Vit. B_2 Mg.	.13	.19
Niacin Mg.	16.2	4.8

Children and adults like peanut butter best when eaten with jam or jelly in the popular sandwich combination. Over 50 per cent of all peanut butter sold is used in this manner. Peanut butter also can be used as an ingredient in sauces, salads, beverages and soup.

Organically Raised Lamb

"Poor little lambs who have lost their way" is a more meaningful lament than intended by the songwriter. Today, in addition to antibiotics, dips, drenches, shots, medicated feed, confined rearing and other "factory-farm" management techniques, sheep may even be treated with strong chemicals to defleece them. The latest insult is a plastic spiral intrauterine contraption that provides its own disinfectant. And the so-called "spring lamb" sold through regular outlets may turn out to be tough old mutton.

And what about naturally produced lamb? Our survey brought back comments such as: "Sweet and fresh, tender, never tastes like mutton." "The sweetest meat the family ever had." "Out of this world."

These are some of the high praises sung by people who have been eating organic lamb. Have you ever had this pleasure? Once you have savored the flavor of well-raised animals, slaughtered young, you will never again be content with supermarket lamb. What is the difference?

RAISING LAMBS THE ORGANIC WAY

Just as organic gardeners learn which soil amendments make plants thrive and how to meet emergencies of plant pests with non-toxic materials, so do organic lamb-producers display wise management with their livestock. At Benson, Illinois, Edward Johnson grows all the feed for some 40 to 60 head of his blackface HAMPSHIRE and SUFFOLK lambs on 160 acres. Other organic lamb-raisers also succeed in growing all their own feed.

Some organic lamb-producers supplement feed with natural materials such as bran, oilmeal and minerals. At West Bend, Wisconsin, Bernard Johnson's lambs are born as early as January and February, weaned before the ewes go out to pasture, then fed ground corn, bran, some oats and good second-crop alfalfa. He says this food produces good solid lamb meat.

On the other hand, at Brunswick, Maine, Earl Blackstone prefers to have lambs born as late as April or May, raising them on their mother's milk, and then turning them out to run all summer in rich, well-fertilized pasture. In addition to the tender green grasses, Blackstone values the benefits from summer sunshine, good air and pure water to help make good meat quality.

Among other problems, sheep are prone to parasites and ticks. For controls, organic raisers use safe approaches. Since Johnson's lambs are born so early in the season, they never get onto pasture, and therefore don't pick up parasites. Weaned and put on dry food, they never need antibiotics, either. Bob O'Brian of Tunbridge, Vermont, finds that he does not have to dip his sheep, since he controls the tick problem at its source. "Usually ticks are introduced into a flock by the purchase of animals from a flock already infested. Since our purchases are limited to an occasional ram to prevent inbreeding, we do not have ticks. An arsenic base is often used in dipping, and arsenic is highly carcinogenic for a person susceptible to skin cancer. I don't want to take such chances, so I am especially careful when buying sheep from an outside flock. I make inquiry and closely inspect their condition." O'Brien adds he does not worm his sheep by drenching them with chemicals. Instead he controls any parasitic problem by pasture rotation, about every three weeks.

For backyard lamb-raisers, Mrs. Joan Lindeman of Hornell, New York—who's been the adopted "mother" of at least eight lambs—says she's found "bottle" raising a pleasant and inexpensive way to beat high living costs while feeding her family top-quality meat. Orphaned lambs are readily obtained from regular sheep farmers, she writes, because they don't have either the time or the inclination to bother with bottling.

AVAILABILITY

Frozen organic lamb is sold in some health and natural food stores. Depending on suppliers, it may be available year round, but is more apt to be available seasonally or irregularly. Since most organic lamb-raisers have their animals slaughtered when only five to seven months old, the meat is tender and delicately flavored, never like strong mutton. Store prices for lamb are somewhat higher than supermarket ones. Usually the meat is lean, with little waste. Customers agree that such organic lamb is worth the extra cost.

Some organic lamb goes to special buyers. At Metamora, Illinois, Robert Adams, who considers himself "a strict natural farmer," sells all of his lamb—plus a large portion of his other products such as pork and beef—through a distributor. His poison-free foods reach highly allergic patients who depend on them as a lifeline. At Maplehurst Farms and Gardens in Hampshire, Illinois, Thomas Barry also sells organic lamb and other uncontaminated foods to highly-sensitive allergic patients.

If you are able to go directly to farms to find organic lamb, sources are available. By experience, many raisers have found that the most satisfactory way of selling their product is to deal directly with interested individuals. This eliminates the expense and problems of packing, shipping and distributing, and such savings can be passed along to the consumer. Sometimes the price is competitive with the supermarket, or only pennies above the prevailing top market prices.

At Loganville, Wisconsin, Harold Kruse has advance orders for organic lamb from his customers by the first of each November, selling through the co-op lamb pool. He used the convenient services of an abattoir two miles from his farm. There, with the facilities of meat inspection on the premises, as well as a frozen food locker, the lamb is prepared—either fresh or frozen—according to the customer's wishes, and picked up by Kruse's patrons. Although he sells whole lambs (far less poundage than for beef), sometimes he finds two buyers who wish to share half a lamb each.

Similarly, Bernard Johnson's lambs are slaughtered by a nearby butcher, who cuts them according to the customer's specifications, then wraps and sharp freezes the individual portions. Johnson also sells whole or half lambs to individual customers.

PRIDE PRODUCES QUALITY

Earl Blackstone points out the advantage as well as the economy of direct raiser-buyer relationships. "When the customer goes directly to the producer, talks with him, judges him for honesty and sincerity and can check the surroundings where the lamb is raised, he can get a first-hand impression. With organic farming and husbandry, pride in your product and 100 per cent guarantee of it go hand in hand."

Recent federal meat inspection legislation succeeds in further restricting the organic meat market, and keeping it at the farm. For example, O'Brien had hoped to sell some of his Vermont-raised lamb to the co-op food store, just a few miles away, across the state line at Hanover, New Hampshire. But the new law prevents it. "To cross the state line," he said, "our meat would have to undergo federal inspection before slaughter. There is no federal meat inspector in our area. If we had to truck our lambs to the nearest one at Woodsville, N.H., our costs would become too high for the co-op to sell our meat competitively. Although a state inspector checks the lambs when we have them slaughtered in Norwich, Vemont, this inspection is unacceptable to the federal officials."

Blackstone also relates why the most likely market for organic lamb will probably remain at farms. "Trucking 70 miles to a federally inspected slaughterhouse, then having to pay to have the meat cut up, packaged and frozen, buying dry ice and shipping, all end up with prices too high for the buyer and no profits for the raiser." He now sells his lambs live at his farm preferring to have customers arrange for slaughtering and processing.

Blackstone finds the rewards of sheep-raising difficult to translate in terms of dollar profits. "The aesthetic value of having lambs in a pasture by the house cannot be measured in money," he said. "I feel that I have other profits, even if I only break even financially."

—Beatrice Trum Hunter

Organically Raised Beef

Sink your teeth just once into a club steak, a rib roast, a stew or even a hamburger fashioned from naturally raised beef. You'll never be content with going back to supermarket meat—cut from cattle fattened on chemically grown feed, doused with pesticides, and pumped full of hormones and antibiotics.

When it comes to flavor and downright good eating, there's really no comparison. As for nutritional value and common-sense health protection, this meat stands head, shoulders and tail over the artificially hurried, "doctored" fare.

Actually, says one rancher, organic-minded people ought to be just as concerned about the quality of the meat they serve themselves and their families as they are about vegetables, fruits or any other foods. If insecticides, chemical fertilizers, weed-killers and all pose a threat to their well-being in seasonal produce, how can they be disregarded in the beef or other meats eaten regularly?

IT'S AVAILABLE

There's no need to "look the other way" on this important aspect of food quality and health. Some 40 or 50 farms, homesteads, natural-food stores and cooperatives were contacted in an *Organic Gardening and Farming* survey. These people are making organic beef available, and they insist to a man that the supply will rise with the demand. All that's needed is more folks wanting chemical-free top-quality meat.

Take the way Norman and Marjorie Aamodt have been building a following for their Black Angus at Snowhill Farm outside of Coatesville, Pennsylvania. On 280 acres—kept at peak fertility with cover crops, sludge, chicken-house litter and yearly applications of two tons of rock phosphate per acre—they grow the corn, soybeans, hay, oats and barley to feed 135 pure-bred Angus steers and cows. Nothing but some molasses is added to the ration, plus a little vinegar for brood cows to encourage milk. Whole soybeans, rich in vitamins A, D and E, which Aamodt says help prevent colds or other illness, are in the feed, too.

The Snowhill beef, all USDA inspected, is cut, well-wrapped, then frozen and sold in 42-pound boxes or sides and half-sides from the farm. Individual cuts go to several stores and a few institutions. Delivery and shipping have made the Aamodts' organic meat available throughout the country, and they have a number of "long-distance" customers who want nothing less than the fine taste of this Black Angus. Aamodt—a young man who left an engineering post to take up organic farming —hopes a boost in trade will make beef-raising more practical.

"Buying patterns are, to a large degree, a matter of habit," writes energetic Marjorie Aamodt, mother of two youngsters and a diligent "farmhand." "We are encouraging health-minded people to break the supermarket habit by establishing a new habit of ordering for and eating from their home freezers . . . . However, before encouraging more growers to service the 'organic market', a more effective buying climate should be established. The buyer must recognize, first, his own need for organically grown, natural products, and he must support the producer of these products."

INFORMING THE CONSUMER

Carlton Barnes, a veteran of organic beef raising, answered in similar fashion from his 115-acre farm at Sykesville, Maryland: "It's hard to encourage anyone to raise or to eat better beef who doesn't know the whole story—and even many who do know better don't put it into practice." Barnes says he now tries to produce all the meat he can find customers for and keeps a small herd of Angus and Hereford. He markets some beef in a shop near Washington, D.C., and expects government inspection to enable out-of-state shipping soon.

Further south, at Gordonsville, Virginia, is the largest beef operation adhering to natural methods, the Sylvania Organic Angus Ranch. Here, on 1,400 acres, Richard C. Allen raises close to 500 head, marketing about 165 a year in the state, all as ground, trimmed beef in frozen two-pound packages.

Allen, who's developed a spreading "organic community" around his ranch, has opened a health-food store and bakery. He lectures widely, seeking to publicize the benefits of naturally grown foods and to alert people to the rise in degenerative diseases which has followed a comparable rise in the use of agricultural chemicals. This sort of program for education, plus cooperative advertising, he feels, will propel the whole idea best.

Another organic beef man with strong words for consumers is Lawrence M. C. Smith, also an Angus raiser, whose 350-acre Wolf's Neck Farm stretches along the coast at Freeport, Maine.

He suggests "a test for chemical residues be made on meat bought at each of the country's five major food chains" as a way to wake up the public. He insists the consumer isn't getting the quality in food—particularly meat—that he pays for.

FARMS EVERYWHERE

Other organic beef farmers dot the map, many of them combining cash crops, poultry or other livestock. In Michigan, for instance, Ron and Sandra Davis have 160 acres at Laingsburg, raising Holstein-Hereford or Holstein-Angus crossed stock, along with hogs. They sell about a dozen head a year, having them processed to order at a local plant, then delivered to customers' freezers. They run a small community newspaper ad and feel they've helped educate people by trying to explain why natural beef is better. "Perhaps the next time they hear or read something about poisons, additives or pollution, they will stop and think. Not until people are convinced that they don't want to eat poisoned food will farmers really become interested in raising organic livestock."

There are many other organic meat raisers throughout the country. The Davises, the Aamodts and the Smiths are typical of them. Their techniques and the scale of the operations vary, but the premise is unequivocating. And their lot is striding forward.

Our cross-section look into the organic beef picture has shown considerable progress over the limited availability of just a few years ago. It also shows a lot of room ahead for improvement in letting people know the *why's, wherefore's and where* of seeking better meat.

Quite likely, increased sales through expanding big-city organic markets will also help bring more organically raised beef to health-conscious consumers.

—*M. C. Goldman*

About Buying Beef

It's often not easy to find beef you can feel safe to eat these days. Used to be a piece of beef either was good (it looked good; it smelled good) or bad (it looked and smelled bad). Today it all looks good under those special meat-case lights; you don't see any chemical residues in the meat; you don't smell much through the plastic wrap.

Stay away from it all. Buy organically grown beef from someone you know and trust, if at all possible. This is especially important today for a number of reasons:

—First, of course, is that you're getting quality beef, raised freely in pastures, and fattened in nature's own time, without any chemicals. This means better health for you and your family, as well as real beef flavor so often missing in commercial cuts.

—Second, the beef industry is in a state of flux, with new rules from the FDA on antibiotics and other drugs. A lot of beef growers just might turn to producing organic beef if enough people demand it and the factory-beef industry is ever-more plagued by restrictions on the chemical demons it has summoned to help it grow more meat faster.

—Third, organic cattlemen need all the support they can get. USDA action in Nebraska recently forced an organic beef distributor out of business. But governmental policies can't stop the production of clean meat if that's what the people want. Here are the ways to procure the best quality beef:

You can raise it yourself. Then you know exactly what you're getting.

Find and get to know a reliable producer of organic beef. You might make it a family outing for a day to visit the farmer and purchase the meat you've arranged for ahead of time by phone. If he's taking the time to raise organic beef, he'll be glad to tell you about his methods.

There must be a farmer somewhere near you who is raising beef cleanly. Compare these farmers' grass-fed naturally grown cattle to the feedlot variety and the difference in taste is more than striking: cattle are ruminative, and while they enjoy grain and get fat on it, the fat often covers tasteless lean; many experts consider beef the best when the cattle get a mixture of grain and hay during the non-foraging months of winter, and forage freely during the summer.

Buy organic beef in retail stores. Ask the store owner where the beef comes from and the name of the farmer. He should know. If he doesn't, ask him to find out. It's important for the link between grower and consumer to be maintained. In this way, someone is accountable for the quality of the meat. By contrast, try finding out who raised the beef steak on the supermarket shelf.

DEALING WITH A SUPERMARKET

If you must buy meat at the butcher or supermarket, there are still ways to find beef that may not have been treated with diethylstilbestrol (the growth hormone) or antibiotics or the host of other chemicals used in the feedlot. Here's what you should know:

The least expensive hamburger is apt to be the cleanest. Usually, this is made from fresh-frozen beef imported from Argentina (all grass-fed and very hearty), Australia, New Zealand or Ireland . . . beef grown on grassland without DES or other drugs. It may not meet the requirements of being organic, but it is natural beef. You may be able to specify cuts from imported carcasses. However, U.S. cattlemen have lobbied a tough import quota law, and this holds down the amount of clean beef from overseas.

Commercial grade beef is much more likely to come from older heifers, and while it might not be as marbled with fat or as cherry-red as young beef, it's usually just as good and leaner. The USDA grading service first grades beef on the hoof. After slaughter, it is regraded as a carcass. So the farmer who gets paid for a lower grade may see his beef end up being sold at a higher grade. The official grades are Prime, Choice, Good, Standard, Commercial, Utility, Cutter and Canner. Grade determination is supposed to be based on many factors, including shape, amount of rib eye, fat, color, texture, age, marbling.

But as Vance Bourjaily points out in the March 1972, *Harper's:* "Steers spend eight months in the feedlot . . . until they reach the

---

Standards For Organically Grown Meat

Organically grown meats are products of stock raised on land which is managed organically. Animals are free to run and get adequate exercise for physical fitness. Both feed and environment are free from pesticide and herbicide residues, DES, antibiotics, growth hormones, and irradiation. All young stock must have daylight and well-ventilated housing. All cattle, sheep and hens shall have free range; permanent housing is prohibited. Routine use of drugs and antibiotics, urea and synthetic proteins is not allowed. If an animal requires drugs or antibiotics due to illness, it is not marketable until chemical analysis proves that all such drugs are no longer in its body. Food supplements include seaweed, bonemeal and other natural supplements. Animals shall not be sterilized chemically. Grass grazing is encouraged as opposed to heavy grain feeding. Animals shall be periodically examined for vitamin and mineral deficiency. Ninety-five per cent of the feed should be grown and harvested on the farm itself. Beef is raised with the view of minimizing, not maximizing the fat content, and this fat content should be 30 per cent less than that of commercial beef of the same quality. Meats should be graded carefully, and the highest-quality packaging should be used.

—*Dick Townley*

---

weight of 900 pounds (Good), 1,000 pounds (Choice) or 1,200 pounds (Prime). That's all the grading system is any longer; once it reflected whether an animal had matured properly, and therefore it meant something in terms of meat quality. Now all it tells is . . . how grossly he's overweight." He suggests that a more appropriate grading system might be "U.S. Fat," "U.S. Fatter," and "U.S. Fattest."

Young steers taken to Midwestern feedlots are fed chemicals to improve growth so they finish off at Prime or Choice weights for the supermarket trade. But the mothers of those steers usually wandered the grasslands and are much more natural than the feedlot beef. These cows often end up as Commercial beef. Feedlot beef is in reality overweight baby beef, usually less than two years old. One good, old encyclopedia of cooking says the best beef for roasts comes from five-to-six-year-old grass-fattened cattle.

Madeline D. Seim of Shade Hill, south Dakota, wrote us to call attention to this more natural if older, beef. She said, "Why doesn't the consumer who truly doesn't want beef implanted with DES, just ask for it? All you have to do is tell your butcher you're going to buy Commercial grade beef until feedlot operators stop this business. Help us ranchers out."

"The lack of clean meat may not be as acute as it seems," says Robert C. Lantis of Maudlow, Mont. "There are still some cattle ranches scattered about the states of Oregon, Washington, Idaho, Wyoming, Montana and Colorado which have not had the land contaminated by the chemical syndrome nor the cattle messed up by medical madness all in the name of production.

"The valleys of the high mountains of the West produce grass of the highest quality for the growing of beef. The Big Hole Basin of Montana is perhaps the best known, but there are many others. The animals grown on this grass finish off in a manner that is hard for even an expert to tell from grain-fed beef. These cattle are allowed to roam the range at will, feeding where the grass suits them best . . . . I believe that a bonus of a few cents a pound would be enough incentive for a lot of ranchers to clean up their operations and stay that way," Lantis says.

These excellent range-fed steers may end up as Commercial beef, however, because they are not raised under feedlot conditions. So ask for Commercial beef if you must patronize the supermarket.

A Quick Eye-Check For Quality Beef

In a nutshell, here are a few of the most important things to look for when inspecting a piece of beef:

—*The bone should be ivory-white, not chalky or yellowed. Ivory-white bones indicate a young steer. In the supermarket, though, the ivory-white bone of the young steer probably means he's come from the feedlot.*

—*The fat should be white, not yellow. Again, this is an indication of age. Avoid over-fat meat.*

—*The finest-tasting meat is cherry-red to red in color. The darker the meat, the older the animal. The meat should be velvety rather than coarse.*

GRADING AND INSPECTIONS

Once upon a time it was possible to say that veal was a good buy. But no longer. This meat from very young cattle has been upgraded by the USDA, according to Sid Goodman who tipped us off. What the USDA has done is raise all veal one grade. What was once Choice is now Prime; what was once Good is now Choice and so on. Veal has become so costly it's out of many people's reach. The regrading was confirmed by USDA.

Another grading system, called the Yield Grade, is also in use today by the USDA. A carcass is graded from 1 to 3, depending on the amount of fat. An animal with a Yield Grade of 1 might have a quarter-inch of fat over the rib-eye; a 2 might have a half-inch, and a 3 might have an inch. So if you want leaner beef, specify meat from a carcass with a low yield grade. Some fat is desirable though.

The USDA also runs an inspection service. We spoke to one meat inspector who told us that some major chain stores buy ungraded beef (the USDA grading service must be purchased by the slaughterer) to avoid the payment for grading.

The inspectors cover some areas of inspection thoroughly, but the rules miss great areas where inspection is needed. For instance, while the inspectors maintain the slaughterhouse in a neat and clean condition, they allow sodium nitrite and sodium nitrate into processed meats —and both are poisons. While they examine head, tongue, liver, heart, kidneys and lymph nodes for disease, the rules say that some carcasses with cancer tissue can be used for food after the cancer has been removed.

Tissue samples are taken by USDA veterinarians on the kill floor, but only randomly, and animals with hormone and antibiotic residues do get through.

According to the "Federal Meat and Poultry Inspection Statistical Summary for 1971," some 10,000 of the 31 million cattle inspected failed the on-the-hoof inspection; 86,000 were condemned after both on-the-hoof and carcass inspections. Of these 86,000, about 17,000 were totally condemned because of malignant tissue. There were over 3 million cattle carcasses passed for food after disease was discovered and the affected parts removed—including 92,209 cancerous cattle and 101 containing drug and pesticide residues. We wonder how one removes the part affected by drug residues and passes the rest as clean. And we wonder if those meat inspectors really got all the cancer.

ANTIBIOTICS AND DES

Some of the drug residues found were antibiotics, upon which the feedlot industry depends. A lot is happening in the area of antibiotics now, since the Food and Drug Administration has recently proposed steps to limit the use of antibiotics in animal feed. This must be shocking news indeed to feedlot operators since without antibiotics, the cattle which are crammed tightly into pens full of their own excrement and plagued by flies, would soon fall prey to disease. Basically, the FDA wants to stop the use of antibiotics which are also used in human medicine, since their prolonged use can build a transferable resistance to the drug into the meat tissues. Humans who eat the tainted beef can find that when they desperately need antibiotics to fight an infection, their microbes have developed a tolerance for the drugs.

"There is not going to be a ban on the use of antibiotics in animal feed. It would be a catastrophe. The industry has become geared to the use of these substances," a drug industry source told *Supermarket News* (Feb.7, 1972). The article also quotes a member of the FDA's task force which recommended curtailment of the drugs. and who asked not to be identified, as saying, "the value of antibiotics to livestock growers is estimated at $414,135,000."

He said antibiotics were growth-promoters as well as disease-preventers. They promote growth by eliminating growth-retarding infections. Over the last 15-20 years, the time it takes to bring cattle to market weight has been reduced from ten to seven weeks because of antibiotics, he said.

Then *Supermarket News* asked a drug company spokesman, "Are the risks of antibiotic livestock feeding to consumers greater than the advantages to producers?"

"No," said the spokesman. "It's all a game of chance. You have to go with the odds, and the odds say the danger is minimal."

The ironic part of the antibiotic hassle is the evidence that animals may be worse off taking them. Dr. Richard Bristol of Iowa State University studied 174,000 feeder cattle three years ago. He compared a group fed antibiotics before shipment to a group that endured shipment with no treatment. He found that 64 per cent of the treated groups developed sickness in transit, while only 51 per cent of the untreated groups got sick. These are groups, now, not individual animals. Death losses involved 44 per cent of the groups on antibiotics and only 22 per cent of the groups not using them.

Another fattening agent is DES, the growth hormone, about which volumes have been written.[37] At one time, an estimated 90 per cent

---

[37] See *Sowing the Wind* by Harrison Wellford, a Nader Raider, published by the Center for the Study of Responsive Law, Washington, D.C.

Feed Additives & Pesticides

These are the most common chemicals your sirloin steak may encounter on the way to the supermarket. There are many others.

Antibiotics and Hormones	Pesticides
Arsanilic acid	Co-Ral
Carbarsone	Ruelene
Diethylstilbestrol	Rotenone
Melengestrol acetate	Toxaphene
Phenothiazine	Korlan
Roxarsone	Lindane
Thiabendazole	Ciodrin
Tylosin-sulfamethazine	Pyrenone
Chlortetracycline	
Chlortetracycline-sulfamethazine	
Penicillin	

of the cattle finished for market in this country were fed this substance, which can cause hormonal changes in humans if residues are retained in the meat. The European Common Market countries, among others, banned the importation of U.S. beef as unfit for human consumption because it was raised with DES. Our FDA doubled the permissible amount of DES for use in fattening cattle, while extending the withdrawal time from 48 hours to 7 days. This means that growers are supposed to stop using DES a week before slaughter. Let's pray they do.

The recent move by the U.S. Food and Drug Adminstration to eliminate DES from livestock feed shouldn't be construed as a move to eliminate the use of DES. Implanting DES in livestock is still permitted, and the practice will now undoubtedly grow. The DES does have a restriction on its use; the growers still have DES.

Growers wouldn't even *need* DES if they'd raise bulls instead of steers. Bulls grow the fastest; then steers; then heifers. So, in order to make steers (castrated bulls) grow like bulls, they feed the hormones that stopped when castration occurred. Some growers say that bulls aren't as manageable as steers and especially can't be handled in the feedlot, and that's the reason for castration. But some cattlemen report little trouble with most bulls. Most important, docility in the cattle is hardly worth the human woe from DES. The real reason is that for no good reason, bull meat sells for less than steer meat.

FEEDLOTS, USDA AND THE CONSUMER

There's more about feedlot beef: Some managers feed the cattle plastic pellets for roughage. These pass through the digestive tract and act solely to provide bulk when grain is fed. Some managers also feed urea, or high-nitrogen supplements. The cattle convert some of this to protein by their ruminative processes. But it's horribly unnatural and of possible danger to humans. Experimentally, newspaper and poultry-floor litter has been fed to cattle. The grains are fed solely on availability: in Iowa, cattle eat corn; in Texas, sorghum; in Idaho, potatoes.

For those who think about such things, feedlot cattle are not happy cattle. They are not treated as living animals, but as potential dollars. Meat from such animals must contain gland secretions out of harmony with the natural balance which the animals would achieve if allowed to roam free.

Stronger federal meat inspection and consumer orientation might help improve the beef situation. Such an agency, responsible only for meat inspection and quality control was recently proposed for the USDA. Assistant Secretary of Agriculture Richard E. Lyng turned it down. Lyng was the official accused of hiding data on DES residues found in cattle.

There are other abuses in the selling of beef which you'd be wise to know about. Two may occur when you buy meat for the freezer. Sometimes meat dealers will advertise a USDA Choice carcass at very low prices. When the customer sees the carcass, it may be overfat and wasty. The dealer then trots out a leaner, better carcass which he says is what the customer *really* wants . . . at a higher price, of course.

Another practice is substituting forequarter cuts for hind quarter. One customer complained to the USDA about the amount of chuck roast he received with his hindquarter. Chuck comes from the fore-quarter.

Some suppliers offer a "beef bundle" or a "steak package." Unless the grade of meat is specified, and the kind and amount of cuts, you'd do well to avoid such "bargains."

Even though organic beef may cost more these days, it's still a better buy because the money you spend goes to the man who really earned it—the farmer. This is especially true when you buy directly from the grower. A lot of your meat dollar goes to middlemen when you buy supermarket beef. For instance, of the typical supermarket beef dollar, the retailer gets 15 per cent, the wholesaler gets 11 per cent, 5 per cent goes for trucking of the carcass, 4 per cent goes for other marketing costs. The rest is split between rancher and feedlot operator.

To sum up: the closer you can get to the producer of the beef you want to buy, the better. Make sure it's organic. If you have no recourse but to use the butcher or supermarket, buy imported beef, or Commercial grade beef, and ask for a low yield grade. Most important of all, demand clean meat.

—Jeff Cox

2

The Organic Grower Certification Program

Is It Really Organic?

The promise of new confidence for the troubled consumer, new status and security for the small farmer and new hope for the poisoned soil, air and water of America is involved in a new program to certify farms as sources of organic food.

The undertaking is being carried out through *Organic Gardening and Farming* magazine. Basically, it entails chemical, visual, and per sonal investigation of farms claiming to be organic to make sure that what they grow is in fact organic.

Farmers who are approved will be given the right to use the registered Organic Farmer trademark, and a statement that they are "Certified by *Organic Gardening and Farming* magazine." In addition, the identifying label will bear the name and address of the producing farm, so that the consumer knows not only what he's buying, but whom he's buying it from. Even when the produce is distributed by an intermediary, the label will identify the source farm.

To get the program underway in its fledgling stage, the costs of the certification program are being absorbed by Rodale Press. Even laboratory fees are being spared the farmers. No advertising or any other requirements other than good farming practices are made of the producers.

What does all this mean to *you*, the consumer hungry for good food? Here are some of the ways you'll benefit:

First of all, you'll be able to shop with greater confidence. With the demand for organic food increasing tremendously, the door has been opened for hustlers to make a fast buck. A few unethical distributors and retailers have cast a shadow of doubt over the whole field. Certain fearful commercial interests have made it a point to claim—ridiculously—that 95 per cent of "organic food" isn't organic. And who's to say—authoritatively—that they're wrong, dead wrong? That's where the Organic Farmer seal comes in. When you buy food bearing the Organic Farmer certification, you'll know it's organic: grown without the use of chemical pesticides, herbicides or fungicides. You'll know your food has been grown without the use of chemical fertilizers that destroy the natural ecology of the soil and make minerals unavailable to plants. You'll know your food wasn't grown in soil nutritionally exhausted by years of monoculture and erosion. Likewise, you can stop worrying that the grain you buy has been unfrocked of its bran, shorn of its vital germ. A chicken from a certified farm will be a chicken, not a chemochicken—stimulated, medicated and hormone-treated. The same goes for all organic livestock. They're treated as living creatures; steers roam to graze, putting on protein instead of fat, hens walk around in the sunlight and scratch the ground.

In a positive vein, you'll be sure that the food you purchase from a certified farm has been grown in soil systematically enriched with living humus, soil that has been analyzed and found to contain available nutrients you and the plant need. You'll know your system will be cleaner and healthier for eating purer, more naturally grown and ripened food. And that food, by the way, will taste better—fantastically better. Tomatoes will be a revelation, carrots startling.

Consumers won't be the only ones to benefit from the Organic Farmer certification program. Retailers stocking foods from certified farms will gain new acceptance by their clienteles. Doubting Thomases who don't take the seal at face value can simply read the label, note the farmer's address, and if it isn't too far away, drive out to see for themselves if he is legitimately organic.

NEW HOPE FOR AGRICULTURE

Tremendous benefits accrue to the organic farmers, especially small farmers, as most of them are. Few can keep up with the kind of mechanized farming done by gigantic corporations today. If they don't have at least several hundred thousand chickens, they can't compete price-wise with an outfit that has a million. If they don't produce green peppers by the car-lot, they're at the mercy of distributors and middle-men. For these families, the Organic Farmer seal opens up a premium market that recognizes quality instead of quantity, and rewards their many hours of extra work with the extra profit they need to stay on the land. Equally important, it gives them a new sense of dignity. Creeping anonymity will be replaced with sudden responsibility. All their food is marketed under their own farm label and address. They're centrally registered. If their pears or roasters are especially tasty, they'll earn a deserved reputation. If not, they'd better try harder, because they won't last long.

There's even a psychological advantage involved. Floyd Allen, the West Coast editor of *Organic Gardening and Farming*, who's already established the certifying system in California, puts it this way: "In my travels I've found that most organic farmers are actually hungry for some kind of contact with the people who eat the food which they produce. Farmers, really good farmers, are like fine cooks. They like to know that other people enjoy their food."

In a wider focus, it becomes clear that this new chance for the small farmer has profound sociological meaning. Thousands being forced off the land their families farmed for generations now have a viable option that just didn't exist before. The very smallness that had spelled their doom may now become a saving grace, because raising 500,000 fryers by the organic method is all but impossible in the present state of the art. The medium-sized conventional farmer may be more likely to wind up in the slums of a city than his smaller, but organic neighbor. Migrant agricultural workers who have been the virtual slaves of large landhold-ers may find that organic farming, with its need for personal attention to every plant, is precisely suited to the "labor intensive" farming they have specialized in (so unprofitably) all their lives. Still another part of the picture is the chance of a better break for the many who have left the teeming, violent cities to return to the soil, worked their hearts out, and failed utterly just because they were too small to buy all the ma-chinery and get all the credit an industrialized, chemical-oriented farmer needs to exist.

RESTORING THE LAND

The very soil of America will receive benefits commensurate with those given its farmers. It's no great secret that typical American farmland has lost between 25 and 75 per cent of its ability to retain water as a direct result of modern farming techniques. The rate of loss accelerates as exhausted top soil gets blown away, washed away, or compacted by elephantine harvesting machines. This theft is already measured in the millions of tons. There are further losses. Wheat in the mid-west is reported to have lost 10 per cent of its protein content just in recent years; vast stretches of other croplands have been nutritionally ravaged by monoculture and chemical fertilizers.

Organic farming changes all this. It restores good structure and balance to the soil, by returning to it large amounts of the organic building materials it would get in the natural state from decaying vegetable and animal matter. The organic farmer deals with his soil as he does his bank account: he puts in first, then takes out. He makes deposits of organic wealth regularly, refrains from writing bad agricultural checks and at season's end draws out his interest in the form of top-quality crops. Neither he nor his children nor his children's children will ever have to move on because their land is worn out. Rather, the more he farms it, the stronger it becomes.

The promised growth of organic farming will have other benefits for the land. Because he does not use pesticides, the organic farmer must make certain he is in tune with nature; he becomes both farmer and conservationist. He encourages birds to feel at home by leaving some brush or building bird houses. He introduces insects that prey on harmful insects but don't become pests themselves. He doesn't shoot hawks or owls and doesn't stamp on snakes because he knows they're natural rodent killers. His farm is truly alive, an ecosystem. Additionally, his farm is not going to be responsible for pesticides poisoning the food chain, endangering man and animal alike, downstream, downwind, down to the depths of the ocean and down to Antarctica where penguins who have never seen a man are toxified with his DDT. To farm organically is to practice preventive medicine on a global scale.

The farms that have already been given the right to use the Organic Farmer seal range in size from less than one acre to 3,000 acres. Expansion of the program will be made as quickly as possible without lowering the standards.

STANDARDS AND TESTS

And just what are those standards? As outlined by Floyd Allen, each farm is visited several times a year by a sampler who does not give advance notice. In California, this is a representative of Agri-Science Laboratories. He takes samples of soil, produce and water, which are then analyzed for a number of characteristics. Among them are the amount of extractable humic acid (must be at least 3 per cent), the amount of extractable nitrate, potassium and phosphorus, total organic nitrogen, total organic matter and total trace minerals. These are only a few of the tests made. Others zero in on pesticide residues and contamination by industrial pollutants. The testing program is dynamic and will be modified and improved. The results, incidentally, are also of great value to the farmers themselves.

Beyond the chemical testing, investigators with years of experience in farming poke around each farm and look for tell-tale signs of inorganic practices. A sprayer hidden in the barn? Old fertilizer bags? At the same time, they'll be available to offer advice to the farmer—if he asks.

No system is fool-proof, of course. Nobody can give you an iron-clad guarantee that the eggplant you bought contains the optimal amount of trace minerals. On the other hand, food inspection carried out by the Federal Government, with all its vast resources, is no model of efficiency. Certainly, no certified organic farmer will go on his merry way, unchecked for four or five years, as do some huge food processing operations.

Perhaps, the Organic Farmer certification program will bring order and science to a rapidly growing but somewhat chaotic development— not only in agriculture, but in eating and nutrition. It is young, just getting on its feet, but fortunately, attracting an increasing number of intelligent, dedicated people—pioneer types, nonconformists, farmers with their backs against the wall and young people just starting out— people who never saw a farm in their lives, but who are refusing to go on paying good money for tasteless, degenerate food. They're rallying around the idea of an Organic America.

THE PHONIES AND YOU

But they need help, Primarily, they need some way of purging the parasites, the unscrupulous minority that seizes upon every new idea that fresh minds create and bleeds it white. Already, chain store produce managers are being urged by their trade magazines to "get on the organic bandwagon," without being given any idea of why, where or how organic food is grown. All they know is that it's the latest thing, a hot item. TV commercials are hawking "organic shampoo," one magazine ad offers "organic furniture."

Inevitably, these crooks and phonies will be exposed, and when they are, a lot of honest people may be brought down with them. Before that happens, though, they may have so cheapened and corrupted the idea of "organic" that there will be nothing much left to bring down. An Organic America not protected against these parasites is a risky investment of work, money, and enthusiasm.

The Organic Farmer certification and labeling program, we feel, provides that protection. First, the very word "organic", as *you* mean it, is defined in display signs which are being offered to appropriate retailers. The seal itself, on bags, boxes and crates, will distinguish those farms which are proven to be organic from those which are at best unproven. The consumer will know exactly where he stands when he makes a purchase. If he buys food which is not certified, he has no basis to blame anyone else if he discovers the product is not what it's supposed to be. The reputation of honest people and the entire organic movement will not be sullied.

At the same time, the Organic Farmer seal will provide a way for you to encourage the growing of truly organic food by purchasing only those items properly labeled. In this manner, the organic farmer and the organic-minded consumer will literally nurture each other by their cooperative efforts.

Eventually, you will be able to insist that the "organic food" you buy be certified with the Organic Farmer seal. That day is not yet here, but there are ways in which you can speed its arrival.

Let your retailer know that you do not automatically assume everything he sells is truly organically produced. Ask him where he got those apples. How about the oranges? What about the frozen piece of beef? How does he *know* they were produced organically? Has he seen the farm? The grove? The ranch?

If you're new at a store, play dumb. Ask the man just what does "organic" mean? How does he know there's no DDT on the celery? How can he know?

In all likelihood, even the most responsible merchant won't be able to come up with satisfactory answers. You can't really expect him to—not yet—so don't press him too hard. The important thing is for him to realize that his customers want to be sure of what they're buying. If enough people ask him, you can bet he'll start worrying about it, thinking of ways to provide some meaningful assurance. Before long, the Organic Farmer seal will be providing that assurance.

What The Seal Means

This seal means what it says: the farmer is organic. He is using recognized organic growing practices to raise his crops. The seal and certification have already been awarded to many farms.

What Is Organically-Grown Food?

Organically grown food is food grown without pesticides; grown without artificial fertilizers; grown in soil whose humus content is increased by the additions of organic matter; grown in soil whose mineral content is increased with applications of natural mineral fertilizers; and food that has not been treated with preservatives, hormones, antibiotics, or other synthetic additives, etc.

That definition is the heart of the Organic Farmer program. It spells out clearly the way his food is grown and produced. It defines the methods used in raising wholesome food, not in processing or manufacturing anything else.

Display cards with this definition and the Organic Farmer seal are being sent to over 3,000 health food stores, shops, stands and markets. It is part of *Organic Gardening and Farming's* program to get grower and public together—right.

T.M. REGD.

Organic Farmers Need Action—From You

Next to growing your own, the best way to boost the organic idea is to shop for foods you *know* are organically grown—and to insist that whoever sells them to you does the same. That's the one vital thing every consumer, retailer and distributor of natural foods must do to make certain the organic food movement continues its surge. What's more, it is the one essential step toward making sure those same enterprises aren't squeezed out of business—whether by a drop in public confidence, manipulation and pressure from chemical agriculture or a staged series of court actions aimed at smothering trade that has begun to cut into big commerce.

The Rodale Press newsletter for the health food trade, *Organic Food Marketing,* has been emphasizing the importance of this in its editorials. It's equally important that you, the consumer, understand the importance of *knowing* that the organic food you buy is truly organically grown and that you pass the word along where you shop. As OFM editorialized in mid-1972:

> *It's up to you.* The number of large-scale organic farmers has been increasing. Floyd Allen, the West Coast editor of *Organic Gardening and Farming,* reports some truly significant developments. "A few months ago I was told that organic farms in the Texas Panhandle have now reached a total of 50,000 acres, with individual farms averaging about 1,500 acres. In California, we certify 720 acres of the Whiskey Slough Farm in the Stockton Delta area, and John Zuckerman (Whiskey Slough's owner) is ready and willing to commit his entire 6,000 acres to organic production. Moreover, he believes that if Americans really do want a clean environment and are willing to support farmers accordingly, that it's possible to convert the entire 30,000 acres of the Delta area to organic production . . .
>
> "The Lundbergs of Wehah Farms (Richvale, California) produce approximately 820 acres of organic rice each year (maximum the law allows them to) on their 3,000-acre farm, and this year they have encouraged their neighbors to convert another 900 acres to organic production, and they have a waiting list of farmers wanting to go organic . . . Talking to them I imagine that most of the area involving hundreds of thousands of acres could be put into organic production, and into an environmentally safe and sound form of agriculture, over a period of ten years if, as consumers and citizens we are willing to help pay for it. And not too far from Sacramento, Jack Anderson of Knights Landing is growing 400 acres of tomatoes . . . now that's pretty large-scale farming . . . no pesticides contaminating the environment . . ."

One strong example of how the organic food trade might tackle the problem is with rice crops. Discussing this with Homer Lundberg of

Wehah Farms, Floyd Allen makes it clear that "if all unquestionable organically grown rice could be positively identified for the market, I doubt that there would be nearly enough to go around. This condition in the past has created part of today's problem. Our objective at Rodale Press has been to help organic food buyers to distinguish the differences.

"We have long been aware that as we promote legitimate organic farmers, we also provide an 'umbrella' for organic phonies," continues Allen. However, he stresses, "If we were able to identify all organic producers for consumers, particularly in the case of rice—that is, to identify all producers of organically grown rice within one easy-to-recognize-and-remember identification such as an ORGA seal (Organic Rice Growers Association) which we could endorse and promote, then we would be operating from a position of considerable strength.

"For example, we could state categorically that if the label (regardless of brand) fails to carry the ORGA Seal, then it is not organically grown." We can inform retailers and consumers of this, he adds. "I think you could see that this would give us some real teeth and it would enable organic food buyers to draw the same lines we do. With this to operate from, we could begin to push out questionable rice (from the existing market) and establish a firm foundation where gains are held while we all work to bring better rice to conventionally grown rice eaters."

IT'S UP TO YOU

And so, here is how we wrapped up our message to the health food marketers—a message you can help deliver with enough force to make it penetrate:

> *It's up to you.* While we've been informing and alerting the public to know and seek bona-fide organically grown foods, it takes the industry to make them available. The merchant—be he producer, processer, shopkeeper—owes it to the consumer to have those foods for sale. He owes it to the grower to translate the public's demand for real food to the marketplace. Most of all, he owes it to himself to support the very foundation of the natural health foods concept—that is, the foods grown and sold without chemicals, poisons, additives. Not only is it sensible for good business, it's absolutely requisite for his business to look into the

future and to last. Supermarket chains might dabble in organic foods, then toss them aside—but the health-food trade today is committed by the consumer's desire for and his faith in these products. Tossing them aside or stomping on that trust would wipe out the entire industry in the long run—including the principles, the hopes and goals of so many people everywhere.

So, it's up to you. The confidence built in the buyer depends on your supplying him with real organic food. The products that stock your shelves and fresh-produce bins, barrels and sacks, refrigerators or freezers can and must be those produced by farmers dedicated to the organic ideal. *Those foods are available.* Many already honestly identified by the Organic Farmer certifying program. If you offer customers something that you are uncertain about, you're stomping on the whole concept of good food, and driving out the growers who have determined that they want to produce it and have learned how. Whether it is wheat or rice, oranges or apples, sunflower seeds or mushrooms—get it from the man who's growing it right. *Now, let's level with the grower!*

Let's have everyone get into the act, too. Don't let down the farmers who want to deliver real food. You can prevent organic farmers from winding up with a surplus harvest by making sure your organic food purchases come from an identified (and preferably certified) organic farmer. Let them and the shopkeepers know by word, letter and organic buying power that it makes a difference to you.

—*M. C. Goldman*

Be A One-Person Food Certifier

I can remember driving down a road near the Oregon coast and seeing the hand-lettered sign "'ORGANIC BLUEBERRIES." We stopped, bought some berries and had a good chat with the wife of the grower. There were many times like that—not just signs along the road but in stores as well. Each time, I stopped, and I knew there'd be lots to talk about.

But now, organic has become a very popular word. Like Voltaire said a long time ago, "What a heavy burden is a name that has become too famous." The burden is heavy upon those who know what the name *organic must continue to mean even after it's famous.* The best way to get really good food today when you go shopping is to use the same standard you use in the garden when you select a variety you like, grow it using natural methods and harvest it at the right time.

When you go into a store—whether it's a health food store or supermarket—apply the same standards uppermost. Don't let your guard down at all. By doing this, you're not only protecting yourself, but you're protecting the future of the entire organic idea and the organic family farmer.

Because organic gardeners know exactly what should go into foods (and what should not), they have a huge advantage over storekeepers, distributors and other elements of today's food industry. I'm sure there are still many people in the health food industry today who do not completely understand what we mean by the word "organic." Many still speak in terms of compromising, "haziness in defining organic foods" and so on. The best way to shape them up is for you to educate them. In just about every business, the truly alert consumer-customer can be the major upgrading factor.

Each of you can be an organic food certifier. Here's how:

1. *Get thoroughly familiar with the Organic Gardening and Farming organic food certification program.* It's been described fully in the preceding pages.

2. *Make sure organic means what you believe it to mean.* Recently we have seen the adjective "organic" applied to sugar, and it did not make sense. To our knowledge, the sugar cane was not grown by organic farming methods. We've also seen the word "organic" applied to maple syrup, shampoo, cosmetics and a few other products—none of which really made sense in terms of the certification program.

In each case, I try to think of organic as an alternative way of growing something. Until I'm convinced that the grower or producer did something specifically different—something that most commercial firms regard as unnecessary and "extra time and effort" —I don't give my *personal* certification to the word organic.

3. *Try to identify a person with the food.* The best way when it comes to purchasing food is to know the farmer. No substitute for this. You can see how and where he is producing the food he harvests, and he in turn learns what you're looking for. It's your best criterion for certification

If you can't know your farmer personally, then your storekeeper or his distributor should. Ask him, and educate him to the points you look for.

4. *Be skeptical about high prices.* There is good reason for higher prices at this stage of the organic market—farmers must innovate, and it often costs more money. America has always rewarded innovators with higher profits, and we think organic farmers deserve to be paid likewise. But sometimes, other elements of the food distribution system want that greater mark-up and this becomes the reason for high-high prices. We advise you to shop around for organic foods when you feel the price is too high.

5. *Skepticism now—a larger market later.* Friendly skepticism on your part is important. This does not mean distrust, but neither does it mean you should be naive whenever you see the words "organic foods" or "natural foods" or "certified organic." A friend of ours says he saw a sign for organic eggs in front of the same chicken factory that he had visited a short time before which uses mass feeding, cages, and extended lighting. In another case, a granola bought in a health food store showed a high residue of pesticides. Though the granola was not described as organic, we still believe that health food stores should strive to carry items that are extra-good for health. We recommend that you continue to shop in health food stores, because—as an alternative to supermarkets—you'll make better choices on an item-for-item basis. But that doesn't mean everything sold in a health food store is as good as you or we want it to be. That same caution applies to organic products you see advertised. Ask the the suppliers the same questions you would ask any storekeeper.

We are at a critical stage in the market development of the organic foods field. We understand its potential for aiding family farmers to reach a special market. We understand its potential for improving the quality of our food. We understand how it can encourage the development of neighborhood food stores. We understand how it can improve the nutrition for all Americans—in the ghettoes as well as the suburbs.

While we understand the potentials, we must also understand the realities. And the realities demand that you and I act as individual certifiers, so that the firms and farms commercially involved will use the methods we want.

We are optimistic that organic foods will be a real force in America. We are optimistic so long as the same people—you, the readers—will continue to exert the same force you have so far.

As a one-person organic food certifier, you can go a long way toward bringing the family farmer back into the American food picture.

The organic idea is already becoming a mass market idea. The challenge—for you and us—is to make sure it continues to help the "small guy"—on the farms and in the cities.

—Jerome Goldstein

3

The Outlets

Shopping in The City

Maybe the notion that you had to be out in rural territory to shop regularly for wholesome, better-tasting produce was true in a bygone day. *Now, there's a remarkable change taking place.* Urban shops by the score are responding to the mounting interest in spray-free, organic foods. More people everywhere are after quality and a steady supply of all the natural products to serve a full menu. And more shop-keepers are responding to the demand.

As a case in point, take Philadelphia. We did—and discovered in a first-hand survey that organic foods are indeed available in a wide selection at many stores within this Eastern metropolis as well as along its suburb fringes.

Starting right in the historic heart of the city, then fanning out in every direction we visited a dozen shops of assorted sizes—all offering some fresh natural foods, and all reporting an increase in the call for them. At the massive old Reading Terminal Market, for example, two "organic stalls" cater to a stream of steady customers. One of these, the Terminal Market Health Center, packs an exceptional choice of produce into its compact aisle corner, along with fresh juices, supplements and refrigerated dairy items. After five years of operating the stand, energetic Alex Wiener exclaims, "I didn't expect it to mushroom the way it has!"

VOLUME AND PRICES

Buying in quantity is the key, according to Wiener. "I must stay competitive—I buy enough at a time from reliable organic growers to price vegetables and fruits by volume costs. For example, I get my carrots in 50-pound bags—50 of them at a time." With a giant cooler right in the market, Wiener is able to stock foods easily, although nearly all his fruits and vegetables—an "all-organic" sign swinging over them—seem to move remarkably fast from bins, cartons or baskets.

Prices—that competitive key Wiener turns into good business—stay equal or very close to the chain markets. "I stay so busy now with folks after spray-free quality foods, I don't know what I'd do if more were to come!" grins Wiener.

Down another cavernous aisle in the Terminal Market is P. F. Baungardt's stand, where he sells his own "Vegetables Organically Grown," as the large sign proclaims. His 92-acre farm in outlying Perkasie, Pennsylvania, has three "truck patches"—one each of smooth IRISH COBBLER potatoes, deep-green asparagus and rhubarb.

Braungardt, an old-fashioned farmer and butcher who hickory-smokes various meats without the usual additives, also offers products from his goat dairy and brown fertile eggs from his own flock. Mrs. Braungardt prepares homemade sauerkraut from the farm's cabbage, selling it below supermarket figures. ("When I price vegetables, I kind of go by what *I* would like to pay.") Every spring, she also has customers for a patchful of wild dandelion, lots of fresh and dried catnip, mints, pennyroyal and other herbs. Meanwhile, along the market wall, the Braungardts post articles and news items about pesticide dangers, pollution and so on—read eagerly by many who come to buy or browse.

THE FUTURE—FRESH FOODS

Uptown, at the Foods for Health outlet, is one of the area's main distributors of organic produce—and a man who saw ahead to the demand building up today. Nine years ago, Dr. Pershing Newman began supplying a number of stores with natural products after making detailed studies of nutrition and organic-method principles. He now wholesales to 60 shops (in Pennsylvania, New Jersey, Maryland, Delaware and New York), besides maintaining a retail trade in his own. Fresh vegetables and fruits arrive regularly from the Southwest, Florida, Ohio ("where the lake-bottom muck soil produces excellent, high-nutritive crops") and other parts of the country. Prices, as well as quality, range somewhat above the market averages. Also stocked for distribution: beef, veal, chickens, ducks, butter, eggs, cheese and baked goods from sources like Shiloh, Sun Circle and Mease.

Dr. Newman, a frequent speaker at health club meetings and conventions, stressed one very significant point: "Several years ago I insisted that the future of health food stores is for those who handle *fresh* foods—and it's happening!"

Back in the city's downtown shopping district are at least three more markets for finding the right menu. On South 11th Street (and in suburban King of Prussia) is Martindale's Health Foods, a spacious, well-kept center managed by a long-time veteran in the field, William M. Martindale, who says the store was established in 1869. In addition to some seasonal produce from nearby Malvern and Paoli organic farms, he offers apples from Virginia's Golden Acres Orchard, carrots and frozen fish, meat and breads from Shiloh Farms. There are also colorful shelves and refrigerator cases of dried fruits, grains, flours, nut meats, cereals, raw sugars, herbal teas and honeys.

Most of Martindale's traffic, though, is for dietetic and body-building specialties, vitamin and mineral supplements. Quite frankly, he stated, "I've found we haven't had the call for as much fresh food as we'd like in order to give it more space and time." But the picture may well change. He added that he believes people today are more willing to pay a reasonable price for wholesome foods.

Along busy Chestnut Street is a Nature Food Centres shop, another that has supplements and packaged products as trade mainstays, but carrying organic eggs, meats, fish and baked goods along with them. Further north is Lahr's Nutritional Food Center, with much the same setup. Supplied via the right sources, both shops could well merchandise much more in the fresh-food line, especially with their established following of health-conscious patrons.

SUBURBAN SHOPS

Continuing our "sample city" tour, we found a generous sprinkling of shops along the Philadelphia perimeter. In the old Germantown sector, Sid and Charlotte Cimente—"better health enthusiasts for 15 years"

—operate the Maplewood Nutritional and Dietary Shop, stocking many seeds, oils, stone-ground flours, herbs, among other foods. They have a realistic pricing attitude and hope to expand the fresh products offered. At Lansdale, there's the North Penn Health Food Center, where Walter K. Wade urges "nutritional logic and natural foods." Organic eggs and raw milk, greens, carrots, cabbage and celery, plus a number of meatless specialties (such as frozen soybean products) for customers who are Seventh-Day Adventists are on hand.

Slightly north of the metropolis, at Southampton, is Bunn's Natural Food Shoppe. Proprietor Thomas J. Bunn, for many years a spokesman of the organic-food way, says their fresh-killed chickens are a standout, along with eggs, lamb, veal and beef. Vegetables (stored in a large walk-in refrigerator) run the full gamut of root crops, greens and beans, while fruits include grapes, pears, apples, plums, cherries, peaches, berries and tropicals like papayas, bananas and avocados besides citrus. Raw goat's milk and goat's milk ice cream are another feature, as is a full selection of organic seeds for sprouting. At Souderton, another town along the Route 309 artery, Feldi's Health Food Center also offers many of these fresh products. Owner John Feldi, one more well-versed advocate of natural nutrition, offers organic beef by the quarter.

And at Ardmore—out along Philadelphia's famed "main line"—is the Main Line Diet Shop, a bustling, attractive market run by Walter and Irma Cleary. Besides fresh produce, there's fine organic honey from Waldron's in nearby Malvern. From the Bringolf Bakery in Radnor, they stock several natural-formula breads, plus the well-known Cornell recipe high-nutrient loaf. Dried fruits from Covalda, grains from Yosemite and beef from Shiloh and W. P. Wear's Enterprise Farm in Cecilton, Md., make up some of the other stock.

Mrs. Cleary, a knowledgeable veteran in natural foods, became interested in organic health ideas while she served in the British army after leaving Germany in 1932. In England she frequently heard Sir Albert Howard lecture and decided to start a shop in New York (encouraged by J. I. Rodale) when she migrated here once the war ended. Now at Ardmore, she has built a steady trade, drawing pleased customers of all ages to the bright, cheerful mart.

Looking into a dozen or so shops this way convinces us that it's *people* who make the organic foods scene. The service and thoughtful attention they offer is a big factor in the success of bringing natural products to the public. Again and again careful, informative explanations of nutritional points are given to inquiring customers, along with facts about foods grown organically. And everywhere, pamphlets and reprints, books and magazines on the natural concept were being offered or tucked into shopping bags.

There *are* shopping opportunities—really good ones—in the big-city area we looked into and in yours, no matter where you live. There are more on the way, too.

—M. C. Goldman

An Organic Supermarket On The Grow

Some people don't know where to begin, but Wayne Myroup's problem is different—he must decide where to continue. Not that beginning was easy; it wasn't.

It was six years ago that Myroup bought Sunrise Farm Stores, Inc., a small, mildly prosperous south Chicago health food operation. He began to specialize in fresh organically grown produce, and the business proliferated faster than you can say, "More and more people want to buy food that isn't poisoned!"

Sunrise is the *only* supermarket where Chicagoans can buy a complete line of organically grown foods instead of the usual apples, tomatoes, and "whatever happens to be in season locally." In fact, the operation is so large that Myroup is shipping in around 3,500 pounds of fresh fruits and vegetables every week.

So, it came as no surprise to discover that the produce bins at Sunrise offer as good and on many days, a better selection of fresh produce than any supermarket.

Here's what was "on hand" during one early April visit: apples, sweet potatoes, lettuce, tomatoes, garlic, onions, beans, broccoli, Brussels sprouts, carrots, cabbage, mushrooms, potatoes, pears, bananas, peas, oranges.

In addition, the store features a busy, well-stocked butcher shop and fish market. Here Sunrise customers can purchase prime cuts of organically raised beef and pork. Fish, all from pure waters, include ocean perch, cod, haddock, flounder, trout and whitefish.

At this point it has become a case of where to continue. The first thing in the Sunrise-continuing process is to meet the need for more space. "That wasn't too hard to decide,," Myroup said, "it's the other things that leave me wondering which direction next?"

PROCESSING AND DISTRIBUTION

One of these "other" things is Myroup's investigation into the practicality of fresh-freezing locally grown organic foods on a mass-production basis. Two of the advantages such an enterprise would bring to the field are a reduction of shipping costs and a more compact package for easier distribution.

A big problem facing the Chicagoan shopping for organically grown produce is the fact that it's "Sunrise or nothing." It's impractical for a shopper living on the north side of the city to make more than one trip a week to the far south where Sunrise is located. If frozen produce were available in addition to the fresh, he could easily stock up for the week on a Saturday.

Further, there's a good chance that more stores would be willing to stock organically grown produce in this form. It takes so much less care, and as a marginal item (for larger supermarket operations), the frozen package is a much more attractive initial investment.

That's one of Myroup's possibilities for "continuing." Another is greater distribution of fresh produce. After talking with owners of health food stores in Chicago, he feels quite a few of them would be interested in carrying a full line of produce if they could get easy distribution.

The natural solution to this problem would be to establish a distribution center where fresh produce could be shipped from California and the Gulf States, then moved out to local retail outlets. Myroup's idea is that "this would allow the purchasing of huge amounts of fruits and vegetables, thus lowering the cross-country shopping charges and allowing us to be more competitive price-wise." One of the difficulties has always been the cost of shipping small amounts of food from the coast. Big supermarkets bring their produce in by the trainload, but most small, organic food outlets are lucky if they can bring it in by the truckload.

CONSUMER EDUCATION

Finally, there is the whole matter of "educating the people." On the back wall of Sunrise is a sign that explains what is meant by "Organically Grown." It's clear that people are becoming more and more concerned about what they put in their stomachs as well as what they put into the atmosphere, and they are more willing to listen than ever before. Unfortunately, "health food" carries a "nut" connotation in the minds of many. If the average shopper were informed, the whole field would probably enter the greatest and most rapid expansion period it has ever known, despite prices that would appear to be somewhat higher.

But, consider the facts. In the Chicago area, most supermarket produce is in a deplorable state. Almost dead before it hits the store counter, it's limp and tasteless before safely in the home refrigerator, a third of it inedible and wastebasket-bound. This means you must "buy more to get as much."

Then there's Myroup's *What Do You Know About That?* test. According to him it works like this: "You take two carrots, for example. Both of them look pretty much alike—same length, same width, and so on. You ask the shopper, 'Which one's heavier?' Well, usually he'll say something like, 'I imagine they're both about the same.' Well, you hand him the two carrots and he'll look kind of dazed. Then you explain that the organically grown carrot is much heavier, has more juices and is just naturally richer in vitamins and minerals."

Probably the only way to begin to educate people on a mass basis would be through advertising. But the small store owner can't afford to compete with the big chains. One solution is for all the local organic food outlets to pool their money and begin a co-op advertising campaign.

The question that Myroup faces of deciding where to "continue" might be summed up in this way: Do you create a demand first (advertising), make food available at more organic food stores (distribution center) or bring in more "normal" retail food outlets (fresh-frozen organic food)? Of course, it's not just Myroup's problem. The whole industry is faced with this question.

The answer is probably: "All of them—now and at once." In fact, it could be that organic foods may become the next "fortune-to-be-made" development in our society. Hardheaded businessmen who don't give a hoot for health are already beginning to cast a serious eye at the increasing demand for poison-free food.

This is one of the facts that makes Myroup's decision of "where to continue" even harder. The small operator (and that's almost everyone now operating in the field at a retail level) could be in serious trouble if he doesn't grow big enough, quick enough. To survive, these shops will have to be well-established before the chains *really* understand the potential inherent in organic food sales.

The Chain Store That Dared

King Soopers of Denver, Colorado, started selling organic produce because their older customers asked the chain for help in living with their allergies. Now the chain expects to stay in the business because their young customers want to live a more natural life.

The Colorado chain of 29 supermarkets (organic produce is sold in six of the stores) started selling naturally grown produce at the requests of physicians and their patients about six years ago.

"These doctors were allergy specialists," says John Darnes, produce specialist for King. "They knew we made our own baked goods from unbleached flour and without preservatives, so they sent their patients to us. Before long, we were persuaded to stock organic foods."

The supermarket chain, which now carries between 25 and 30 organically grown items shipped from California, then contacted physicians and health food stores in their area to let them know that they were stocking the products. Before long, business in those foods began to pick up. The chain claims it has customers from all over the state —even from out of state.

Organically grown foods are sold in two ways at King's, depending on the type of customer. One operation is strictly service, where shoppers come into the produce cooler and buy right from the crates, in bulk.

"This is the type of shopping preferred by our older, our original customers who like the idea of service and who can discuss the fine points of organic foods (as well as their personal problems) among themselves and our sympathetic produce clerks," says Darnes.

On either Monday or Thursday, usually the first day of delivery for different stores, these coolers are packed with customers who think nothing of buying 25 pounds or more of carrots at a time. Before the day is over, most of the supply is gone.

The operation at the downtown Denver store, which is open 24 hours a day, seven days a week, is self-service. Customers in that store are mostly students. They have other reasons for buying organic foods.

These people are well-versed in ecology and don't have to be sold on naturally grown produce.

"We package this produce just like our other and display it all in the same area," Karnes points out. "We put a special sign over the organic variety in the section and use special price labels. We also make available pertinent information about these foods which we get from the supplier, but we don't have to do too much selling. These kids know where it's at.

"Just how far we can go in selling organic produce depends a great deal on the supplier. Right now we sell everything we can get. The problem is we can't get enough to meet the demand."

—*Hy Sirota*

Fresh from the Farm

Americans everywhere are reviving the week-end pastime of combining Sunday trips through the countryside with leisurely shopping from farmers and farm-operated roadside stands along the way. Nearly all states report a phenomenal upswing since 1968 in direct buying, and, if the trend continues, shopping directly from farmers will become an important market.

Recent state surveys indicate that there are multiple reasons contributing to the swing away from "one stop" supermarket buying. Freshness is given as the leading reason. Consumers are indicating their preference for freshness over the "convenience" and "cleanliness" of modern food markets. Mature, ripe fruit at peak flavor is a big drawing factor while farm-fresh vegetables at bulk prices are attracting repeaters who plan their menus—and their budgets—according to the farmer's garden.

Price is definitely a consideration. Food buyers expect and receive more for less when buying directly.

A family outing away from crowded weekend resorts and jammed freeways is directing more Americans from the beaten path and onto quiet back-country roads where leisurely traveling inspires "rambling around." Picnicking in some remote spot along the roadway or perhaps among the trees of a farmer's orchard provides families with an opportunity to spend a day by themselves without the abrasive contact of heavily populated parks and beaches. Small children especially enjoy visiting farms and seeing first hand how food is grown. Consumers state that they prefer the friendlier atmosphere of farms and roadside stands. The high spot of the day's outing is the trip home with a car loaded with good things to eat, everyone munching along the way.

Discovery is an exciting possibility. The happenstance chance of spotting a farmer's appealing roadside stand or sign is a compelling prospect, encouraging many direct food buyers to scout the countryside and see what they might find available while sightseeing.

Freshness, quality, and price, then, are the three major reasons consumers give for shifting their buying preference from convenient one-stop supermarkets to possibly a half dozen or more farms. Distance is not a deterring factor. Food buyers will drive as far as 100 to 150 miles to buy food directly. More and more farmers are marketing entirely through direct customers who return each year to "stock-up" with more pears or oranges, or who return each week to buy quality eggs and fryers.

"Pick Your Own" is becoming a big business. Since 1968, nearly all states showed a sharp increase in the acreage which farmers have committed, on a pick-your-own basis. While strawberries is the big, all-around leader, all deciduous fruits are popular. In California, pears and apples continue to be pick-your-own regulars, and in recent years, venturesome citrus growers are discovering that there are food buyers who would rather do their own harvesting.

Young marrieds and affluent families tend to be the major direct buyers. Consumers with average or below-average incomes who buy from farmers or from farmer-operated roadside stands are most often young married couples in their late teens and early 20s. The trend is continued by couples over 30 whose incomes are above average, and the odds will favor the possibility that the housewife does not work outside of the home.

In the 70's, "organically grown" has become the lodestone which is attracting buyers to buy more food directly. Direct food buyers, given the opportunity to receive straight answers to tough questions, are laying it on the line to farmers who are learning that, as far as food goes in the consumer's mind, "The buck has got to stop here." "How is this grown?" "Do you use pesticides?" "Do you use hormones?" "Do you use any stimulants whatsoever?" Non-organic farmers are finding themselves hard put to give satisfactory answers, and more than one farmer has converted to organics to hold his customers. In the past few years, a number of growers who sell directly through roadside stands have adopted the practice of leaving a portion of their fields unsprayed to advertise some commodities as "unsprayed" or even as "organically grown."

Increasing consumer awareness and the shortage of organic foods is spurring Californians to look for legitimate organic farmers and gardeners who can supply directly. Present demand is creating a situation where organic gardeners find themselves with a waiting list of friends and neighbors wanting to buy their surplus, and large scale gardeners have more customers than they can accommodate once the organic quality of their fruits and vegetables has been tested against the flavorless taste of supermarket produce.

Dissatisfaction and organic shortages have created an explosive trend in 1971. Many urban consumers can now buy organic foods through the mail, direct from farmers and growers. Beef and hog customers sometimes wait several months for a side of organic beef or pork, and frequently haul the meat to the butcher shop themselves for cutting and wrapping.

The concerned consumer and organic farmer have discovered a true rapport through their mutual desire for quality food with strong indications that by the end of the 1970's many Americans will be doing some portion of their regular food shopping directly from the growers. The direct organic market has established a vital and exciting alternative to mass distribution.

—Floyd Allen

Organic Foods In The Cafeteria

College campus cafeterias that up to now have offered only conventional "plastic" meals are likely to find themselves in the middle of a new clamor for natural eating. Students at several West Coast schools launched the organic-food-in-the-cafeteria movement, and the trend is advancing eastward in giant strides.

A large share of the inspiration comes from developments such as the one at the University of California at Santa Cruz, where a student garden project swelled into insistence that the organic foods they were growing be made available in an "alternative choice" cafeteria line.

Now in its third year, the project is expanding and has consistently drawn upwards of 40 per cent of the campus eaters into the organic food line—with many others crossing over to get the better bread.

More recently, the University of California Davis campus cafeteria started offering natural foods. Carolyn Krauss was the moving force behind the Davis kitchen, organizing a drive for student signatures to present to the University's catering service. It took about three months, and then a lot of work to open a closed-off wing of the cafeteria, where volunteers now prepare and serve organic dinners to about 100 students a day.

Taking his cue from the Davis success, Bob Warren sparked a campaign at Sacramento State College. Warren believes in organic foods as a way of life. He says he isn't trying to convert people to his way of eating, but feels that those who like natural foods should get what they want on the college campus. So he began a drive to get organic foods served in the cafeteria by setting up petition stands to enlist the 1,000 signatures needed to bring it to the student senate.

In the East, a classroom nutrition seminar at New College in Sarasota, Florida, led students to seek a change in the college dining room bill-of-fare. They've succeeded—and some of them are growing vegetables organically to help supply the better menu. A similar evolution is taking place at Florida Presbyterian College in St. Petersburg. The manager of the food service volunteered to provide one student the fruit and nuts he wished to include as a major part of his diet. Then another student, who had worked at a health resort, asked if he could switch to the same program. From there on, student interest mushroomed. More and more of the student body showed a preference for the natural foods program which was expended to include cereals, juices, eggs and nut butter. Now 360 students (out of a college enrollment of 900) are in the natural foods program. Some interesting effects on those participating; better weight control, fewer colds, improved complexions, and—because they feel so good—much less use of drugs or stimulants.

THE ORGANIC IVY LEAGUERS

Yale, too, has gone into the health food business—and Harvard's right in back of its Ivy League cousin. At Yale, the decision to shift away from the traditional mushy vegetables came as increasing numbers of students were drifting away from the campus dining halls. In a large section of the university's biggest cafeteria, the old dishes have given way to such delicacies as soybean patties, vegetable chili and Good Shepherd cereal. Along with them go huge bowls of wheat germ, brewer's yeast, organic peanut butter and honey.

The *New York Times* (Nov. 15, 1971) reported that before the switch, "the official excuse many students gave to get out of their university contracts was that they were vegetarians. Some were, but many others just wanted to get away from the gravies, mushy vegetables and fried foods that for years have been so much a part of the American way of eating." There was a time, said Albert E. Dobie, the director of food services at Yale, when he thought of health food enthusiasts as "quacks—a definite minority" and didn't pay much attention to them. But, he went on, "you begin to observe and talk with these people, and you find they have some solid ideas. So you begin to cater to them."

At present the new restaurant offers only the evening meal. But Dobie is considering expanding the dining area and offering lunch. He said he also plans to offer some of the more popular health food dishes like pinto bean goulash and lentil cakes in the other campus dining halls. Wheat germ, special cereals and brewer's yeast—a popular source of protein and B vitamins—are already available in the dining halls of the 12 residential colleges, many of which have also begun to serve brown rice at least once a week.

Student comments on the change at Yale have been simple and direct. They like the new restaurant because "the food tastes good." Peter St. Clair, a sophomore, put it this way: "It's not greasy, it's fresh, and they don't cook it until it dies."

Meanwhile, over at Harvard the food service is similarly "introducing new victuals for the dinner table." According to the university's student newspaper, the move is "to accommodate health food nuts, vegetarians and others who are fed up with the Harvard diet."

The *Harvard Crimson* reported: "Each undergraduate dining hall will have a tray at every meal containing the following foods: raisins, honey, wheat germ, raw oatmeal, peanut butter, cottage cheese, yogurt, and whole-grain breads . . . ."

"Interest in such foods has been growing, especially in the last few years," Charles G. Hurlburt, Jr., Director of Food Services, said. "Students were becoming interested to a point that we thought we would like to oblige as far as we could." In the Freshman Union, where the foods have been served in addition to regular meals from some time, they have been "well received" according to Hurlburt. "A good percentage of students appear to be eating the new foods, but not to the exclusion of other food. The more food put out, the more the students seem to be helping themselves."

THE COUNTERCULTURE'S CONTRIBUTION

"The counterculture is affecting the attitudes and values of many teen-agers in regard to food," said Ruth L. Huenemann, a University of California nutrition expert.

Although it's unlikely that a counterculture cuisine of carrot juice and wheat germ will replace cola drinks and chocolate bars in the stomachs of most teen-agers, Dr. Huenemann said, "there's a shift away from highly-refined foods like candy and soft drinks. Your counterculture kids are eating fewer empty calories."

Dr. Huenemann, at a nutrition-education conference in Washington, said she thought the movement toward organic foods "could have a good effect on our culture," but she took issue with some dietary habits. "Some of the things they're doing are not nutritional," she said. "Where they try to live on cereal alone, as a nutritionist, I cannot condone this. However, with a combination of cereal and legumes— dried peas, dried beans and lentils—you are able to get all the amino acids you need."

Discussing the value of food grown organically, Dr. Huenemann said: "Some of your organically grown fruits and vegetables have slight nutritional benefits. The distance from the field to the table may be shorter. You may have less vitamin loss from storage. Also, they may have been grown more slowly because they're not heavily irrigated or fed with as much fertilizer," techniques often used to make food grow faster. "Therefore, they may have less water content and more flavor."

Dr. Huenemann said she thinks the organic food movement will continue to spread. "A shift away from our over-consumption has to come," she said. There has to be some modification of our wasteful way of life. The counterculture movement's interest in organic food may make a contribution to that effect.

Will more colleges and universities start hearing from students who want natural food? There's no doubt about it. The call reflects a genuine, wholesome aspect of the total environmental awareness today's young people continue to demonstrate—starting with themselves. The prospect is encouraging as well as significant. Would that their enthusiasm and the momentum of what's happening on campus help penetrate the complacency stubbornly remaining in so many other people and places!

4

Co-ops and Other Conspiracies

The Santa Barbara Plan

Santa Barbara, California, is a casual city. Beauty is everywhere—the weather, even the name of the streets are beautiful, soft Spanish names like De La Guerra, or Anapamu. The citizens never forget their city's beauty. It's important to know this, because there is nothing casual about their attitude when it comes to ecology—especially concerning pollution and organic gardening.

Like it is so often everywhere, it took a disaster to awaken the community and move it to meaningful action. After the much publicized oil spill of 1969, citizens of Santa Barbara, scared—and mad—began organizing. Various informal community groups formed. Environmental organizations in the area joined together to seek out ways and means to prevent future disasters. Without a doubt the most important and perhaps nationally significant meeting was a conference held at the Santa Barbara City College. Exactly who called the meeting is not clear—it simply emerged out of the need to do something effective. In any event, an ad hoc committee, now called the January 28 Committee, was created.

It is often the case that ad hoc committees represent only a segment of the community. However, the January 28 Committee was absolutely a whole-community action. The participants represented a cross-section of the entire city. Moreover, there was commitment. An entrance fee was charged—you had to pay to get in—and once in, the participants were asked to make contributions. It is not remarkable that the group collected $1,500.

The main thought of the committee centered around the need to educate the community to all the problems of pollution, to present alternative solutions to these problems, and to focus action—pressure—wherever it would be effective.

A DOWNTOWN GARDEN

It was resolved to establish a community-sponsored agency (which was soon thereafter legally incorporated as a tax-exempt, non-profit entity) called the Community Environmental Council. Combined with its activities were two dramatic ideas: The first was to plant an organic community garden—not just a garden somewhere, but an organic garden downtown, in the business section, and out where everyone would have to see it. The garden was started in May of 1970. The other idea was to establish an Ecology Center—a conveniently located information center, film library, book store, and informal meeting place—that held its grand opening June 28.

The principal idea behind the organic community garden was to demonstrate—to prove—to the community that chemical fertilizers, toxic herbicides and poison insecticides are not necessary in the production of an abundant and safe food supply.

From the very outset the garden was a community commitment. An expensive, vacant downtown lot was acquired at a cost of one dollar for six months. The city provided free water and—when it was needed —the use of a tractor and its operator for two days. Seeds were supplied by the New World Resources Co., and, of course, all labor was voluntary.

Naturally the soil was in poor condition—hard, difficult to work. Leaves were acquired from the park department, hard sludge from the Goleta Sanitation District and a supply of horse manure from a riding club. Then with donated tools, the volunteers worked the soil over well, then planted seeds. Work at the garden project was loosely scheduled; Saturday was a work day but many volunteers liked to stop by and work in the garden whenever they felt like it. The food was casually harvested, as the volunteers simply helped themselves. But the garden was an overwhelming success.

Mrs. Judy Patrick was in charge of the mid-city garden project, which is to say she coordinated its activities and devoted four or five hours or more each day working there and answering questions. By conservative estimate, she converted eleven hundred people to organic gardening. All in all—from the council, the Ecology Center, and to all the volunteers—the garden worked because they all believed in what they were doing and because things were held at a maximum level of productive enjoyment.

Insects and other destructive pests were only minor problems. The only difficulty was created by spotted cucumber beetles, which were easily controlled by hand-picking them each day. There was a small problem with aphids—not much, however, because preventive measures were provided free by the Vitova Company, Inc., who treated the garden with trichogramma wasps and lacewings.

The garden can be described as a fair demonstration of the possibilities of organic gardening, but not necessarily a test of all the local problems. It was located downtown, surrounded on two sides by parking lots and on the other two sides by busy streets. There was no easy access for communicable insects that walk and crawl, such as earwigs, sow bugs and snails. The community gardeners did not have to contend with gophers (the scourge of Santa Barbara.)

A DOWNTOWN FARM

As a demonstration of what can be accomplished using the organic method of growing crops, the garden made its point well. But something was missing. In its operation, it had raised just as many questions as it had answered. It succeeded in convincing gardeners and urbanites, but failed to persuade farmers that the methods were economically as well as ecologically sound in the long run.

What could be done?—a model farm! And in the full bloom of their garden's success, the people made plans to expand.

Within the city's limits and just north of the downtown area there was a vacant city block—4.6 acres worth—owned by the Santa Barbara Art Museum. According to museum plans, a new art museum is to be built there within three to five years. During the interim, however, a lease for the site has been arranged for the establishment of an educational and research center which will operate a variety of ecological systems, both aquatic and terrestrial—in other words, an experimental organic farm.

The emphasis of the farm will be on the "pond," a polycultural system proposed by John Todd of the New Alchemy Institute. The fresh water pond will be stocked with plant and animal life and is integrated with the surrounding terrain in order to create a self-sustaining source for protein food. The farm also includes an insectary, a wormary, a large composting area for treated municipal waste, apiaries for pollination and 2.5 acres of land devoted to extensive organic cultivation of vegetable plants, fruit trees and herbs.

But perhaps the most exciting possibility being explored is a complex insect control ecosystem. Patterns of diversified plantings (including permanent shrubbery) are being designed to provide refuge and breeding sites for natural enemies of potential pests. Intercropping patterns, crop rotations and redistribution of refuge and repellent plants are being integrated and scheduled according to time patterns. By understanding the life cycles and feeding habits of potentially destructive insects, refuge plants and suitable predatory insects can be established before a serious infestation occurs.

Another factor of farm management to be followed is the prime importance of geographic location in the selection of planting crops. In every case, an effort is made to choose only varieties of vegetables and trees that are particularly adaptable to the Santa Barbara climate.

The farm eventually will include limited parking areas, a lath house, a hot house and a large, open-air classroom—all adding up to an expensive proposition.

Those expenses are being met with donations, and volunteers are meeting the demand for labor and services.

However, perhaps the greatest gesture of cooperation and community spirit has been demonstrated by the citizens who occupy the buildings surrounding the farm plot. Many of the buildings are residential dwellings, and considering the large-scale composting project, the potential parking problem and traffic, the cooperation and support of the people living there is quite considerable.

COLLEGE GARDENING CLASSES

These programs have provided Santa Barbara with an unexpected dividend. The Adult Education Department of Santa Barbara City College scheduled a class on organic gardening, and the result was the largest response to any class ever offered by their department. Consequently, four sections of organic gardening were arranged—and where do you think they held their lab classes? That's right—at the community garden.

From its conception, the project received generous supporting coverage from the *Santa Barbara News-Press,* and according to Louis Shauvin, associate director of the center, "Organic gardening is exploding all over the country!" You can see indications of this just about everywhere. Imagine a nursery advertising "Ecology Specials" and giving space in their advertisements for clean air!

Local school districts are all doing something, including class instruction in ecology and, where possible, participation in informal beautification and organic gardening programs. One school district is now considering a three-month experiment which would entail busing third-graders over to Isla Vista where they could develop organic gardening skills by working right along with Santa Barbara students. The Extension Department of the University has also offered an organic workshop.

THE ECOLOGY CENTER

The success of the organic community garden and farm has to be considered in relation to the success of the Ecology Center; all combine to represent a tremendous community effort. Following the January 28 Committee meeting, additional money (about $200) was raised when volunteers set up a downtown booth for Earth Day. Looking around for a desirable location for a center, they narrowed the choice to a vacant building owned by the Woolworth Co. After receiving letters from a number of prominent citizens, including the mayor of Santa Barbara, the company graciously elected to participate in the community's interest, and reduced the rent from $400 per month to $150 per month, which probably barely pays the taxes.

The Berkeley Ecology Center helped out by loaning the Santa Barbarans a $600 book inventory, and somehow, by inspiration and plain old-fashioned scrounging around, the center was put together. It is entirely a self-supporting, community run organization. Operating income is derived through sales of books, pamphlets, posters, contributions, trading-stamp contributions and through the publication of a monthly news magazine titled *Santa Barbara Survival Times.* A regular subscription is $4.00; students $2.50.

The *Santa Barbara Survival Times* is first-rate, sophisticated and comprehensive. It looks like something with two or three years of operating experience behind it. The Center's membership program now includes a subscription. Memberships range from students at $6 per year, to patrons at $500. Periodic talks and films are scheduled for members. In the past they have included topics such as Biological Pest Control, given by entomologist Dr. Everett Dietrich.

The Center operates very effectively, very pleasantly. People coming and going all the time, buying books and posters, seeking information, meeting informally to arrange for various projects. The main theme is cool and helpful; everyone is casual, no push-push, nothing heavy-handed. If someone wishes to express himself through the Center, there's a way for him to do it.

Talk of ecology and organic gardening strikes a progressive, forward note today. Actually, it is a practical matter, and in this respect the Ecology Center of Santa Barbara is essentially quite conservative. They know how to save a dollar and where to cut corners. Their development is, of necessity, very rapid, but careful and extremely well-planned. The focus of their activities is usually low-keyed, persistent and meaningful. They have all the possibilities of becoming a permanently established organization. The only danger is that they might lose the loose cool they have today. If they can avoid political orientations or the entanglements of special interests or the sympathetic clutches of various non-environmental organizations—who'd no doubt like to use them—the Center should continue for as long as it's needed.

The Santa Barbara Plan is working. Allowing for variables, it can work for any community that has the spirit and that sees the problems. The January 28 Committee could have talked about a big operation and the raising of large sums of money—it *is* a rich community—but how is anyone going to get an all-out community participation (in any community) by talking about big deals and large sums of money? What is needed is what they did—and what they have done has made it possible for their community to express itself.

The Santa Barbara Plan incorporates a warning. Will other communities look ahead and take preventive steps, or will they wait for a disaster?

—Floyd Allen

How To Set Up An Organic Food Co-op

"How about trying to find out what you would do and be and think and create if there weren't some corporation trying to sell you on doing everything its way," Federal Communications Commissioner Nicholas Johnson suggests.

Applying his suggestion to finding good, wholesome organic food for yourself and your family, you'd probably come up with something close to an organic food conspiracy—which is simply a cooperative buying effort by private citizens.

Cooperative members by-pass the whole rigamarole of the commercial retail stores: Gimmicks, trading stamps, Muzak, hidden costs for advertising, hyped-up and wasteful packaging, chemical-laden food that comes from heaven-knows-where and may be heaven-knows-how-old—and all the rest of it.

As a member of a food conspiracy, you regain some control in this most important area of your life, rather than leaving the selection of your food to a retailer who may be thinking of profits first.

I've been associated with one of the most loosely-knit cooperatives in America for some months now. We call it the Perkiomen Co-op. Because of it I've eaten some of the best and rarest raw milk cheese, been treated to organic fruits, chicken, goat's milk ice cream, and much more. And for less than I'd pay in a store.

The reason it's so loosely knit is because it's disorganized. It limped from the first meeting, when the participants spent more time playing my records and dancing than they did talking organic turkey.

But you can profit from our mistakes, and from the successes of many other co-ops in this country and Canada. Let's examine successful and unsuccessful co-ops to see how they organized, handled finances, contacted sources of supply, figured out how much to buy, and distributed their food.

GETTING ORGANIZED

It's not exactly simple: you need people willing to work, a person who can handle the accounting precisely and a firm organization with rules and a manager. Otherwise, you end up like us, with a co-op that gets food on a random basis, with the manager showing up at your door whenever he gets a supply of something. Organization is necessary if you intend to supply yourself regularly with the best food at the lowest possible cost.

The first thing you need for an organization is an organizer, someone who's willing to take charge of the first meeting at least, and get things rolling.

The organizer may be you. In Madison, Wisconsin, it was Bill Winfield and some friends who used the talents of some people fresh from the University of Wisconsin to form a nucleus around which "The People's Grocery" was finally built.

The nucleus of a food conspiracy must be well-informed, enthusiastic, and—here's your first decision—either representative of the community as a a whole or limited to some special group, such as friends, people in a specific neighborhood, age group, or whatever. The most successful co-ops (at least the ones that have grown the most) usually attempt to include people from all walks of life. The talents of a local lawyer or accountant or truck driver can prove to be worth more than friendship alone.

Call a meeting in someone's home or have interested people go to their neighbors and talk it up. Sooner or later your core group will meet. This is the time to take the steps to incorporate (and where the lawyer comes in handy).

Without incorporation, you'll have the devil's own time trying to rent property, buy equipment and keep your accounts straight. Some states have special laws for incorporating co-ops. Of course, in my own co-op we didn't incorporate and the big plans soon fell apart into a one-man service for personal friends.

Next you should talk about managers, directors and who's to do the work. If all this sounds like a slavish imitation of the A & P's corporate structure, make up another one. But you'll find that some small, yet responsible group, with or without rotating membership, is necessary to make the quick, minor decisions that crop up. For instance, your buyers may find a source of beef, but may have to rent a cold locker to store it until distribution day. Somebody has to make a quick decision or you'll lose the source.

You'll also decide at this point how large a cooperative you want. Although the organizing group may be small as two people, as it was with the Cuyler-Warren Consumer Buying Club in Brooklyn, New York, final membership typically runs between 100 and 300 in cities, less than 100 in suburban and country areas. It can be much smaller, and in California you find groups of about 10 families running a food-buying service. With such a small group, there's no necessity for renting a storefront and buying cold-storage cabinets and all that. Or it can be larger, as with the Willamette (Oregon) People's Cooperative with 500 members, 30 clerks, and a gross of $800 a day. Just about any size will do, but the larger group can afford a more complete line of items. This is because the larger groups have more operating capital with which to snap up a farmer's supply of organic whatever.

DOING THE WORK

Next you'll have to decide how you're going to divvy up the work. You'll need truck drivers (to say nothing of trucks), loaders, clerks, buyers, a store manager, clean-up people, bookkeepers and so on. A small co-op on Sedgwick Avenue in the Bronx, consisting of 15 wives, has a rather elaborate point system.

Each member is expected to accumulate 15 points during a 20-week cycle, and once he earns 15 points, there's no further call on his time. For instance, a distributor (the person who picks up the food and opens his apartment as a distribution center) gets 15 points. A distributor's helper earns three, a baby sitter earns one and so one.

Another way of parceling out the work is to run a duty roster, just like in the Army. For each job, make a sheet with members' names down one side and days or weeks, as appropriate, across the top. That way you can keep track of who has done what and how often. Per person, it usually doesn't amount to more than an hour or two a week.

Still another way is to give specific and continuing jobs to members who fulfill them periodically. For instance, the buyers may soon learn the best sources, going prices, how to dicker with farmers and gain other expertise that would be lost if buying were rotated throughout the whole group. This has to be up to you and your group.

In our effort here in eastern Pennsylvania, we let the buying up to one man. He soon found that he was saddled with distribution, too. Taking our group as an anti-model, don't put too much on one person. Share and share alike.

One thing we did *right* was to pass out order sheets to everyone who attended the first meeting. These were simply organic shopping lists that included everything we could think of. They can be printed up cheaply, and we intended to use them every week. We asked the members to return them so that our buying committee (of one) could total up how much of each food item was wanted, and thus make intelligent purchases. There's a real danger in ordering too much food, and the shopping list seemed to be the best way to figure our needs.

FINANCIAL ARRANGEMENTS

The next thing to be considered is the type of financing and charging your group will use. There are options.

In Canada, the most common type of cooperative is the "direct-charge" kind. Under this arrangement, food is sold to the members at cost. The by-laws specify that there is to be no markup on food, except a bit for spoilage. Operating expenses, such as rent for a store-front, repairs, supplies, insurance, inventory losses, even salaries if you're into that, are totaled and divided among the members equally, no matter how much food a person buys.

This usually comes to no more than $2.50 a week, according to an Ottawa co-op.

This covers the cost of food and operating expenses on a week-to-week basis, but the co-op also needs a slush fund—enough capital to purchase equipment or special food items. It also allows the co-op to buy with cash and avoid credit. Although many co-ops use credit, I think it is something to avoid.

One way in which the Ottawa co-op avoids this is to sell shares to incoming members. Members are required to purchase $10 worth (two shares) when joining and one $5 share quarterly thereafter. If a member leaves the co-op, the corporation buys his shares back from its capital fund.

At the People's Office in Berkeley, California, new members pay a one-time kitty fee of $2—a less complicated arrangement and one suitable for smaller groups. The larger the group, the more you need a cushion of quite a few thousand dollars. The People's Grocery in Madison started with $1,500, but they all later agreed that $1,500 was cutting it too close.

The advantage of a direct-charge co-op where food is sold at cost and members divvy the operating expenses is that buyers know exactly what they're paying for food. This separates expenses in a handy way for the bookkeepers, too. "At cost" includes any delivery charges and perhaps that little extra for spoilage.

At the Berkeley Food Co-op, the other method—marking up the food—is practiced, with good results. They generally mark up as follows: one cent a pound for items under 10 cents per pound; two cents per pound for items under 20 cents a pound; three cents for items under 30 cents, and so on.

A co-op of 300 persons should find operating expenses running somewhat over $600 per week, or slightly more than $2 per member.

ALTERNATIVES—SOME TIPS

There's another type of co-op that's beginning, one which you might consider if your goal is to get wholesome, organic food to the people in cities. The Devcor Farmer-Consumer Co-op, for instance, is part of the International Independence Institute and plans to help create flourishing markets between organic growers and buyers. As buyers and farmers both contribute toward a capital fund, both are entitled to draw out money to be used for improving farms and homes at one per cent interest or less. This makes the food co-op a spark plug for economic gains within cities and a spur to organic farmers. When the trade is established, Devcor pulls out. If you're interested, write to Devcor, Route 1, Box 129, Freeland, Md. 21053.

Only when this preliminary work of organizing is done properly is it time to actually look for food.

You might want to set up a group of two or three members to check out the food co-ops nearest you. Visit them, talk with the principals, find out how they do things and where they're having problems and successes. Nothing will help your effort get off to a smooth start like contact with an already-existing co-op.

During the organizational phase, the buying committee should go to work locating organic farmers as close to home as possible. Rodale Press publishes a list of all the certified Organic Farmers and other non-certified organic farmers we know of in a book called *Organic Farming: Methods and Markets*. One of the reasons co-ops have been so successful in San Francisco is not only the progressive attitude of the city folk, but the tremendous availability of organic food year-round in that locality.

If you live in the temperature zones of the upper Midwest or East, the winter will pose problems. Large cities, though, such as New York, have farmer's markets. These huge halls of agricultural commerce may have an organic food wholesaler from which you can buy the usual winter vegetables and food. Check with the largest farm markets in the nearest big city.

Co-ops can often find a small businessman or woman who is turning out a line of organic products. In our area of eastern Pennsylvania, our fledgling co-op found a good source of organic sauerkraut (Pennsylvania Germans abound here, you know) and pickled red beets from a Bernville organic farmer. We intended to purchase this packer's entire line if the co-op ever got off the ground. But remember all that dancing when we should have been planning? So it fell through.

Some farmers are strictly organic but don't use the term. When checking with local farmers, you might ask whether they use chemicals and pesticides. Organic is as organic does—despite labels and names. We found a source of fertile scratch eggs and home-cured bacon (you never tasted anything like it) at reasonable prices from a woman who's been farming without chemicals since before they invented most of them.

The Sedgwick Avenue co-op in the Bronx ran into trouble when it started to offer non-food items to its members. One item offered was toilet paper, but members wanted all different colors and they couldn't get that together. So stick with food, unless you have an unusually amicable group.

Don't forget the large wholesale outlets of organic food such as Walnut Acres. It's not like finding a local farmer, but it's one way to procure rice, other grains and such in bulk, on which you get the bulk break.

Bob Dylan wrote about Daddy in the alley "lookin' for food." You might not have to look as far as the alley, but your buying committee should expect to spend time phoning and driving around. You have to search out sources of supply.

BRINGING IT OFF

Okay. You've lined up your sources, you know what to buy and how much of it. Your distribution day is Saturday. What will you need?

You'll need a truck to pick the stuff up and deliver it to the store-front or home you're using as a distribution center. You'll need at least one good scale to measure things out, knives and table space for cutting and wrapping cheese or meat (if you buy parts of carcasses). It's best to have two or three scales if you expect a volume of business. Baby scales do fine if you can't find any old Toledos for sale, reports the Berkeley co-op. You'll also need paper bags and boxes, unless you in-struct members to bring their own re-usable bags. Labor is much cheaper when volunteered, but the work is difficult enough that you may ultimately want to pay wages.

Timing is essential because food, in hot weather especially, spoils fast. Most co-ops soon rent a store and watch the classifieds for old coolers. A Colorado co-op found two scales, two cold cases and a large freezer for $200, cash and carry.

Without proper refrigeration equipment, the distribution is much simpler because you can purchase food as you find it and store it fresh until distribution day. Some developed co-ops, such as the one in Madi-son, stay open weekdays, and some, like the Berkeley co-op, offer sales to passers-by as well as members.

Another possibility, and one which our one-cylinder effort here at home tried, is to rent a booth at a local farmer's market one day a week to serve as a distribution center. Member's orders can be packaged beforehand and any leftovers sold to the public.

But most likely your co-op won't be selling to the public immedi-ately, and you'll find yourself with some damaged and some leftover items. One answer is a grand mulligan stew of all the leftovers (but hold the anchovies) served to the people who've manned the co-op on distri-bution day.

If you've planned wisely and your co-op is an integral part of the community, you'll be free of the fabricated "necessities" of the mass media—and you'll be providing a real service and real food.

There was an editorial in a local newspaper the other day complain-ing about rising prices. As the editor scoured the countryside of his mind looking for someone to blame it on, his thoughts stuck on con-sumer groups. "These warlike consumer groups are taking business away from the mass-distribution system that American business has developed. This drives up prices. We need to return to the efficiency of the large chain stores. We don't need less goods, we need more supermarkets," our editor opined.

Doesn't talk like that make you want to start your own food conspiracy?

—Jeff Cox

Likely Farms—Unlikely Places

If Americans want to return to the land, there's still plenty of land for them to return to. There are 3,615,211 square miles of river and hardpan and topsoil and rock supporting the most outrageous extremes of climate imaginable. Some of these acres, though in unlikely spots, are waiting for an organic farmer to work his magic.

There are mountain valleys high in the Sangre de Cristo range in New Mexico that grow exquisite wild grasses. The fields are dotted with crumbling abode huts—legacies of long-vanished farms. They could grow food and flowers and herbs once more, if someone would farm them. There are fertile valleys in northeastern Washington that'll knock your eye out. The four- and five-thousand-foot mountains are dry and the valleys are lush with streams; the area gets more sunshine per year than the Caribbean. While there are a lot of fruit growers there, good farmland stretches unused down 10-mile vistas.

There's a canyon in north central Colorado with topsoil 40 feet thick that no one is farming. And there's enough water there, too.

JUST A FEW ACRES

While it's true that the superb farmlands of the U.S. generally tend to be exhaustively farmed, that's only true for large land areas. A single farmer, however needs only a single farm—it might be just a few acres. And single parcels of superb farmland are found in the most unlikely places.

Take Colorado, for instance. You don't generally put Colorado together with farming—at least not the mountainous part. But on a drive from Ouray to Durango—over 11,000-foot passes and through scenery so majestic it can hardly be described—there are bits and pieces of land that chance to be at a lower altitude in good position for sun and water. Some are being farmed, many grow only what nature sows.

A happy circumstance can bring together good farming conditions almost anywhere—even on the fringes of the desert. But only in small amounts.

It's dug into these priceless little farms that you'll find some of the hardiest farmers in the country—many of them organic.

High in the red mesas of New Mexico, Bob Houle, formerly from Arkansas, raises goats. He's got 18 in a fertile little valley he found 8,000 feet high and 20 miles from nowhere. "Usually you have to keep goats in a pen," Bob drawls. "But mine . . . I just let 'em loose. They wander up on the hillside during the day and come down to sleep at the cabin by night." He added that he came to New Mexico because he is a Capricorn, astrologically, and Capricorn is also the sign of New Mexico. Capricornus, of course, is a goat.

Herb Ruhl found a choice spot in the winter-blasted regions of northern New Hampshire where the temperature often gets to 40 below. His four-acre farm is tucked halfway up a mountainside with a flat face to the south, and sheltered on two sides by higher hills. He says that his growing season is at least a month longer than his neighbors' because he recognized the worth of the land configuration.

The Oregon coast can be just miserable—certain spots get up to 25 *feet* of rain a year. But 40 miles inland, it can be hot, sunny and dry. Occasionally, the way mountains are built causes a hot, sunny, dry climate over a parcel of land as close to the sea as 10 miles. These scarce but choice pieces of land would make excellent farms close to the sea, yet without all the fog and cold.

There's land for the asking out there. In West Virginia, a poor state that has lost in population recently, 100-acre farms are selling for $5,000. Northern Idaho and adjoining territory in Washington also have rich farmland for sale cheap.

A prospective farmer might find a perfect bundle of land almost anywhere. Near hot and arrid Missoula, Montana, is a range of hills and mountains richly forested and interspersed with small dairy farms.

America is full of surprises to a traveler with an eye for farming. There are fertile-looking stands of corn in Arizona and little green valleys along streams throughout the dry Southwest. The deserts of California, Oregon and Washington all have their oases.

Up in North Dakota, the "badlands" don't look so bad at all. Most of the area is grassy hills in shapes straight out of a Martian fantasy— cones and cylinders, mounds and rings. The soil is dark and humusy—a gift from the millions of buffalo that lived and died on the land. There are a lot of farms, but plenty of open space.

Albert Garrett has been farming organically in a little piece of Arkansas' Ozarks for many years. He remembers when land was cheap—$5 an acre. It still stays about $100 an acre and less in many places. He concedes there are a lot of rocks, but he says "these are strange rocks. They'll grow things that dirt won't."

A farm-minded traveler notices evidence of the pioneer passage (across America), too. The Indian is gone. The buffalo is gone. In many places the trees are gone. Much of the topsoil is gone and the land eroded. For almost a hundred years vast stretches of the West were cleared of their timber and farmed until an exhausted soil gave up and died.

SAVE THE LAND

Organic farmers know best how to stop the erosion and build up a humus-rich topsoil—an absolute necessity when water is less-than-plentiful. Organic farmers make compost and mulch their soil, crack open the hardpan and bring bacteria and earthworms back to the ground, grow crops or sweet grasses on it to protect it from the wind. The dull, gray-green scrub covering much of our wasted land could frame the true vibrant greens of the organic farm. It shows in state after state— much of the ground looks poor in the remote areas until you see the brilliant green of a farm. The farmer's working acres are clearly delineated with color. Today's unlikely farm area may be tomorrow's farm.

Organic farmers would heal the wounds opened by the still-recent march westward, when we ate all the best nutrients off the land, buried them in the sea and put nothing back.

To respond to this need in nature—that of replenishing the soil and refreshing our city-worn souls—Americans are discovering this land in remote areas. It's why some observers say that within the past 10 years the farm-to-city movement has been reversed and now people are trickling back to the country.

Well, they can't have the country . . . not the secluded idyll of virgin forests and streams so many are fond of dreaming about. The country has been used and its virginity gone to the limbo all virginity reaches when man touches it. If they want wilderness, they're going to have to work for it.

Organic farmers know that you can't exploit the soil or try to force it to grow crops for you—not if you want good, wholesome food. A true farmer, standing on his ground, is a part of it. He's made of the elements of the ground and his body will return to the ground. He cherishes the ground as the medium through which life is quickened in him.

If all men treated nature with the same respect she affords them (healing their wounds, growing food for them), our wilderness would return. Since that's not going to happen in the foreseeable future, persons who want to get back to a garden or farm must do the best they can. It's a start. But it's also a fight.

In Bozeman, Montana, Chet Huntley and a large corporation are developing sections of mountain for a $19-million sports resort. On the remote mountain roads of the Ozarks and in the cool, mile-high glades in the Southwest people are selling lots—an acre and under.

Everywhere America is under development. This is a back-to-the-land movement of the first order—but it doesn't help the erosion if the lot owner puts up a mobile home for weekends. What this country needs now are real farmers.

—Jeff Cox

Part Four

In the Kitchen

1

For Better Cooking

My Ideal Kitchen

The natural food cook spends more time in the kitchen than the ordinary cook because she does most of the chopping, grinding, blending, slicing herself. Her kitchen is important—and different from many others.

If money were no object, what are the things I would consider most desirable in planning my kitchen? As a natural food enthusiast, what are the special requirements I most devoutly desire? Unhesitatingly, I answer space, efficient equipment, comfort, safety and beauty.

COUNTERS AND CUTTING BOARDS

I want adequate counter space. Basic equipment such as the electric blender, seed grinder, vegetable shredder and flour mill should each have its own stationary place and be ready for use. Let's face it. When space is limited, these appliances are apt to be disassembled and tucked away in deep recesses behind other items which must first be removed. The appliances don't get used as much as they should, simply because they aren't handy.

Counter space is needed to hold jars of sprouting grains, beans and seeds, in continuous production throughout the year. We enjoy a daily crop of sprouts. Because I use a dish-draining rack to invert the jars of sprouts I need a larger than average dish-draining area.

Adequate counter space is important because of other special requirements. As a natural fooder I am involved with more cleaning and
cutting operations of foods prepared from basic materials than the
person who depends on the can opener. A generous amount of work
surface, a large sink, and an efficient colander are all musts. I crave a
variety of good cutting knives, held in readiness on a large magnetic
wallboard. I can quickly select the proper knife for a specific job. The
magnetic wallboard has a safety feature, too. By removing sharp imple-
ments from a drawer full of other kitchen tools, my fingers will not be
exposed unexpectedly to cutting edges. This work area should be well
lit with a recessed light, so that the occasional green worm can be
dislodged from the crinkly kale, or the cornworm removed from the
husked corn.

The counter ledge should project outward sufficiently from the
closed cabinets or drawers built below it, so that I can sit comfortably
on a stool while working, without bumping my knees. A good portion
of my day is spent in the kitchen. If I remember to sit down as often
as possible, while cleaning and cutting food, I can eliminate unnecessary physical fatigue. This is especially true in hot weather.

For this work area I'll settle for three separate cutting boards, of
closely-grained durable hardwood. No, I don't consider three boards a
luxury. They are a necessity in any kitchen. Let me explain. I'll use the
first board for dry materials such as for slivering almonds or slicing
bread. This board can be brushed dry. (As a frugal New Englander I'll
add the crumbs to cereal or feed them to the birds.) I'll keep the second
board for cutting fruits and vegetables. This board will be washed and
air-dried. The third board, however, will be reserved solely for cutting
and trimming raw meat or poultry. Then the board will be scoured
thoroughly. The importance of this has been impressed upon me by Dr.
Oscar Sussman, Chief of the Veterinary Public Health Program for the
Department of Health of New Jersey, who contends that despite new
laws, "No present method of U.S. meat or poultry inspection can assure
disease-free, non-contaminated raw meat or poultry products. Reliance
by the housewife on the U.S. inspected legend alone has, can and will
cause countless cases of food infections such as salmonellosis and trich-
inosis."

Dr. Sussman suggests that the hazards of bacterial contamination can be controlled by the housewife who is aware of the problem and careful in her food handling and cooking techniques. Although proper cooking will kill the bacteria, the danger is that they may first be *transferred* to other foods such as fruits and vegetables which are served raw in salads. Thus, to avoid contamination, the housewife who has handled raw meat or poultry must remember to wash her hands thoroughly before touching other foods. For the same reason, it is necessary to cut fruits and vegetables on a different cutting board from that on which raw meat or poultry is handled.

COUNTERS AND SINKS

In my dream kitchen the height of the work counter will be given careful consideration. I want it built at a level to suit *my* height, not that of the "average" homemaker. If it were to be too low, I should have to bend unnecessarily; if it were to be too high, I should have to elevate my arms unnaturally. Either posture would result in needless fatigue. I have been made aware of the importance of having a comfortable height for a working surface when I have demonstrated food preparation before women's groups. Using unfamiliar kitchens in other persons' homes, schools and churches, and sometimes demonstrating on a bridge table in a living room, I have encountered various heights of work counters. At times I have resorted to make-shift arrangements, especially to mix dough or batter. I have placed the mixing bowl in an empty sink to lower the height of my working surface. On other occasions, finding the height too high, I have stood on a foot stool to raise myself. Surely the factor of a comfortable working height should be considered in any plans for a new or remodelled kitchen.

Mention of sinks reminds me, if money is no object, that I'd like to requisition two separate sinks in my dream kitchen. The main one would be exclusively for my use, since I am the preparer of food. The other sink, preferably near the outdoor entrance would be to clean the untrimmed produce brought in from the garden. This supplementary sink could also serve all intruders in my sacred domain. This list includes the handyman who gets thirsty just when I am using hot water, as well as members of my family who need to wash grimy hands at the very time when I am trying to clean lettuce. Do these situations sound familiar?

STORAGE—COOL AND COLD

The average American kitchen requires storage space for the canned, bottled and packaged goods which keep at room temperature—nearly forever. My needs differ, with requirements to store mainly perishable foods. I'd like to have a large storage pantry. This room, attached to the kitchen, would include a walk-in refrigerator, lined with shelves. This would solve the problem of adequage storage for the usual perishables, as well as the bulk shipments of whole grains, dried fruits, nuts, crude vegetable oils and certain food supplements. All these items have limited shelf life and need cool storage. I can dream, can't I, of the walk-in refrigerator? However, I can visualize the architect shaking his head negatively. All right. If a walk-in refrigerator is out of the question, I might settle for *two* refrigerators. The first one would be used for the day-to-day perishables—fresh fruits, vegetables, meat, fish, poultry and eggs. The second one could store all the semi-perishable items. And, hopefully, the supplementary one would have enough space to store the occasional summer watermelon which, when brought home, sends me into a flurry of excitement in rearranging the refrigerator to make space.

As for a freezer, I am the modest creator of what is known within inner scientific circles as Hunter's Law. It goes as follows: "Buy a freezer at least twice as large as you think you'll need." To date, in repeated tests to judge the validity of this law, I confess that it seems to be flawless. Regardless of how the capacity of the next freezer purchase is increased, it never seems to be greater than my ability to fill it.

A large freezer offers an inducement to grow or obtain more organic produce and to raise or seek more organic meats and fowl. A large freezer makes it possible to enjoy the extras, such as strawberries in December or cranberries in July. I continue to find added uses for my freezer, which in turn demand more space. For example, I skim off all congealed fat from cooled stews and soups, pack this waste into containers and freeze it. At a later date I render it for soapmaking. Similarly, I trim off all visible fat from steaks before broiling them. This fat, frozen, is later used for winter bird feeding.

Then there are unusual uses for the freezer. I've been told that the freezer is run most efficiently when it is as full as possible. I strain my imagination to cooperate. As the food dwindles I can mothproof the woolens and furs in springtime, without using hazardous materials, wrap them in plastic bags, and store them in the freezer. I've also discovered that the freezer serves as an excellent fire-retardant vault to store temporarily a half-finished manuscript, favorite jewelry and my last will and testament.

In addition to cool and cold storage, I want an area where foods can be dried under ideal conditions. Perhaps this can be a nook somewhere in the pantry. In such a place I will be able to festoon sprigs of herbs, strings of mushrooms and apple rings and leave them unmolested until they are dry enough to be stored.

ATMOSPHERE

Adequate window space is important in my kitchen, I would place the kitchen location in the house so that I could enjoy bright sunshine from sun-up to sundown. I would consider using the special glass, described by Dr. John Nash Ott in *My Ivory Cellar* which allows beneficial rays from the sun to penetrate the glass. Deep windowsills would house potted plants. Some could yield salad garnishes year round, including basil, chive, parsley, rosemary, pot marjoram and mint. If space permitted, a small window green house for winter lettuce would be welcome.

A cheerful atmosphere in my spacious kitchen would be important. The windows should face agreeable outdoor scenes, since I enjoy watching trees, bushes, the antics of birds and other small creatures, as well as the changing of seasons while I scour the pots. The pleasure of music in the background, from a radio or tape, could lighten the monotony of culling berries or podding peas.

I admit that my dream kitchen reflects my tastes and values, which may differ vastly from yours. I am country-oriented, while you may be city or suburban bound. However, some of my suggestions may arouse your own interest, especially if you are planning to build or remodel. Perhaps a thought has been sparked. Possibly you have been stimulated to formulate ideas about your own dream kitchen. Maybe you will have answers which continue to stump me. For example, have you solved the ever-present problem of storing those brown paper bags which accumulate from shopping? How do you cope with the used plastic bags, washed out, hung to dry, and ready for re-use? How do you store your freezer jars efficiently, as they continue to accumulate when food is thawed out? Have you found a good method of filing recipes, household hints, innumerable and valuable clippings from *Prevention* and *Organic Gardening and Farming* and addresses of organic food sources, so that you can find them immediately when you want them? Have you been able to devise a practical dispenser for food supplement tablets without the daily count and inevitable spills? If you've licked these problems, please let me peek into your dream kitchen before I build mine.

—Beatrice Trum Hunter

2

For Better Meals

Cooking for Nutrition

Do you feed your sink and garbage pail better than you do your family?

Even if you are carefully heeding a food value chart in attempting to prepare well-balanced meals, your foods very likely suffer depletion of their nutrients in your own kitchen. This is true of practically all home cooking. It is true of yours, unless you know how to prepare your foods for the table as carefully as you select them for their food value.

After decades of neglect, the facts about nutrient losses in the kitchen were once more brought to light when renowned nutritionist Robert S. Harris, Ph.D., of the Massachusetts Institute of Technology's Department of Nutrition and Food Science, testified before the Food and Drug Administration's public hearings on their proposed new food supplement regulations.

In his testimony, Dr. Harris submitted evidence that improper methods of food preparation cause vitamin and mineral losses in large-scale cooking. He said that small-scale cooking has not been scientifically tested, since the methods of preparation vary from kitchen to kitchen. Even so most of the evidence he cited can be applied by the woman of the household who wants to establish better methods of cooking in her own kitchen.

"Essentially all studies have indicated that considerable losses of nutrients take place during cooking," said Dr. Harris. "Some of these losses are unavoidable. Food that contains cellulose must be cooked in

249

order to be digested and absorbed by human beings. During the first few minutes of cooking, when the temperature is being raised, the enzymes in the tissues of these foods are activated and rather rapid losses of nutrients occur. After the food has been cooked, these losses become minimal because the enzymes have been destroyed, and most of the oxygen has been driven out of the tissues. The extent of these losses varies and is often much greater when poor methods are used in preparation for eating."

FOOD AND HEAT

The reason for stopping this enzyme growth at all is that what is good for the plant may turn into something that is not good for you. Remember that as far as the plant is concerned, its purpose is to reproduce itself and not to provide food for human beings.

The purpose of a peach is not to be eaten but to grow a peach tree. The tree develops in such a way that it grows a seed for reproduction and surrounds it with a pulpy substance which we know as a peach. If the peach is not picked, the enzymes responsible for its growth continue to do their work by breaking down the pulpy fruit, decomposing it so that it can provide food for the seed. This happens when the seed falls to the ground, pulp and all.

Now we consider the peach to be a delicious food for ourselves. But even when we pick the fruit off the trees, the enzymes keep working. So we must eat the fruit before the enzymes decompose it, or stop the enzyme action by preserving the food through a method such as cooking and canning.

Of course, raw fruits and vegetables are more nutritious than any type of cooked plants. The enzymes are still alive, and as long as the food has not yet gone into the spoiling stages, the enzymes in the raw foods actually have nutritional value. However, if the same fruits and vegetables—or meats—are stored raw or improperly cooked, these enzymes, in the course of their work, destroy the value of other nutrients.

Cooking is an essential part of food preparation since the enzymes and also other microorganisms, which help plants and animals to grow, are also responsible for breaking them down. As a result, plants decay and meats putrefy. And that's where cooking comes in. Proper cooking not only destroys these two kinds of spoilers by its intense heat but also makes many kinds of food much more palatable.

NUTRIENTS AND HEAT

But heating foods has disadvantages, too. While enhancing proteins, fats and carbohydrates by chemically changing them into foods that man absorbs more quickly, it does play havoc with vitamins and minerals.

According to Dr. Harris, laboratory tests on foods showing degrees of nutrient loss during preparation were reported by Nagal and Harris in the *Journal of the American Dietetic Association* (19: 23, 1943). Nine different vegetables are checked at various stages of preparation and storage.

Vitamin content was measured, in the raw vegetables prior to any preparation, before cooking, after cooking, after an hour of steaming and the next day, after being refrigerated overnight. The vegetables studied—string beans, red cabbage, carrots, cauliflower, peas, potatoes, spinach, squash and turnips—were measured for effects on thiamine (vitamin B_1) and ascorbic acid (vitamin C).

Thiamine losses ranged from 5 per cent to 82 per cent after cooking, and those vegetables which sat on the steam table for one hour lost between 29 per cent and 89 per cent of their original thiamine content. Except for cauliflower, potatoes and turnips, which momentarily "gained" during cooking, ascorbic acid losses of 9 per cent to 77 per cent were measured during cooking. Even the gains went by the way-side at the steam table, where the vegetables lost from 61 per cent to 96 per cent of their ascorbic acid.

Basic rules for good cooking are as follows: Destroy enzymes by rapid heating; avoid oxidation—which destroys vitamin C—by leaving vegetables unpeeled wherever possible and covering bruised surfaces with a dab of oil; displace oxygen in the utensil with steam; cook in the shortest time possible; save and use all the cooking liquid which now contains much of the vital nutrients; serve these hot foods immediately after preparation to avoid unnecessary nutrient loss.

The water soluble vitamins—C, P, and B complex—suffer most from cooking, and hence from improper cooking. Many minerals are also lost in the cooking water—another reason to save the cooking water which, unfortunately, many modern housewives don't do.

While **water** is by no means the only depleting influence upon nutrients during preparation and cooking, it is by far the most common one. Foods that are washed, soaked, or boiled stand to lose much of the vitamins and minerals they contain—especially the water soluble ones.

According to Munsell, *et al. (Journal of the American Dietetic Association*, 25: 420, 1945) cabbage, which was boiled, gave up 72 per cent of its ascorbic acid, half of which was left in the cooking water. Thiamin retention was recorded at only 59 per cent, two-thirds of which was found in the cooking water. When the cabbage was steamed, the ascorbic acid loss was only 33 per cent.

Further evidence comes from Streightoff, *et al.*, who tested carrots for vitamin retention by comparing results of boiling with steaming. According to the results published in the *Journal of the American Dietetic Association* (22: 511, 1946) 73 per cent of the ascorbic acid was lost when carrots were boiled, and only 38 per cent escaped when steamed. Niacin, thiamin and riboflavin content dropped 40–50 per cent during boiling; smaller losses occurred in the steaming process. The evidence indicates that steaming is a superior form of cooking for vitamin retention.

HEAT WITH CARE

You might consider preparing your vegetables in an oriental cooking utensil called a wok, a conically shaped vessel with a small flat bottom. It takes only a minimum amount of water to cover the bottom of the wok, so you can cook most of your vegetables to tenderness by steaming them, with little of the vegetable touching the water. This type of utensil is becoming more popular and is becoming widely available.

Provided you keep an eye on the cooking time, steaming in a pressure cooker is another good method of preparation. The length of time that each kind of vegetable should be cooked is included in the directions with the equipment. Only a few tablespoons of water need be used, and the remaining liquid should be served with the vegetable.

Have you considered cooking vegetables in the top of a double boiler? Try it. Put a few tablespoons of water into the top of the double boiler, and bring it to a boil over direct heat. Add vegetables and steam to destroy enzymes. Then place the top section over boiling water in the bottom of the boiler to finish cooking.

The best method of cooking vegetables is the waterless method. Fresh vegetables contain 70 to 95 per cent water, which is sufficient for cooking them if the heat is controlled so that no steam escapes. The utensil must have a tight-fitting lid, and the heat should be evenly distributed. A tablespoon or two of water should be put into the pre-heated utensil to make steam that will drive out any oxygen that is present. The important thing to remember in this method is to keep the heat low after the first few minutes so no steam escapes.

If you must boil your vegetables, keep them refrigerated until you bring the water to a rolling boil. Then drop in the vegetables and keep them there only long enough to soften them: don't overcook them. Make sure that you conserve whatever water is left in the pot for use in gravies, salad dressings and soups.

SAVE THAT WATER

Not only the water soluble vitamins, but minerals such as iron, copper, potassium, magnesium and manganese spill out into cooking water. So do even the vitamins which do not dissolve in water. How? When vegetables containing vitamins E, K or carotene are chopped or cooked to the point that the cell walls give way, the minerals simply drift into the cooking water, then you also toss out an abundant reservoir of nutrients.

The water need not even be hot to drain your foods of their nutrients. Soaking foods—especially vegetables—in *cold* water will often have much the same effect. Vegetables and fruits for salads and desserts deserve the same precautions as those which are to cook in hot water, in order to prevent losses of vitamins C and P and the B-complex.

Ideally your vegetables should be bought immediately before using, but if you must buy them some time before, wash and dry them and put them into your refrigerator as soon as you get home. Exceptions to this rule are soft-textured fruits and vegetables such as lettuce, berries and watercress. They should be refrigerated until serving time, then washed in a colander or sieve and served. Don't bruise the surfaces by drying them with a towel.

The reason for chilling your fruits and vegetables is that while they are on the kitchen counter, just waiting, they've got more enemies than friends. The combination of oxygen and light at room temperature will take its toll of nutrients in a matter of minutes. Vitamin B_2 for example, is particularly susceptible to destruction by light.

You must remove your foods from heat and sunlight because these two forces will cut down nutrient content. Fortunately, you have an appliance that is ideally suited for the job—your refrigerator. Don't underestimate its importance, and keep your foods inside it until it's time to prepare and serve them. The cold and dark of the refrigerator discourage enzyme activity.

If you must store foods for any length of time, freeze them taking the proper safeguards to preserve their freshness. The freezer will slow down the natural process of change even better than the refrigerator.

PEEL WITH RESTRAINT

Next to soaking in water, peeling is considered the second greatest threat to your family's nutrition. Unfortunately, because pesticide spraying has become so wide-spread, peeling food has become a sensible health precaution, even though it means throwing a lot of good nutrition into the garbage. It is an important reason why you are often better off to lose some of the nutritive value of food and take a vitamin supplement instead.

Feeding a household well takes more thoughtfulness than just getting the foods together. Even if you religiously plan your meals from a food value chart, your foods may be losing out on three counts.

Two of them are beyond your power if you are not raising and picking your foods from your garden. First of all, mass distributed fruits and vegetables may be nipped off their plants before they ever get the chance to ripen into their full nutrient potential. The foods displayed for your selection in supermarkets may never come close to the food value specified on the chart you follow. Secondly, those foods that are processed and packaged before they reach you lose a lot more of their nutrient content. The inviting picture on the package may well be the best thing about them. Neither food charts nor tempting packages mention that many vitamins and minerals are sacrificed during mass production and storage. Your family cannot thrive on appetizing photographs.

The third way your foods can loose their nutrients is in *your* hands. Many an American housewife accidentally reduces her family's nutrient supply by improperly preparing meals.

How can *you* avoid these vitamin pitfalls? Shop for the freshest foods available, and when you get them home waste no time in storing them. Then follow the above suggestions for cooking and preparing your foods. Don't waste vitamins and minerals on the kitchen counter and stove. And don't cook your family's foods to death.

Enjoy Your Vegetables

We are not a nation of vegetable eaters. We tend, in fact, to avoid them—and, not so incidentally, the myriad vitamins and minerals they contain—because they seem so dull. But the reason they bore us happens to have nothing to do with their inherent qualities. It's our fault—we really do not know how to cook them.

Our culinary vocabularies are curiously lacking in ways to make vegetables elegant. And no matter how popular carrots, for instance, may be with your family, serving them the same way all the time is sure to make their popularity pale, if not disappear. Another, more basic cause for the lack of enthusiasm greeting platters of vegetables all over America is our lack of restraint in cooking them. That is, we simply do not know when to stop. The longer they stay on the stove or in the oven, the shorter they are on taste, texture, color and nutritional content.

Americans are not alone in the tendency to make pablum out of perfectly good beans, turnips, asparagus, etc. The British have made mushy brussels sprouts a national institution as unavoidable as fog. The French are more subtle—they conceal their vegetable casualties under exquisitely seasoned sauces. This does make it possible to enjoy them, but not exactly for themselves alone.

The only place in the world where vegetables are traditionally venerated, where their individual personalities are extolled, rather than concealed or destroyed, is in the Far East. The Chinese are champions at this particular art (among many others) and there is much to learn from what goes on in their woks—as well as what goes into them.

The Chinese have gentle methods for sautéeing and boiling vegetables. They are adept at throwing together seemingly incompatible kinds of food in a way that makes the combination seem predestined. And they season things lightly, bringing out the flavor of each ingredient rather than creating a pungent, but amorphous, whole. Their emphasis is on simplicity and harmony.

In the Rodale Press' Fitness House Kitchen the stress is, of course, on health. But simple foods combined harmoniously are intrinsic to a healthful diet. So you could say that we've adopted the Chinese outlook naturally, as it were, although our meals are by no means strictly Shanghai or Peking or Cantonese oriented.

CHINESE VEGETABLE CUISINE

Recently, however, an expert on Chinese cuisine visited our kitchen, and our resident experts on nutritious cooking were introduced to the Sino style of preparing vegetables. Stir-frying, which is more or less the nucleus of Chinese culinary art, is called *Chow* in the native tongue (as in Chow Mein). It's not frying as we know it, but more closely resembles intense sautéeing. You cook sliced or chopped food in a bit of very hot oil and stir it non-stop until all surfaces are browned, lifting from the center so that everything gets evenly cooked. The Chinese usually add sherry or dry wine, cover the pot to allow the liquid to permeate and then proceed with the final cooking. The alcohol evaporates, leaving the wine flavor.

In the case of plain vegetables, however, simply add a little water to them, cover the pan and steam for about three minutes or until they are tender—but not too tender. Stir-frying is an ideal way to cook vegetables because the initial absence of liquid and the speedy cooking process allows neither flavor nor nutrients to escape. It is infinitely preferable to submerging vegetables in boiling water, the typical American procedure.

Speed is one of the crucial factors in Chinese cooking—a Chinese chef at work is energy incarnate. Therefore, they find it useful to cook vegetables ahead of time, when including them in a meat or fish dish, so that the final moments of cooking will be uninterrupted by last-minute fuss with individual ingredients.

The method used for pre-cooking vegetables is blanching or par-boiling, and it is equally effective for Western dishes. You clean the vegetables and cut them as desired, and then put them in a little boiling water *briefly* until they are half done. The vegetables are then immersed in cold water, stirred so they cool evenly and quickly, drained, and set aside for later use. By blanching vegetables and then adding them to the dish when the rest of the ingredients are just about done, you completely eliminate the possibility of soggy, dead vegetables.

Chinese vegetables dishes can be extremely complicated, though few approach the so-called Buddhist's Feast, which involves about 20 different kinds. Here is a delicious recipe which is easy, but still provides ample opportunity to develop your stir-frying skill:

3 large radishes, sliced very thin
½ cup sliced fresh mushrooms
1 medium onion, sliced
1 cup snow peas
1 cup shredded baak choy (chinese
    cabbage)—plain old American
    cabbage can be used if this is una-
    vailable
2 slices shredded, fresh ginger

1 clove garlic, minced
½ teaspoon honey
¾ cup chicken stock
2 tablespoons Tamari soy sauce
1 tablespoon cornstarch
¼ cup cold pressed oil
pinch of salt
½ cup diced celery

Mix honey, chicken stock, soy sauce and cornstarch together and set aside. Put dry saucepan on heat until very hot, then add oil and salt. Turn heat to medium and brown garlic and ginger, stirring constantly. Add onion and stir-fry for about a minute. Turn heat to high and add radishes, mushrooms, celery and cabbage, and stir-fry until vegetables are just tender. Add snow peas and sauce mixture. Stir until sauce has thickened. Remove from heat and serve immediately on brown rice.

VEGETABLES—PLAIN AND CAREFUL

Nancy Albright, chief chef and nutritionist of the Fitness House Kitchen, was extremely enthusiastic about China's arrival on the premises (it was, incidentally, just about the time Mao's men came to the U.N.). But Nancy has never had to coax dining room guests to eat their vegetables. They are always too good to turn down. There is nothing inscrutable about Nancy's own methods—and nothing difficult about them, either. She finds that plain vegetables become irresistible when steamed *briefly* and seasoned with a harmonious blend of sea salt, kelp, balanced mineral salt and your choice of herbs. Nancy has dozens of tricks to suit various vegetables. She has found that non-beet eaters become instant converts after trying them her way—steeped in orange juice. "It's not exactly original," she admits. "I got it from *Joy of Cooking.*"

The following special treatment for green beans hails from the Fitness House Kitchen—and it's a favorite in our dining room:

1 pound fresh green beans
2 tablespoons peanut oil or other cold
    pressed oil
½ cup sunflower seeds
½ teaspoon basil
½ teaspoon marjoram
½ teaspoon chervil
1 tablespoon snipped parsley

2 tablespoons freshly chopped chives
    (or 1 teaspoon dried chives)
⅛ teaspoon savory
⅛ teaspoon thyme
1 small onion, chopped
1 clove garlic, minced
1 teaspoon salt
¼ teaspoon freshly ground black pepper

Wash drain and trim beans and steam them, along with onion and garlic, until crisp tender. Meanwhile, combine herbs in small bowl. Add oil to heavy skillet and place over medium heat. Add the mixed herbs and sunflower seeds; stir until thoroughly heated (about two or three minutes). Add beans to mixture in skillet, heat briefly, add salt to taste and serve immediately.
Yield: 4 to 6 servings.

Nancy has also come up with some interesting escapes from the steamed-and-salted squash syndrome. Acorn squash is delicious when cut in half, basted with honey and cold pressed oil, and baked. And yogurt is an intriguing topping for yellow summer squash. A simple— perhaps the simplest—way to prepare pumpkin for pie is to cut it in pieces and steam, skin side up, in a 350 degree oven for an hour and 15 minutes—or until the pulp is fork tender.

Then scoop out the pulp which, incidentally, can be frozen for future use.

BREAK WITH TRADITION

In the Fitness House Kitchen, pumpkin and pie are not necessarily synonymous. You might try our non-traditional treatment for the traditional pumpkin next Thanksgiving. Cut a one pound pumpkin in one-inch pieces and place them in a saucepan, covering each layer liberally with honey, cinnamon and nutmeg. Add a very little bit of water and cook over medium heat, stirring occasionally, until pumpkin pieces are tender. Serve garnished with walnuts and almonds. An alternative cooking method, which eliminates the "syrup," is stir-frying honeyed pumpkin pieces in a little oil until tender.

A lot of the charm of vegetables can be brought out not only by judicious seasoning, but also interplay with other vegetables. Turnips, for instance, are good on their own but great when combined with carrots and zucchini—and then steamed or stir-fried until just after they lose their crunch. One of the most popular dishes in the Fitness House dining room is a mixture of carrots and onions—cooked, to be sure, in a rather unique way. We cut the carrots in elongated slices and sauté them, with chopped onions, in chicken fat or cold pressed oil. No water is needed but shake the pan often.

Curried vegetables are a great complement to plain meat or fish— and they can be a superb main dish, especially if you throw in a few soybeans for protein. This is a basic recipe which allows for lots of innovation on your part:

Peanut oil or soy oil
1 onion, chopped
1 teaspoon chili powder or dried chilis
   (optional)
1 teaspoon cumin
1 bay leaf
¾ teaspoon turmeric

6 crushed cardamom seeds
enough water to cook your choice of
   vegetables (cauliflower, tomato,
   eggplant, carrots, green peppers,
   peas, potatoes, green beans or any
   combination of these are all suitable)

Sauté onion and spices lightly in oil. Add vegetables cut in desired size, bay leaf, and as little water as possible. Cook until just tender.

Ratatouille, a Mediterranean dish, is perhaps the most famous vegetable mix of all. Here is the way we make it.

3 tablespoons cold pressed oil
2 small eggplants
2 small zucchinis, washed and thinly
   sliced
2 medium green peppers, washed,
   cored and cut into one-inch strips
5 tomatoes, washed and quartered
2 medium onions, sliced
1 clove garlic, minced

1 tablespoon freshly snipped basil or
   ½ to 1 teaspoon dried basil
2 tablespoons fresh parsley
1 teaspoon salt
1 teaspoon powdered kelp
¼ teaspoon freshly ground black pepper
3 tablespoons raw wheat germ

Sauté onions and garlic in oil for about five minutes. Add zucchini, eggplant and green pepper, and sauté for ten minutes, stirring occasionally. Add tomatoes, basil, parsley, salt, kelp and pepper. Reduce heat, cover skillet tightly and simmer for 15 minutes more.

Place the mixture in a 2-quart casserole and top with wheat germ. Bake in 375 degree oven for a half hour. Let the casserole cool for about ten minutes before serving (the longer it stands, actually, the better it tastes).

STARTING ADVICE

Before you get started on your own adventure with vegetable cookery, here is a bit of advice on selecting and preparing the raw materials. The ideal source of fresh vegetables is, of course, your organic garden—or someone else's. But if you can't pick them yourself (and few of us can), rely on a health food or other store which keeps organic vegetables in a chilled case and receives new shipments daily. Freshness is of the essence. Tired vegetables will not revive no matter how kindly you treat them.

Vegetables should be washed quickly in very cold water. Never soak them. Chopping or slicing should be done directly before cooking to prevent moisture (and vitamin) loss. Most vegetables which are traditionally peeled shouldn't be, because the skins of carrots, cucumbers, tomatoes and the like are loaded with nutrients and flavor. But if you must peel, do so as sparingly as possible because there are a lot of vitamins and minerals lurking just under the skin as well.

If you can't get good, fresh vegetables at certain times of the year, choose frozen ones rather than canned. But stick to the plain frozen vegetables, not the ones mummified in sugar, salt, butter, cornstarch and food dyes. Seasoning vegetables yourself requires little labor, so there's no excuse for buying them with built-in, but artificially induced, flavor.

Vegetables, as you have seen, can be a dynamic contribution to your diet. And by making the most of them, you can, in turn, improve their droop image—at least in your own home. When your family starts fighting over the last crumbs of broccoli, you'll know you're on the right track!

—Shelagh Jones

For the Salad Days

A salad, by nature is a hodge-podge of things; a hodge-podge, by definition, is a diverse mixture; and in diversity there is always room for the unexpected. A salad can be the simplest of combinations (lettuce plus lemon juice springs to mind) or the most complex. It can be hot or cold (though most are cold), all-vegetable, vegetable-plus-fruit, or all-fruit. Grains, nuts, eggs and meat may also be involved.

"Salad" is one of the loveliest words in the English language: light, crisp, sprightly and fresh—which is, appropriately enough, just what a good salad should be. Leader of the common garden variety is the Green Salad, which can be great but often becomes the bane of an otherwise pleasing meal.

The reason? There are really a number of them. A lot of people think that a good salad, once devoured, should leave a pool of dressing in its wake. But dressings are meant to coat and flavor, not act as a floating agent.

Others think that it is perfectly all right to chop the vegetables and douse with dressing way ahead of serving time. But while this may save last-minute hassle, it destroys the final product. Vegetables can be safely washed and refrigerated, but once cut they lose moisture (and therefore crispness and vitamins) rapidly. Dressing them in advance increases the sogginess. A green salad should never be marinated.

START WITH THE BEST

The most glaring error of all is also the most basic—careless choice of vegetables. A green salad should contain nothing but the finest, freshest, organically grown vegetables you can find. There is nothing that you or the world's best dressing can do to revive dead vegetables. If you think lettuce is tasteless, as many people seem to do, then you've never had organic lettuce.

In our Fitness House Dining Room the salad is always outstanding. And, although we make some interesting dressings, comments we receive usually include some amount of surprise over the quality of the vegetables—which are, of course, all organic.

Nancy Albright, head of the kitchen staff, recommends using a variety of greens, to provide color, texture and taste contrasts. Try a combination of romaine, watercress and Belgian endive, for instance. Experiment with raw spinach, bronze lettuce, dandelion greens, beet greens, chicory and collards, as well as the standard iceberg and butter lettuces. A green salad need not, of course, always be greens through and through. Tomatoes, onions, celery, carrots, avocado and cucumbers are obvious additions—and then there is a whole medley of vegetables, usually served cooked, which are sensational raw (zucchini, mushrooms, cauliflower and turnips, for example).

The next thing to remember is that all ingredients should be completely dry. Wet, or even damp, vegetables are dressing-proof and no matter how much sauce you slather on, it won't stick. It is a pretty fair assumption that the reason so many salads end up afloat is that so many cooks use wet vegetables and then think that overdressing them will compensate. It won't.

DRESSING—THE CREATIVE PART

And now we come to the most creative part—the dressing itself—which is, naturally, creative only if you make it yourself. It has been our experience that a really delicious bottled dressing has yet to be produced, and bottled dressings are, in addition, often laced with preservatives and other unnatural things that do little for your salad and less for your health. Making a dressing is easy, and allows you to unleash some of your wilder herbal fantasies.

You've no doubt seen that T.V. commercial in which the victim (salad-eater) screws up his face at the villain (salad-maker) and the latter wails, "But oil and vinegar don't mix!" The solution, of course, is to use Brand X oil, which dissolves beautifully in vinegar. Brand X also happens to be processed (i.e. the real villain). But this advertisement can be criticized for more than the nature of the product.

Oil and vinegar don't have to mix. The proportion of oil to vinegar in the ideal dressing is three to one. The touch of vinegar adds a little spark, but most of the flavor should come from herbs—and not so many (or in such quantity) that the taste of the vegetables is lost. Salt is probably the most important single seasoning for a salad. The word "salad", in fact, derives from the Latin "sal" (for salt, which was used to preserve vegetables). Today, successful salad-makers use it to really bring out the flavor of vegetables.

Some people like to add oil and vinegar to the salad and then season it directly, adding each flavoring individually and tossing in between. This free-form method is nice if you're a real pro, but the rest of us are probably better off making a pre-seasoned dressing. First of all, you can make enough for more than one salad, then refrigerate what remains for later use. Secondly, you can taste it before it goes on the salad, thereby making sure that all is well.

Any number of herbs will do wonders for an oil-vinegar base. Tarragon is a favorite, as are basil, oregano, dill, rosemary, parsley, thyme, and sage. A few drops of rosewater add interest, as does a pinch of dry mustard and/or cumin. You can also add a tiny bit of lemon juice or dry wine (but cut the quantity of vinegar accordingly). If you use garlic, don't overdo it. Rubbing your salad bowl with a cut clove of garlic will provide ample flavoring—or add a little crushed garlic to the dressing itself.

ENDLESS POSSIBILITIES

Beyond basic green, salad possibilities are endless. The following two Fitness House Kitchen favorites are unusual and give some idea of how creative the salad-making process can be. The importance of being uninhibited cannot, in fact, be stressed enough.

SPROUTED LENTIL, BEAN AND RICE SALAD

¼ cup lentils, sprouted
½ lb. pinto beans, soaked, cooked, cooked until tender
½ lb. pink beans, soaked, cooked until tender
2 cups cooked brown rice
1 cup celery, diced

½ green pepper, diced
¼ cup pimiento, chopped
1 medium size red onion, sliced thin (for garnish)

1. Soak pinto and pink beans overnight in water to cover. Do not drain. Use soaking water to cook beans, thereby saving the vitamins and minerals. Cook the beans in salted water until just tender. Don't overcook. Drain.
2. Combine beans, rice, celery, pepper, pimiento and lentil sprouts.
3. Toss above ingredients in dressing and top with the onion rings.

DRESSING

½ cup soy or corn oil (cold pressed)
½ cup wine vinegar
1 tablespoon raw honey

1 teaspoon salt
1 teaspoon pepper (fresh ground)

Note: Fresh green beans can be substituted for one of the dried beans, or added to the recipe as is. Also, kidney beans can be substituted for pinto or pink beans. And soy beans, chick peas, and/or lima beans are all welcome additions—or substitutes. Yield: 10 servings.

MACEDOINE OF VEGETABLES

2 cups cold cooked cubed potatoes
2 cups cold cooked peas
2 cups cold cooked green beans, cut into one-inch pieces
2 cups cold cooked small lima beans
2 cups cold cooked cubed carrots
1 teaspoon salt
½ teaspoon kelp powder

½ teaspoon freshly ground pepper
1½ tablespoons wine vinegar
1 tablespoon fresh lemon juice
¼ teaspoon dry mustard
½ cup pignolia nuts or sunflower seed kernels
3 hard-cooked eggs
2 medium tomatoes
1 cup mayonnaise

1. Wash 4 or 5 medium potatoes. Place in medium saucepan, cover with water and cook until tender. Drain potatoes and when cool enough to handle, remove skins and cut into small cubes.
2. Prepare remaining vegetables and cook each one separately in very small amount of water. Do not overcook. Drain well. (Do not cook vegetables in salted water).
3. Place cooked vegetables in large mixing bowl. Combine wine vinegar, kelp, dry mustard, salt and pepper in a small bowl. Blend together and pour over cooked vegetables. Toss gently and allow to cool at room temperature.

4. Add one-half cup pignolia nuts or sunflower kernels to mixed vegetables. Sprinkle one tablespoon of lemon juice over top and stir in enough mayonnaise to moisten the vegetables well. Taste and correct seasoning.
5. Cover and place in refrigerator and chill for several hours before serving.
6. Pile macedoine of vegetables on a serving plate lined with greens. Garnish with hardcooked eggs and tomato wedges.
Yield: eight to ten servings.

NEVER TOO MANY COOKS

Salad-making is one culinary art in which there are never too many cooks. In other words, invite members of your family to invent their own salads—and get guests in on the act, too. Next time you have a buffet-style party, serve a huge bowl of mixed greens, surrounded by smaller bowls of various dressings and "accessories'." Among the accessories could be: chopped nuts, scallions, radishes, raisins, fresh parsley, chives, shredded red cabbage, assorted types of pickles, or chopped bananas—yes, bananas. One of the most intriguing salads we've ever come across consisted of bananas—plus shredded chicken, watercress, butter lettuce, raisins, cashews, pecans, pickled watermelon rind, fresh shredded ginger, unsweetened coconut, raw mushrooms, fresh mint, tomato and fertilized egg. It was served with a remoulade dressing and, in addition to its unforgettable taste, left an indelible message; never be afraid to experiment!

In addition to inventing your own combinations, investigate foreign cookbooks for the classic salads of other countries. Indonesians make lettuce almost cosmic by dousing it with a very tart dressing and sprinkling it with chopped peanuts. Simple—but exotic. In Japan, they mix cucumbers, scallions and shredded cabbage and top it with a dressing of rice vinegar, soy sauce, sugar (substitute honey) and sesame oil. You can also toast sesame seeds and then add them to any cold pressed oil. The Turks make a splendid salad (also known as cold soup) called cacik (pronouced: ja-jook). Chop cucumbers, salt them, and pour on a sauce made of one cup of yogurt, a tablespoon of vinegar, and dill and garlic to taste. Garnish with fresh chopped mint and a few drops of oil.

Our final salad suggestion comes, as is only proper, in the form of a dessert. Fruit salads are the ideal way to finish off a meal, particularly a heavy one. The following recipe is known as "Heavenly Salad"and with very good reason:

1 cup orange sections
1½ cups pineapple cubes, unsweet-
ened
1 cup seedless green grapes, halves if
desired
½ cup fresh blueberries
½ cup fresh strawberries, halves (fro-
zen strawberries may also be
used—buy whole, unsweetened
ones)

2 bananas, peeled and sliced
2 teaspoons fresh lemon juice
1 teaspoon orange rind
2 tablespoons raw honey
1 cup unflavored yogurt
1 cup flaked or coarsely shredded
coconut, unsweetened

1. Prepare fruit; drain well.
2. In large bowl, combine orange sections, pineapple cubes, grapes, blueberries and coconut. Add lemon juice, honey, orange rind and yogurt. Toss together lightly. Cover bowl and place in the refrigerator for at least one hour before serving.
3. Remove fruit mixture from refrigerator and add strawberry halves and sliced bananas. Mix lightly.
4. Serve in a large dish or individual dishes, garnished with fresh mint.

—Shelagh Jones

Cooking Proteins

Protein is the substance of which living cells are largely made. It consists of carbon, hydrogen, nitrogen, oxygen and sulfur, thus differing from the carbohydrates which contain only carbon, hydrogen and oxygen. Since the chemical composition of protein is different, the method of cooking it is different, too. Only one piece of advice remains the same as for vegetables—the lower the heat, the better.

Many of us have been accustomed to cooking proteins with high heat. We "sear" our meat, to "hold in the juices." We fry eggs in very hot fat; we broil cheese; we bake fish to a state of leathery toughness. If you stop for just a moment and think of your own experiences with protein substances, you will realize the necessity of using low heat at all times when you are cooking protein.

Have you ever tried to wash out a bloodstain with hot water? Can't be done. The heat coagulates and toughens the blood. Ever try soaking an egg dish in hot water before you wash it? All you manage to do is make the egg stick more tightly to the dish. If you would wash milk easily from a container, use cold water, never warm! Milk is largely protein.

TEMPER THE FIRE

Why is it, then that so many of us ruin our protein by overcooking them and cooking them at high heat? Steaks sizzled to a crisp under a blazing broiler are tough and leathery. Roasts seared and then baked in a hot oven are not only tough but have no flavor, for most of the meat juices have been lost. If you would cook economically, and if you would keep your family healthy and if you would be known as a good cook, keep one cardinal rule in mind—cook proteins with low heat.

Meats—roasts, steaks and so forth— are made of muscle fibers. These fibers are held together by what we call connective tissue, the substance from which gelatin is made. The juices of the meat, which contain the flavor as well as all the vitamins and minerals, are held in these connective tissues. When you cook meat at a low temperature, the proteins of the muscle itself gradually become firm. The connective tissue gradually softens. Tender cuts of meat contain little connective tissue, hence they need a shorter cooking time. The less-tender cuts like stew meat contain a great deal of connective tissue—you can see it sometimes in thick layers which you call gristle. So the less tender cuts must be cooked longer, to soften all this connective tissue. This does not mean, however, that you should subject the tougher meats to high heat!

When you cook meat at high temperatures, the protein substances of it are made to shrink and shrivel, so that you end with only a small part of the meat you started with. In addition, the connective fibers break down completely. Instead of merely softening they may dissolve completely into gelatin and leave long strings of fiber not held together by anything and impossible to slice. You have seen chunks of boiled meat that look like this. You know, too, that such a piece of meat has little or no flavor. All the juices have been cooked out of it.

Now doesn't it seem silly to spend money buying meat, which is the most expensive food we buy, and then ruin it by improper cooking? What about searing meat to "hold in the juices?" As the high heat is applied to the meat, proteins break down and juices spill out. When you sear meat you hear the fat sputtering violently in the pot. Fat sputters when it comes into contact with water. The sputtering of your seared meat represents meat juices lost.

Salting meat while it is cooking or before it is cooked is another crime against a good food. Of course we hope you don't salt meat, either in the kitchen or at the table. But if you must use any salt, for goodness sake use it just before you eat the meat. Salt attracts water as we all know. When you apply salt to uncooked or partly cooked meat, you can expect the salt to draw unto itself most of the meat juices. Where do they go? Out into the pan to evaporate. Actually, the best way to keep the juices in the meat is to brush the meat carefully with fat before roasting or broiling it.

Cooking proteins—not just meat but other protein foods as well—at low temperatures does not harm the amino acids—the protein building blocks that are absolutely essential for good health. But high heat breaks down some of these amino acids and makes them unfit for use by the body. It also, of course, destroys vitamins. The B vitamins are especially sensitive to high heat. Low heat does not destroy them to any great extent. But what sense is there to buying liver once a week, for its B vitamin content, and then heating it to such a temperature that most of the B vitamins are lost?

THE SLOW SIMMER

How, then, should you cook meat economically and most healthfully? A friend of ours used to notice that the Sunday roast beef was always more tender and tasty on Sundays when she went to church. Sundays when she stayed home, the roast was tough and tasteless. What was the reason? Days when she went to church she put the roast on early turned the heat low and let it roast slowly until church time. Then, just before she left the house, she turned the oven fire off and left the roast cooking by its own heat until she returned, when she lighted the oven fire once again. When she stayed home from church, the roast cooked at oven heat for the whole time. And was tough.

The best method for cooking meat is to use a meat thermometer and cook the meat only until the thermometer indicates that the internal temperature is right for eating. Broiling and roasting are preferable to other ways of cooking meat. Boiling meat results in tough tasteless meat out of which all juices and valuable elements have been driven. Frying meat involves cooking it in the very high temperature of hot fat. If you must ever fry meat, coat it with flour or crumbs so that *they* will be browned and fried and the meat itself can have slower cooking inside the protective jacket.

One of the reasons so much excellent and nourishing protein is lost today is the efficiency of our modern stoves. The high gas flame, the bright searing hot electric grill spell destruction to valuable proteins. The same is true of pressure cookers where the heat generated is extremely high. If you are planning to buy a new stove, do not be concerned about getting heat from the burners. Try instead to get a stove that has a real "simmer" burner, so that you can cook protein foods for long periods of time at a temperature considerably below boiling. And, if you can, get a stove whose oven can be regulated exactly to a very low heat which it will maintain hour after hour.

The best discussion of cooking meat in a modern cookbook is in Adelle Davis' *Let's Cook It Right,* published by Harcourt Brace Jovanovich. Miss Davis is an outspoken champion of the low-heat-for-protein school. She tells in this cookbook of once cooking a turkey for 24 hours over a pilot light. And she claims it was the best turkey she ever ate.

What we have said about meats applies to other protein foods as well. Fish is very tender and delicate and needs little cooking at very low heat. What about eggs? Every cook knows what happens to a souffle put into a hot oven or an omelet left for even a moment over a high flame. You might as well try to eat leather. Keep the flame turned low. Let little heat over a long period of time be the catch phrase when you are cooking proteins!

Converting Your Old Recipes

If you're at all like the average housewife, you won't want to give up all your family's favorite dishes for organically grown foods. You're going to want to prepare those favorites in a new way, the organic way. But how?

It's really quite simple.

Instead of all those processed, refined and chemically treated foods, you'll use natural foods. Instead of refined white sugar, you'll use honey or raw sugar. Instead of refined, bleached white flour, you'll use organically grown, stone-ground whole wheat flour. You'll use carob instead of chocolate.

It won't be as simple as the following substitutions will make it seem. You'll have to experiment a bit, varying the quantities slightly until you get the results you want. Then just jot them down with your recipe.

Flour: The easiest substitution is flour. If your recipe calls for a cup or two of flour, be sure to use that quantity of whole wheat flour. You can use whole wheat pastry flour, but use only ⅞ cup for each cup called for in the recipe.

You can boost the nutritional value of your flour-based recipe by using wheat germ to replace part of the flour. For example, if the recipe calls for a cup of flour, use ¾ cup of whole wheat flour and ¼ cup of wheat germ.

Sweetener: Substituting for sugar in your recipes will call for the most experimentation. Some substitution charts suggest using 1-1/3 cups of raw sugar as a substitute for a cup of refined sugar. But a straight one-to-one substitution works fine, and a ¾ to one or 2/3 to one works even better. The less sugar you consume, raw or not, the better off you are. Remember, too, that the less sweetener you use, the more the full, rich flavor of the whole wheat flour will assert itself.

A better replacement for sugar in your old recipes is honey. While some substitution charts suggest quantities up to 1½ cups of honey in place of a cup of sugar, you're much better off using ¾ cup of honey for each cup of sugar. In addition, cut the amount of liquid in the recipe, be it milk, water or other fluid, by ¼ cup. If the recipe has no liquid requirement, add about four tablespoons of flour for each ¾ cup measure of honey. The reason for these changes is obvious. The honey is a liquid rather than a dry substance, and will upset the character of the recipe unless accommodations are made.

Carob: Another important substitution is to replace chocolate with carob. For each ounce of chocolate, use instead three tablespoons of carob powder, a tablespoon of milk or water and a tablespoon of vegetable oil. In cocoa powder applications, use four tablespoons of carob powder and a tablespoon of vegetable oil for each three tablespoons of cocoa powder.

Natural foods: There are other substitutions you should make, replacing empty foods with natural foods. Virtually all of them can be made on a one-to-one basis. For example, you should use powdered kelp instead of the ordinary salt. Instead of bread crumbs, use wheat germ or whole wheat bread crumbs. Use brown rice instead of the convenient but worthless white rice. Use cold-pressed, unrefined vegetable oils instead of butter, margarine or solid shortening. On the table, use butter instead of margarine.

Enrichment: Moreover, you can bolster the nutritional content of your old recipes by including some additional ingredients. Use sprouts in salads, soups and stews. Add wheat germ to cakes, breads and cookies. Lace your dishes with brewer's yeast.

There's no end to the substituting and fortifying you can accomplish with natural, organically grown foods. The important change will be in your family's nutrition. But you'll get a new satisfaction from knowing that you're doing some creative cooking, too. So don't throw out those old, family recipes. Add a bit of yourself to them. Convert them, too.

Grinder Cookery

You really have to be on the defensive in vying with food manufacturers who rob much of the food you eat of its natural goodness. Since a good offense is the best defense, the best way to defend yourself against their nutritional thieves is to process your own food.

Prepare as many foods as possible right in your own kitchen so that you know exactly what is going into your food. This is where food grinders can be your best friends. Just like backyard grinders which help you use natural soil builders to feed your garden, kitchen grinders let you prepare natural foods to feed your family. These little helpers allow *you* to do the chipping, grinding, grating, and shredding instead of some food factory. The old-fashioned meat grinder your grandmother used, the small electric or hand mill, and the blender all have a valuable place in your natural foods kitchen. They save you money —and nutrients!

It's a well-known fact that most flours at the supermarket have the very life milled out of them. Wheat germ, the heart of the wheat where all the vitamins and trace minerals are, is removed, and the flour is bleached to achieve that corpse-like whiteness. Those snazzy cereal boxes are filled with lifeless grains, most of which are coated with excessive amounts of refined sugar and artificial flavors to mask their tastelessness.

Grind your own grains instead of relying on the not-so-super market varieties. Grind them fresh each day for hot, nutritious cereals and whole-grain breads. The full-bodied flavor of these unrefined grains remind you of the rich food value with which they were endowed.

To preserve the most nutritional qualities as possible in cooked, whole-grain cereals, grind them first in a hand or electric mill. Ground grains take less time to cook, and since cooking robs much of the E vitamins, quick-cooked cereals are more nutritious—providing the grains are freshly ground. Cooking takes only a few minutes, which is something to keep in mind for morning rushes.

Ground grains may be added to cold water, or stirred into boiling water. Cook only until the mixture starts bubbling, stirring continually. Take the cereal off the heat and let it thicken a few minutes before serving. The hard grains, like corn, brown rice, millet and soybeans, are cooked in four parts water to one part grain. Softer grains like oats, flax, barley, wheat and rye, are best cooked in two parts water to one part grain.

CREATIVE GRINDING

Grinding grains isn't the only thing these little devices can do for you. If you have imagination, there's no end to their usefulness. Like the taste of peanuts and want to improve your family's diets? Then try making your own peanut flour by grinding raw or dry roasted peanuts in a blender or mill. Peanut flour is nutritionally superior to all other flours. It has four times the protein, eight times the fat and nine times the trace minerals of whole-wheat flour! Since it is a heavy flour with a strong peanut flavor you will need to try it on your family by using different quantities in various recipes. Peanut flour can successfully replace small quantities of whole-wheat and other whole-grain flours in breads, cookies, crunchy pie crusts and fruit crisps.

Speaking of peanuts, peanut butter is easy to make at home. Grind dry roasted peanuts into a flour. If you use a mill, remove the flour from the mill and put into a bowl. Add a little oil—just enough to make the flour hold together and form a paste—and salt to taste. If you are using a blender, grind the peanuts in it, and while blending add oil slowly, drop by drop, until the mixture reaches the right consistency. Be careful not to add too much oil. Peanuts contain a lot of their own oil and if excessive oil is added, the butter will taste too thick and oily. If you make your own peanut butter you can be sure that nothing has been added to it, like the hydrogenated vegetable oil (hard-to-digest saturated fat), corn syrup and dextrose found in many commercial peanut butters.

Other nut butters can be made just as easily by grinding different kinds of nuts. Try walnuts, almonds, cashews and brazil nuts, or a combination of these. Such nut butters are made in the same way as peanut butter but may not need additional oil.

Sesame and sunflower seeds, two of the most nutrient-packed little foods you can eat, can be made into meal by running them through a home mill or blender. Tahini, sesame seed butter, can be made just as the nut butters.

GRIND IN NUTRITION AND FLAVOR

When you just don't have the time to bake from scratch and *must* use prepackaged cake, cookie, biscuit and pancake mixes, make sure that you compensate for what's missing nutritionally. Put goodness into these convenience foods by adding wheat germ. But before you add the wheat germ, run it through your blender or mill first. This reduces it to a finer consistency so that you can add it to packaged mixes without anyone even suspecting it's there. The fussiest of eaters won't know that they're getting extra B vitamins and minerals when you add a tablespoon or two. Finely ground, wheat germ makes a great garnish for desserts, salads and cereals. It takes the place of breadcrumbs on casseroles and is a good extender for meat loaves and meat balls.

White sugar is refined to such a point that it is a non-food; it has absolutely no nutrients left in it when it has gone through the washing, boiling and crystallizing processes. Brown sugar is no better because it is only white sugar with caramel flavoring and coloring added. One way to avoid using white or brown sugar is to make date sugar—yourself —with your mechanical helpers. Dates are extremely high in natural sugars; a fully ripe date's sugar content may be from 35 to 75 per cent of the whole fruit. To make sugar, remove the pits from hardened-dry dates and grind them. The product will be a dark natural sweetener far superior to the commercial brown sugar it resembles. Date sugar may be substituted for white or brown sugar in most all recipes. It is especially good for toppings on fruit crisps, puddings and in cookies. Remember when using it that date sugar tastes like dates, since that is all it is, and it is not as sweet as regular sugar.

If honey, molasses, maple syrup, maple sugar or date sugar just won't do as a sweetener in some of your recipes because you need powdered or confectioner's sugar, run Turbinado sugar through your blender or mill until it is fine and powdery. If you grind it up before using it to sprinkle over a dessert, it will go further as a garnish. You'll find yourself having to use less of it.

Coconut is a good, wholesome food, provided it's not sweetened commercially. Stay away from those plastic packages of coconut that have extra sugar, salt and preservatives. Better yet, buy a whole coconut and grate it at home. It will save you money and you'll know that all you're getting is the real thing. Split open a coconut and save the milk for fruit drinks. Cut away the shell, but not the smooth, brown inner skin which contains many minerals. Cut the coconut into small chunks and put a few through the blender or mill. Add more until you've ground up the whole coconut. Ground coconut will keep very well if it's put in a glass jar and frozen. You can take out just the amount you need each time because frozen coconut scrapes off easily. Avoid keeping it in the refrigerator for more than one week once ground as it may start to mold.

When you're finished with an organically grown orange or lemon, don't throw the peel away. Let it dry out in a warm spot in your kitchen and when it's completely dried grind it into a fine powder. Place it in a jar with a tight-fitting lid to protect its aroma and flavor, and keep it as a natural flavoring that can be added to frostings, cakes, cookies and breads. Make sure you use organically grown fruit. The skins of commercial fruits are sprayed heavily with pesticides that don't all come off with a good washing. There's also a very good chance that orange skins have been dyed with Red No. 2, so suspected of being a carcinogen that it's banned in Canada, Great Britain and elsewhere.

MEAT GRINDING

Don't forget a grinder for meats—that old-fashioned meat grinder that clamps on the end of a table or kitchen counter will do nicely. Meats bought in one piece and ground at home bring a better assurance of quality than those purchased already ground in a market. After all, it's not so easy to determine the quality of prepackaged ground meat ambiguously labeled "lean" or "extra lean," or "sirloin," "round" or "chuck." Not only are you likely to have fresher, better meat when you grind your own, but you can also eliminate the costly addition of excess fat which finds its way into bulk-ground market meat.

Unfortunately, the most nutritious meats are usually those least palatable to the average family—the organ meats. They are richest in minerals, vitamins and nucleic acids. A grinder can help you add them to meat dishes without anyone objecting to their looks, taste or smell. Grind kidneys, brains, heart and sweetbreads (thymus) and add them to your usual ground meat. About one pound of organ meat to every three pounds of ground round or chuck will boost the nutritional value of your meat loaves, hamburgers and meat balls and will go undetected by people who usually shun them. Ground organ meats help you extend your chopped meat, too, because they normally cost you less than other cuts.

When you think of kitchen equipment, don't leave out the grinder. It will pay for itself over and over again. And it will help you, when processing your own foods, to get nothing but the real thing.

—*Carol Stoner*

Gourmet Cooking—Organically

Eating properly, our style, can be as exciting as dining in a fine French or Italian restaurant. In fact many of the fine points of gourmet cooking had their origin in time-honored medicinal advice.

Take garlic, for example. Cultivated for thousands of years, it was known as a food and medicine by every ancient race. Today we recognize that garlic is an important anti-bacterial agent, which can work wonders in controlling stomach upsets. In France to this very day, minced garlic is served in a mayonnaise sauce as a tonic.

My husband and I adore the flavor of garlic, perhaps to the dismay of our friends. We find that nearly every meat, many vegetables, and, of course, salads are vastly improved by a subtle suggestion of garlic. Several hours before roasting or broiling a chicken, I always rub crushed cloves of garlic both on the inside and outside flesh. The chicken then is left at room temperature for a least a half hour to allow the flavor to penetrate thoroughly. In this way garlic can be a delightful substitute for salt.

A roast leg of lamb is never complete without a generous rubbing with cut garlic cloves before cooking. Its pungency blends extremely well with the mild yet distinct flavor of lamb. When roasting beef, I suggest plenty of garlic with the less tender cuts. Really fine prime rib roasts, however, need very little seasoning—a sprinkling of paprika and a trace of garlic, if wanted.

A long-standing rule in making appetizing salads is to rub your wooden salad bowl with garlic. For a more penetrating flavor, I suspend two halves of a cut clove in my salad dressing—a 3 to 1 mixture of olive oil (the finest I can get) and red wine vinegar. It is easy to make up a good sized batch of dressing to have on hand at all times. Those who want to cut down on their oil consumption might try mixing up a half-and-half portion of olive oil and wine vinegar.

Sometimes, the housewife finds it tempting to by-pass fresh garlic by adding a dash of garlic powder. Not only are you cheating yourself of food value lost in the drying process, but also the full, rich garlic flavor. It simply is not the same.

Help yourself to use fresh garlic by keeping it in a convenient place near the stove and by investing in an inexpensive garlic crusher, which saves you time and tears in mincing the cloves.

THE USEFULNESS OF PARSLEY

Another herb which has been greatly neglected by American house-wives is that symbol of luxury—parsley. Of all the greens we use, our treatment of parsley is scandalous, indeed. Let's knock it off its pedestal as a deluxe vegetable. Let's take parsley to heart and make it a staple in our diet.

In the Middle Ages writers of herbals believed that parsley had the power to "fasten loose teeth, brighten dim eyes and relieve a stitch on the side." Today we know that parsley is extremely rich in vitamins A and C. Night blindness is cured with doses of vitamin A; the gums depend on vitamin C for perfect functioning as a seat for the teeth. The Ancients were not very far off this time.

"But parsley chokes in your throat," you say? Who can swallow enough sprigs to make a whit of difference in vitamin intake? Even one large sprig provides you with some part of your daily need of vitamin A.

Chopped parsley, however, can be put to any number of uses by an enterprising cook. Popping ½ cup of parsley into a four pound stew will mean 10,000 units of vitamin A on the credit side. Broiled hamburgers, meat balls or a meat loaf are naturals for chopped parsley. Mix with raw ground meat before shaping, for an extra-special, spring-like flavor.

Parsley is unequalled in bringing out the true flavor of mild fish, like haddock or bluefish. Nothing can spark up a seafood dinner so well as a liberal sprinkling of this herb in combination with chives and tarragon.

For most soups, parsley is indispensable. When the broth is partially cooked, add a parsley bouquet, tied with white thread. Do not allow parsley to fall apart in clear soups: rather remove it and serve with fresh-chopped parsley. A handy parsley chopper now on the market will make short work of it.

If you can't grow your own parsley, buy only very crisp, fresh bunches. Wash thoroughly and quickly, drain and refrigerate in a closed glass jar.

FRUITS AND NUTS FOR DESSERT

For dessert, take a hint from the French. Serve a fruit-and-nut course for a refreshing treat, especially during the summer. For those who have to coax their family to eat fruit, serve it the continental way with a fine glass bowl for washing. My husband enjoys a bit of huckstering, too. I place the fruit and nuts in a large glass underliner, around an oversized brandy snifter, 12 inches high, which is one-third filled with water. The fruit is washed directly at the table by the eater, making a charming and healthy dessert ceremony. Since washed fruit spoils quickly, it is much better to save the washing for the dinner table. The remaining fruit will last days longer.

An assortment of almonds, Brazil nuts, peanuts and black walnuts are especially nutritious for a dessert course, high in minerals and protein content. Be sure to have the nut cracker handy.

TAKING YOUR VITAMINS

Another pleasant ceremony for the family group is "giving of the vitamins." An easy method is to keep the vitamin bottles on a good tray (even a silver tray) in the refrigerator. At mealtimes, place the tray at the head of the table if Father likes to officiate, along with a row of small cups. Egg cups work out very nicely. Children, especially, enjoy taking their vitamins with a bit of pageantry, along with the adults of the family. This has been a patriarchal tradition for years in the Rodale family.

Why not be healthy and still serve up meals fit for a gourmet. The extra effort is much more than repaid when every member of the family greets you with "more!"

—Ruth Rodale Spira

Make Your Own Baby Food

The mother who makes her own baby food from foods that have not been contaminated with additives nor treated with nitrates and pesticides is giving her child something of far more value than the traditional silver spoon. She is improving his chances to grow and mature in uncomplicated good health, both mental and physical.

True, when baby foods were first marketed they spelled a sort of emancipation for the busy mother. Today with a blender and a freezer, making baby's foods is no more of a chore than making your own food, and it gives you an opportunity to enrich your baby's food with the highly nutritive ingredients like wheat germ and brewer's yeast.

Judith R. Hinds, a mother who makes her own, calls it "dab cookery." With a minimum of planning, she says, baby meals in the form of dabs can be made in advance and frozen.

To make dabs, you steam or simmer fruits and vegetables, preferably organically grown, just as you would for your family, using very little water and being careful not to overcook. Puree the foods in the blender using all of the cooking liquid, which is rich in minerals. If the mixture is runny, add wheat germ. Meats can be steamed or lightly sautéed and then finely chopped. Or you can make a meat and vegetable combination in the blender. The vegetable juice will provide sufficient liquid for proper blending.

Once the puree is ready, simply drop the mixture like pancake batter by the tablespoon onto a plate. The size of the dab is determined by your baby's appetite. For his first food a teaspoonful may be enough. As he grows, increase the amount and blend for a shorter time. This will encourage chewing. Next put the plate in the freezer for several hours. When the dabs are frozen solid, store them in a covered container. Presto! Baby can have pure unadulterated food with no more trouble than going to the store to stock up—maybe even less.

Mrs. Hinds suggests that when you are ready to use the dabs, you simply thaw them in a covered pyrex dish for several hours in the refrigerator, then heat on a warming tray or a yoghurt maker or simply over warm water in a double boiler. You can even take dabs along on trips; simply keep them cold in a portable cooler.

DAB COOKERY RECIPES

Here are some of Mrs. Hinds' recipes. You can adapt the same procedure to any other food such as apples, prunes, pears, squash, sweet
potatoes, eggplant, anything you grow in your garden and to such meat
as beef heart, calves' brain, liver or fish.

For iron-rich apricot dabs, simmer one or two pounds of sun-dried
apricots for 30 minutes in pure water to cover. Let stand until cool.
Blend the apricots with the liquid until smooth. Then make and freeze
dabs as described. You can double the number of dabs, give them a nice
change of flavor, and increase the nutrients by stirring into the puree
half again as much yoghurt. Baby will love the creamy consistency and
the yoghurt will help him develop a good healthy intestinal flora.

To make chicken liver dabs, Mrs. Hinds suggests that you cut up two
carrots, four stalks of celery and one small onion and steam them for
about ten minutes. Place in blender with liquid. Now sauté one pound
of chicken livers lightly, or steam them until they change color. Chop
coarsely. Now blend with vegetables by flicking switch on and off at the
start. This will make a quite a few dabs. Mrs. Hinds leaves three-fourths
of the mixture in the blender, adds nuts, hard-cooked eggs, one
chopped onion and curry powder for a delicious dish for the whole
family.

You can fix meat for baby by scraping a piece of raw beef or liver
with a knife. In this way you will get off much of the soft, tender part.
The tough muscle and gristle will be left. You can use this part in soup.
Make the scraped meat into a little patty and cook in a custard cup set
in a pan of slowly boiling water until the color of the meat changes. You
could prepare several little custard cups in one kitchen session and
freeze for later use.

When you grow your own food organically, the 'dab' method can
be a wonderful help to you. You can prepare baby's winter menu as
soon as the crops come in when they are richest in nutrients.

EATING WITH THE FAMILY

Another way to feed your baby healthfully is to give him the same
nutritious food you give to the rest of your family. Simply put baby's
share through the blender to get a consistency he can manage. Other
foods baby can manage very nicely just as you serve them to the family.

Chicken soup with brown rice? Baby will love it. Hamburger? Let him crumble his own. If you're having stew, put the chunks of meat and vegetables through the blender. Are you having steak or lamb chops? That high chair thumper will have a ball with a meaty bone. The same vegetables you're serving to the family can be pureed for a few seconds in the blender and given to baby. While the family is eating salad, baby can go to town on a stick of celery or a carrot stick. He can join you for a mashed baked potato right out of the jacket. For dessert, try fresh fruit. Baby's share can be pureed in the blender. It's far superior to the fruit that is processed and sweetened and sold in jars.

If you have a source of organically grown apples, pears, or apricots, cook up a batch with their mineral-rich skins. Use a little raw honey as your only sweetener. Use no sugar. Freeze. Defrost on a winter's day and serve it chunky to the family and pureed for baby.

Use your own ingenuity. Be creative. Why relegate the vital task of providing your baby's food to some manufacturer whose first consideration is profit? If your pediatrician tells you that baby foods in the jars are the purest foods you can possibly get, he hasn't been doing his homework.

Use your good old common sense and your inborn maternal wisdom; give your baby tender loving care and nutritious foods you have prepared yourself. There's no greater source of satisfaction and no better investment in your baby's future.

3

For Better Nourished Families

Be An Organic Housewife

If you have been trying to introduce your family to good nutrition, you know that while the results are indeed rewarding, sometimes the venture can be mighty frustrating.

I well remember the time when one of my small fry said to me at the dinner table, "Mom, why can't we be like other people and have soda?"

Now that's a question which sooner or later everyone of us good-nutrition mothers has to face.

"You can't have soda," I told him, "because I love you."

"Gee that's funny," he said. "Jimmy has soda all the time. Doesn't his mother love him?"

"Maybe Jimmy's mother doesn't know that soda doesn't make you strong and healthy."

"Gosh," he said, "sometimes I wish that you didn't know so darn much."

You are probably among those who know so darn much that you're concerned. You know that our food supply is over-sweetened, over-salted, over-processed, full of chemicals and low in the important elements of nutrition.

Well, how can a mother bring to her family the kind of meals which not only look good, and taste great, but bring to her family lots of zip and zest, beautiful complexions, lovely teeth, pleasant lovable dispositions and the ability to cope? What can a mother do in the kitchen that will help her loved ones fulfill their greatest potential? Can she do it with what is available in the market place?

It isn't easy, but it can be done.

How? Well, come to dinner at our house. I promise that you will be healthier when you leave than when you came. My specialty is making people healthy when they're not looking. You won't know, for instance, that the grapefruit has been scored to include some of the white inner rind to give you a bountiful supply of bioflavonoids. You won't know that the chow mein was made with a supernutritional meat mixture, spiked with brewer's yeast and served on brown rice. You might notice that the tea had an interesting flavor and, if you asked, you would learn that there were rose hips in it for extra vitamin C.

I confess. I am not a conventional cook. I approach each session in the kitchen with a nutritional leer on my mug and a secret health-building ingredient behind my back.

You know why? Because I found out the hard way that with children and with husbands, at various stages of their development, like from toddler right up to the coronary stage, anything that smacks of health is a dirty word, square, or faddist. You can't force them either. But you can sneak it. *You can make them healthy—when they're not looking.* Throughout the various stages of raising four kids from diapers to dungarees to college degrees, I developed a big bag of sneaky stratagems. I'd like to share a few with you.

TRAP THOSE APPETITES

First, just before dinner when the children are ravenous and will eat anything that doesn't move, put out a large tray of crisp, raw vegetables—celery and carrot sticks, turnip slices, pepper rings, raw cauliflower, raw beets, raw sweet potatoes or any other vegetable in season—preferably organically grown. Raw foods have enzymes that start digestive juices flowing. Deftly remove from the premises all the pretzels, potato chips, corn curls, gum drops, jelly beans, chocolate kisses, lollipops, candy and throw them out.

The next step in your campaign to make them healthy when they're not looking is to enlist your butcher's cooperation. My butcher has been in cahoots with me for years. When I order my hamburger—you-know-what mixture—he knows what I mean. If he didn't, I'd have a terrible time placing my order over the phone. Children have big ears.

You see, the meats that are most important to health are the organ meats—liver, kidney, brain, thymus and heart. You can just imagine what kind of closed-mouth strike you'd have around your table if you tried serving these foods frequently, unless you could serve them by some other name. For some strange reason, many people have an emotional hang-up about organ meats.

But you can serve hamburger every night of the week in a different guise and never get a complaint. So, hamburger is the natural medium for your organ meats. Your butcher grinds up whatever you wish to conceal, with your round or chuck. My standing order is two pounds chuck, one pound heart—all ground together. That gives me three pounds of wonderfully nutritious meat—and at practically half the price. My butcher, who, incidentally, now uses this mixture for his own family and can't thank me enough for the idea, gives me valiant service. He wraps it for the freezer in one pound packages so that it's always ready to go into one of my chopped meat dishes. It is a juicy, tasty mixture which the children love and so do their friends who come to dinner. Though they have asked me many times why our hamburger tastes so good, I have never told them what was in it. One of the first rules of sneaky cooking is *never* reveal your strategy. Take the fifth.

Here are some more steps you can take to make your kitchen one that builds good health and promotes vitality. Take a good hard look at your pantry shelves. Read the ingredient list on each package there. You may need a magnifying glass. Does it say BHT or BHA or freshener preserver in packaging materials? Throw it out. Does it have added sugar? Throw it out. If it has none of these and nothing else with a long unpronounceable name, but has been popped, exploded, flaked or crackled, then add wheat germ to it—a good heaping tablespoon to each serving to compensate for what was lost in the processing.

The philosophy of good-health cooking is to add to each food those nutrients which would have been there in the first place if the food had not been emasculated in the refining process.

If your children are hung up on dry cereals, why not make your own? You can make delicious dry cereals using whole grains, dried fruits, nuts, raisins and coconut. Some supermarkets carry a Swiss cereal that combines these ingredients. Another excellent food that is generally available in supermarkets is buckwheat groats. It is rich in nutrients, unprocessed and still not contaminated with preservatives. Wheatena and Quaker Oats are also free of additives. But if you can get your kids to take wheat germ and fruit, as their cereal, you've got it made. If you can't get them to take it, take it yourself. You'll have that much more strength with which to cope with their crazy notions. Know how I got mine to take wheat germ? I changed the label on the jar. After all, if you're cramming for exams or are facing a spelling bee or an arithmetic test, can you resist "anti-stupid molecules" or "high I.Q. granules"?

One of those rare doctors who considers nutrition in his practice tells his patients to avoid the four whites: white flour, white rice, white sugar and refined white salt.

Any mother who serves foodless white rice is committing a big dietary sin. She is filling her family with weight-producing calories without health-building nutrients. Brown rice, on the other hand, is an excellent food—full of good B vitamins and minerals. It is easy to prepare, inexpensive, and your family will actually prefer the good wholesome flavor of the brown rice. It's available at many supermarkets.

What else is available at your supermarket which is good wholesome food and uncontaminated with chemicals? Precious little.

LOBBY FOR WHOLESOME FOOD

How can we make the food industry understand that we want pure unadulterated food without any of the emulsifiers, stabilizers, softeners, color improvers, extenders, flavor intensifiers, texture modifiers and thousands of other chemicals which they pour in by the ton? You must raise your voice, and educate your relatives, friends and neighbors. You who know must educate those who do not know. Do it calmly, rationally and with deep concern—so that you earn their respect, their confidence and their gratitude. Wouldn't they be grateful to you if you pointed out a fire smoldering on their premises? Well, there's a chemical fire smoldering in each of us.

Educate your grocer and baker. Talk to your fellow shoppers in the supermarkets. If the opportunity presents itself, point out the dangers of dyes, emulsifiers, waxes—all of them completely unnecessary from the consumer's point of view.

Make it a point to ask the manager of your supermarket if he has any produce that was organically grown. If enough people ask for organic produce, he might just contact a local farmer who is gardening in this way and contract for his crop. As their demand increases, more farmers will throw away their sprays and chemical fertilizers and start producing real food with that old-time wholesome flavor.

Another group of people you must work on is your legislators in Congress. Lawmakers depend for much of their information on letters from the folks back home. Write a good forceful letter and they may even include it in the *Congressional Record.* Write letters to your local paper. This is one of the best ways to arouse interest and get your neighbors on the bandwagon.

The food and chemical industries have powerful lobbies in Washington. You, however, have no lobby in Washington. You have no weapon with which to counter this expensive well-equipped, highly trained team except your own conviction, your own determination and your own pen and stamp to get through to your Congressman.

TAKE ACTION IN YOUR KITCHEN

Meanwhile, back in the kitchen, what can you do?

1. Buy organically grown food, if possible. Some organic farmer near you may be glad to sell you produce. Contact local organic gardening clubs for sources. Visit your health food store. More and more of them are putting in a line of organic produce and even meats and poultry raised without antibiotics and without hormone injections. If you can't find what you want in your health food store, consult the *Organic Directory* (Rodale Press, 1971) for sources that ship by mail.

2. Shun processed foods when you buy groceries. Buy fresh fruits and vegetables in preference to canned or frozen and buy frozen in preference to canned.

3. Buy meat, fish and poultry as fresh and unprocessed as possible. Unless you are able to locate a source for organically raised meats, you probably cannot avoid the hormones, the antibiotics and the other chemicals that go into animal feeds. But you can avoid the dyes, the preservatives, the fillers, emulsifiers and so forth that go into processed meats like the canned ones, cold cuts, frankfurters, corned beef.

4. Avoid all bakery and confectionery products, candy, soft drinks and ice creams. These are the foods that are most heavily doctored

with chemicals. They are also the foods which contribute least to a good nutritional program.

5. Avoid the pre-cooked convenience foods like instant mashed potatoes, TV dinners and cake mixes. These foods are loaded with chemicals. One brand of cake mixes listed as many as 15 additives.

Every time you give up a chemical-laden food, write a letter to the processor and tell him why. His name and address appear on the label. Urge him to join you in the battle against chemicals in food—he has loved ones, whose life span he would like to prolong. Tell him you are crossing chemical-laden foods off your list. You'll be surprised at the respectful letter you will get in reply. Food companies are very sensitive to consumer reaction.

Besides eliminating chemicals from your food, if you would like to live to be 120 in good health, throw away your salt shaker and your sugar bowl. Both of these substances tend to destroy the chemical balance so vital to good health. Having taken these measures, is there a decent snack in the house?

Is there nothing you can nibble while watching TV? Is there anything you can serve your guests in good conscience? Can you throw a party without white sugar? You sure can. You can serve snacks that not only promote health, but are taste treats. All you need are fruits, nuts and seeds! Seeds have what it takes to turn you on and no side effects.

If you are a smoker, seeds in the shell keep your hands and mouth so busy you don't get much chance to reach for the nicotine. If you're a snacker fighting the battle of the bulge, you can munch happily and in good conscience.

For entertaining, serve little bowls of sunflower seeds, pumpkin seeds, soy beans, raw peanuts, cashews, almonds. Mix them all together with unsulphured raisins, unsweetened coconut and chopped dates. You'll have a truly delightful nibble dish that supplies vitamins, minerals and conversation.

Here's another important step you can take to improve your family's health. Wean them away from sweet desserts. Instead, serve sliced apples, oranges, pears, melons, strawberries or whatever fruits are in season. Try to get unsprayed fruit. Then you can serve it unpeeled.

SCHOOL LUNCHES

Now what can you do about school lunches? Is it possible for school cafeterias to serve nutritious lunches? Can parents and P.T.A.'s influence school authorities to inaugurate nutrition into school lunch programs? It's being done. Mrs. Gena Larsen, director of the cafeteria at Helix High School in La Mesa, California, has enough experience behind her now to be able to point to these results:

—A reduction of 75 per cent in minor injuries and virtual elimination of broken bones.

—Substantial decrease in cavities.

—Production of champion athletes.

—Increased scholarship level.

The key to Mrs. Larson's success is that she has adapted her resources within the framework of the federal-state program. For instance, instead of feeding the youngsters the sugar-syrup in the canned fruit, she drains it off, washes it and serves the fruit plain. She buys water-packed fruit when there's a choice. She stretches foods, uses wheat germ, nutritional yeast, soy flour and carob powder. She makes her own mayonnaise and catsup. Mrs. Larson has prepared a kit, available for a nominal fee, which outlines how to go about introducing nutrition into school lunches. It contains recipes, a brochure on kitchen methods and procedures, a list of food sources (their French dressing powder, for instance, comes from a manufacturer who makes it without sugar) and helpful hints on how to incorporate nutrition into school lunches.

Many of our young people today are gung-ho about health foods. Students at Laguna Beach High School, for instance, elected as president the candidate who campaigned for a health food program on campus. As a consequence, school officials have added large chef's salads, crisp greens, carrot and celery sticks, sliced hard-boiled eggs, fresh apples and bananas to the regular fare. The regular lunch is still offered but even that consists of items such as fresh broccoli, salads, brown rice, whole wheat bread and giant fresh baked cookies with rolled oats or wheat germ to bolster their nutritive value.

The snack bar, too, is well stocked with yogurt, chilled juices from organically grown carrots, papayas, oranges, boysenberries, grapes, raspberries, guavas, pineapple and coconut nectars and snappy cocktails of green vegetables.

The effects of the new program are spreading. Many students, excited by clearer complexions and increased energy, are introducing health foods to their homes.

Feeding teenagers, as you will know if you have any around the house, is not easy. They're always rushing somewhere and will pick up whatever food is handiest, usually an overprocessed snack that's been robbed of essential nutritional values.

But the Laguna Beach experiment proves that when young people are made aware of the results of good diet—and, most importantly, have good food made available to them—they are happy to take advantage of healthful eating.

Many of you are asking, "How can we get organic foods?" One way is to continually seek out sources of organically grown fruits and vegetables. As the demand increases, more farmers will get the message and garden without sprays and synthetics.

GROW YOUR OWN

If you have a little patch of ground, grow your own. If you live in an apartment, grow your own herbs, at least, in a windowbox. Parsley, chives and basil make lovely plants and provide many important micronutrients. And, by all means, be a *kitchen farmer*. Grow your own vitamin-rich sprouts free of insects, insecticides and artificial fertilizers. A sprouting grain is unique. It is the only foodstuff which we can consume, *humanely,* while the life force still is vibrant. A seed that is sprouting has within its kernel the essence of life—it is still steeped in self-creation and produces in abundance all life-giving elements.

While natural grains are sometimes nutritionally incomplete, when these same grains are sprouted, they undergo organic changes which greatly increase their vitamin, mineral and enzyme content.

Sprouts are your wisest investment—not only from a nutrition standpoint. In the face of rising costs, sprouts offer first aid to your soaring food budget. They make great snacks and you can raise a crop in three days.

All of us are hoping for, and working toward, the day when chemical sprays and additives will be banned, when food will again be unprocessed and wholesome.

Until then, you can make an important contribution to your family's well being, if you master the skills of the sneaky cook. Sneaky cookery may be just what you need to recharge their batteries—and your own.

Of course, you run a risky course, too. For one thing this kind of cookery makes your children so sharp it gets harder and harder to fool them. You also run the risk of making your kids different from their soda-pop friends.

One morning, one of mine who was going on 13, after a careful study of his face in the mirror, said to me: "All the kids in my class have pimples. How come I don't?"

Maybe when he has kids of his own, I'll tell him.

—Jane Kinderlehrer

Part Five

Looking at the Big Picture

1

Where We Are Now

Nutrition in the United States

Can a country—any country—achieve its full creative potential if its people are sick and weak? Can a government—any government—be stable and secure, maintain harmony within its borders and avoid the consequences of social unrest if its people are suffering the mental and physical imbalances of malnutrition?

The United States Government and the United States Army believe not. "It was clear to the U.S. Army officials that food inadequacies were likely to become a prime cause of unrest and insurgency," say Drs. Jacques May and Hoyt Lemons in the *AMA Journal* (March 21, 1969). The U.S. Army Office of Research and Development thus undertook an exhaustive study of how to bring better nutrition to the peoples of the Far and Near East, Europe and Africa.

There is one very important area in the world where the United States Government did not seem concerned about improving the nutritional status—*the United States of America.*

Wouldn't it be nice if we had shown as much concern for the deplorable state of undernutrition and outright malnutrition right here. There is hardly a village, town or metropolis in the U.S. that does not have its quota of malnourished, undernourished or starving men, women and children.

Somebody in the Pentagon must have overlooked the fact that if food inadequacies can cause unrest in Cambodia and Uganda, Rwanda and Tunisia, food inadequacies can also cause unrest in Watts and Newark, Chicago and Detroit, Indiana and Ohio.

THE SCHAEFER REPORT

In January 1969, Arnold E. Schaefer, Ph.D., chief of the nutrition program of the Health Services and Mental Health Administration of the Department of Health, Education and Welfare, told the Senate Select Committee on Nutrition and Related Human Needs that preliminary reports of the first Federal nutrition survey in this country "clearly indicates an alarming prevalence of those characteristics that are associated with undernourished groups."

"Our worst fears were realized," Dr. Schaefer told the Senate Committee. "We found every kind of malnutrition that any of us has seen in similar studies in Central America, Africa, and Asia. . . . It is a sobering experience to discover such malnourishment in an affluent society."

For instance, one third of the children under six had hemoglobin levels diagnosed as anemia and requiring medical attention, and many of the older people had hemoglobin levels indicative of poor nutritional health.

One third of the children under six had less than adequate serum levels of vitamin A. These findings are not dissimilar to reports from areas of the world where vitamin A deficiency is known to be a major problem.

Riboflavin and thiamin levels were also low in many of the people studied.

In one group of preschool children in a Head Start program, as many as 92 per cent were found to have serious vitamin A deficiencies. Of 1,500 four- and five-year-old children in Louisiana, Alabama, and Mississippi, 72 per cent were below the normal growth curve. In fact, Dr. Schaefer said, 10 to 15 per cent of all the children thus far examined show retarded growth levels and therefore present a high risk in retardation of mental and physical performance.

While the figures on malnutrition are certainly deplorable, as Dr. David B. Coursin, Director of Research at St. Joseph Hospital of Lancaster, Pennsylvania, pointed out when he testified before the Senate, "figures alone do not convey the real consequences of the potential effects of malnutrition—the major concern is with the possible impairment of physical and mental ability and performance which are usually the consequence of so-called hidden hunger."

The saddest thing is that many of us subsisting on less than optimal diets, don't even know it. For years we have been soft-soaped into thinking that our food supply is the best in the world, that our foods are fortified so that deficiencies are almost impossible, that we don't need food supplements if we eat balanced diets.

NATIONAL MALNUTRITION

The publication *Hunger, U.S.A.* was greeted with shocked disbelief. Even medical and professional people were quick to downgrade its importance. In their search for bacteria and viruses as the main culprits causing disease, medical men very rarely take seriously the possibility of nutritional deficiencies in our affluent society. When a local physician reported that a patient who had suffered a nervous breakdown showed signs of vitamin B deficiency, another retorted, "That's impossible. She's a rich woman."

It was not the physicians who discovered the extent of malnutrition in this country. It was largely a volunteer group. "And this is a sad reflection on all of us, myself included," Dr. Jean Mayer said in an interview reported in the *Medical Tribune* (August 18, 1969).

Dr. Mayer is a well-known physiological chemist and nutrition scientist of Harvard University's School of Public Health and the man chosen by President Nixon to organize the White House Conference on Food, Nutrition, and Health that was held in the Fall of 1969.

Dr. Mayer took *Hunger, U.S.A.* very seriously. It triggered the first national nutritional survey conducted by Dr. Schaefer and Dr. Ogden C. Johnson, formerly with the Council on Food and Nutrition of the American Medical Association; the report showed beyond any doubt that we are indeed faced by two problems: Hunger and malnutrition in poverty areas because there is no money for protein foods, and undernutrition and deficiency disease among the affluent and indeed all classes because of a miserable lack of knowledge about nutrition.

It will knock the props from under many of those who have been depending on doctors to tell them what to eat, what to avoid, and when we need vitamin supplements to learn that physicians, as Dr. Mayer pointed out, know as little as anyone about nutrition.

"Nutrition education is a must," Dr. Mayer said, "and one of the main targets for this education will be the *nation's physicians.*"

NUTRITION EDUCATION

Doctors know a great deal about disease, about anatomy, about drugs and their reactions—but practically nothing about nutrition. Why? Because only about a dozen medical schools in this country teach nutrition at all, and because much of what is taught is part of biochemistry courses and not related to actual foods. While these colleges have the courses available, they are not required courses.

If doctors are uninformed in the field of nutrition, how can we expect the average layman to know how to spend his food dollar to support his health and not his undertaker?

Can we depend on the guidelines handed down by the U.S. Government? Hardly.

As Dr. Mayer points out in the *Medical Tribune* interview, the Department of Agriculture has in the past placed more priority on prices and production than on people, and as *Consumer Bulletin* (September, 1969) reiterates "the Federal government has always widely publicized the matchless properties of certain foods that *need to be sold* in huge quantities in order to support farm commodity prices." (Emphasis added.)

The government's record on specific recommendations in the past would not win any awards either.

The U.S. Department of Agriculture has for several decades vigorously promoted extensive use of fluid milk as a "nearly perfect food" in the face of mounting evidence that, as *Consumer Bulletin* points out, it is essentially a food for babies and definitely harmful to adults in many specific cases. Drinking too much milk has been found by researchers to be an important cause of malnutrition in children causing iron-deficiency anemia, which is one of the conditions which Dr. Shaefer's survey found prevalent among both children and adults. Milk has been found, too, to be the cause of many allergies in children that are frequently misdiagnosed as viral colds, eczema, or asthma.

President Nixon's television address to the nation expressed concern for the plight of the economically deprived with regard to their hunger and malnutrition. However, putting more money into the pockets of the poor is no guarantee that their nutrition will improve. The money could be spent on more calories—empty calories—but not necessarily on more nutrients. You don't have to be poor to be malnourished. Dr. Elmer Severinghaus, one of the country's leading nutritionists, observed in a news release from the Vitamin Information Bureau that "even Americans who can afford to buy what they need nutritionally, often make the wrong choices." The nutritional intake of many who have adequate incomes has been found to be sadly deficient in essential nutrients.

Nutritional education—from elementary school through medical school—was one of the areas explored at the White House Conference because, as Dr. Mayer put it, "Americans have a miserable knowledge of the basic nutrition they need to be healthy."

Because of this lack of knowledge, parents and children suffer from malnutrition. But where does the blame lie for this miserable lack of knowledge?

THE FOOD INDUSTRY

Children and their mothers take their cues from radio and TV commercials and from articles in the popular press which tell them enthusiastically that so and so's bread is whiter than white and eight ways better and will give them boundless energy and a sexy smile. No one tells them that the wheat germ, the source of all the B vitamins, minerals and enzymes of the original grain, has been left on the threshing room floor.

"It's enriched," say the commercials, so mothers buy it confidently, believing they are in some noble maternal way enriching the diet of their families. They feel safe, secure, and *enriched.*

The commercials don't tell them, neither does their doctor, that enrichment means the sacrifice of more than 25 nutrients with replacement of three or four in a synthetic form which the body utilizes poorly. Is it any wonder that the Schaefer survey found widespread deficiency of vitamin B_2 and iron?

So long as the vitamin-rich polish is removed from rice to make it snow white and quick cooking, so long as all our grains have the life processed out of them, so long as our soil is loaded with nitrate fertilizers that rob our vegetables of provitamin A (carotene pigments which can be converted to vitamin A in the body), how can the unenlightened who buy their food in the supermarkets of the country be anything but malnourished?

It might come as a surprise to learn that a dog has a better chance of getting the nutrients necessary to health than the school teacher, police officer or banker who rely on the giant food industry to keep them well fed. The dog food industry employs nutritionists. The human food industry employs food technologists who are well trained in the latest techniques of extending the shelf life of a product—by adding preservatives and stabilizers and eliminating vitamins and minerals. They know how to add eye appeal with synthetic colors, they know how to package foods so that they are irresistible, they know how to apply science and engineering to food production, but they know very little about nutrition.

ANTIDOTE FOR MALNUTRITION

Education of mothers, nurses and doctors is needed, of course. But, if education is to have any effect at all on malnutrition, it must include in the curriculum some eye-opening disclosures on what is happening to our food and why we can't expect to maintain our health and vigor on the foods that sustained grandma and grandpa.

If malnutrition is abroad in our land—and there is no longer doubt that it is—it is not only a lack of knowledge that is responsible, it is so-called technological progress which certainly must take the lion's share of the blame.

Since we have so much more technological know-how now than we had when we first learned how to refine the life out of our grains, why indeed can we not apply this know-how to ways in which we can get the life back in?

Perhaps at some forthcoming White House Conference some bright young scientist will have the courage to stand up and shout:

"Eureka, I have it! Instead of trying to enrich this and replace that, why take the nutrients out of the food in the first place?"

That, indeed, would be progress.

Health Foods—An Industry Burgeons

"All foods are health foods."

Yes, said Dr. George Kerr, no matter what you eat, it is making you healthier. Well, maybe not *physically* healthier, but certainly emotionally healthier, he admitted.

This was testimony Dr. Kerr was giving at a hearing held by the New York City Department of Consumer Affairs to throw some light on the public's current interest in organic foods, natural foods, and health foods. As a nutritionist on the staff of the Harvard School of Public Health, he was substituting for Dr. Fredrick Stare, the famous quackery investigator. Dr. Stare had to leave for Europe, so Dr. Kerr was reading a statement drawn up by the members of Harvard's Nutrition Department.

What about something like Coke? Is that a health food?

Sure, the Harvard nutrition people would reply. Makes you happier, doesn't it? Makes things "go better," too. So Coke is a health food.

Nobody thought to ask Dr. Kerr whether Coke was health food to a diabetic, or to someone with hypoglycemia, to whom even a small amount of sugar is big trouble. Better yet, what is Coke to a small child, who gets jazzed up by caffeine? Aren't most kids jazzed up enough already?

Maybe the Harvard people did have a point about the word health as used to describe food. It is true that nobody eats for the purpose of hurting himself, isn't it? A sandwich of processed meat between two slices of white bread *will* give you the energy to work through an afternoon, won't it? That's true, even though the meat contains additives that may hurt you five years from now, and the white bread is low in chromium, magnesium and other nutrients your body will need in the next few days to keep in shape. But for this afternoon, that sandwich will keep you healthy!

Then along came Carlton Fredericks, Ph.D., a long-time advocate of food supplements, unprocessed food and a vigorous attacker of the phoniness of big-time packaged food.

"We ought to stop calling foods 'health foods,' " Dr. Fredericks testified to the New York group. His point was that you can never be sure that a certain kind of food is going to be a health food for everyone. Maybe you are allergic to something that makes others healthy. And he opposed, in a general way, the vagueness of the term "health food."

"*Better food* is what we should be after," he said. "Let's call them better foods instead of health foods!"

Now the phrase health food was under attack from both sides of the fence. Even a staunch friend of health food stores like Carlton Federicks didn't like the label.

THE HEALTH LABEL

Carlton Fredericks is not really saying anything new. The health food industry tried long ago to hitch its fortunes to other words. The trade organization of health food stores used to be the National Dietary Foods Association. Recently it changed into the National Nutritional Foods Association. The health food label is nowhere in sight.

What about the stores themselves? Very few actually call themselves health food stores. They are "Nutritional Centers," or "Nature Food Shops." Almost any name you can think of, in fact, except "John's Health Food Store."

As much as the industry prefers other labels, though, "health food" is likely to stick around for a long time in the public consciousness. Names have a way of becoming permanent, once they get implanted in the language. Even if all the health food stores *and* the Harvard Department of Nutrition voted to kill the words health food, people would still use them in cocktail party chatter and in trying to tell other people what "better food" to eat.

There's an important lesson to be learned here. It's this: A name achieves quality and value only if the thing it is naming has quality and value. What could be more simple and obvious, yet so often forgotten?

Time and time again, people have tried to give some ordinary or even offensive thing a high status by calling it by a fancy name. A pot belly, for example, is still an ugly lump of flesh, even if you do call it a "bay window." And calling a backside a "derriere" just makes the word derriere sound funny after a while.

Those kind of tricks work for only a short time, if they work at all. The only *real* way to improve the word is to improve what it describes.

Getting back to health foods, the makers of bad food and their allies are out to attack more than just the words "health food." They would like to discredit the whole idea that there is a difference in quality between the ordinary food you buy and the special things you get from health food dealers. They like health food even less than they like *the words* "health food," because the mere existence of health food or "better food" means that there is something else—a kind of food that *doesn't* make you healthy. And if you look at the long-term effects of what people eat, you see that a lot of food does fall into that non-health category. White flour and sugar are two examples of foods that may give you some short-term benefit, but will trip you up sooner or later.

INDUSTRY WITH A PAST

Of course, attacks on health food are nothing new. They've been going on ever since some enthusiastic people began selling brown rice and whole grains in special stores about 40 years ago. Everything from ridicule to search and seizure operations have been used to try to wipe out this growing industry, and at times in the past those efforts were much more intensive than they are right now, when natural food is gaining in popularity.

That very popularity, though, introduces a whole new element into the time-honored controversy between the specialty health food people and the supermarket food industry. No longer is health food the obsession of a small clique of vegetarians and nature-food enthusiasts. It is a routine part of life—something that almost everyone will soon be eating, at least once in a while. And because of that bigness of the industry, new types of regulation are only to be expected.

The New York City hearings, for example, were the result entirely of the growth of the health food industry.

"There are now 70 health food stores on Manhattan Island, by our count," said former Miss America Bess Myerson, who heads New York's Department of Consumer Affairs. That's a lot of stores, and as a result of the growth there have been many questions thrust upon the consumer affairs department. Questions of quality and price, mainly.

It's perfectly obvious that as more people eat health foods, more will be concerned about health foods. Any publicity, pro or con, will receive closer attention and will be more likely to translate into action, such as enactment of new laws. Because of its new-found popularity, therefore, the health food industry should be (and is) very concerned when people start saying that not everything about these special foods is what it's cracked up to be.

HEALTH FOOD OR SHAM

The real problem is to decide which attack is merely vituperative tearing down of health foods by people connected in some way to companies selling bad food, and which criticism of health foods is constructive.

What are the justified criticisms of health food? What problems about this industry, which most of us admire and patronize, should be spotlighted so we can be sure that health foods do, in fact, have a future?

Representation of products is one major concern. The stores imply just by handling a product, that it is not only a health product but something special. And even if they don't represent something specifically, people make assumptions. They assume that there are no chemical additives in the food, that food has not been processed unnecessarily, and that the best possible techniques have been used in bringing that food to the market.

Sometimes, the health food industry handles food that doesn't match in real quality the spoken or unspoken representations that are made for it. For example, until recently there has been practically no pesticide monitoring of foodstuffs that are regularly handled by the health food industry. The assumption has been made that "the Food and Drug Administration is taking care of that." Well, the FDA is too busy—with its limited resources—to do a thorough job of pesticide screening. Sometimes mistakes slip through, and they are just as likely to be found in some health foods as in conventional foods. Unless, that is, the health food people do some screening of their own.

Spot checks for pesticide residues *can* be made for only a small cost, and some companies are starting to make them now. Others should do the same.

Organically grown food is another specific area where representation is a problem—and a very big problem. Hopefully, the health food industry will soon get behind organically grown food certification programs to inspect farms and analyze produce, to make sure that growers who use that powerful phrase back up their words with real quality. If the industry doesn't, there's trouble ahead.

IMPROVING THE PRODUCTS

Better labeling of food in all respects could be a big improvement. Soon much conventional food will carry labels telling what vitamins and minerals it contains. And some labels will even tell what useful nutrients *are not* in certain foods. The health food industry should get on the ball and do the same. In fact, the industry should do it before the supermarket people get around to it.

Origin of food is another thing that is getting more attention. Did you know that XYZ brand of vichyssoise was really Bon Vivant? No, because it's a private label, which makes you think that some local store has its own soup-making plant. Well, those days of mystery foods are numbered. Sooner or later people will have to know where their food is made. And the health food industry could make points by starting now to "tell all" to its customers. What better way is there to make friends and build customer confidence.

All kinds of services that can conceivably be offered to food buyers should become routine to the health industry. That includes clean stores, truthful advertising, informative labels, good education programs, and fair prices.

Oh yes, prices. It's almost a tradition in the health food trade to charge more than the same or similar products sell for in supermarkets. Of course, you get more service. In a health food store you can talk to a clerk or the manager and get much useful information. You get the friendly feeling of going into a store that treats you like a person instead of a punched card. In fact, health food stores are the friendliest of any kind of store, and that's worth something.

Sometimes, though, the price thing gets out of hand. For example, when farmers are getting 90 cents a bushel for corn why should the consumer pay 78 cents for two pounds of corn meal in a health food store? Sure, the health food distribution network is a special thing, sending small amounts of food across the country to stores that offer a unique service. And sure, the law of supply and demand is bound to come into play and even things out eventually. But in the meantime, the health food people are likely to get a reputation for high pricing that will take them years to shake.

Nobody is perfect. But health foods and the health food industry *can* be much closer to perfection than the mass food marketers, who are willing to sell *anything* as long as they can make a profit. And it's up to everyone who buys or sells in the health food marketplace to make sure that the industry does keep aiming toward perfection.

—Robert Rodale

Organic Gardening Clubs Get Action

Action is the word for today's Organic Gardening Clubs—real action that's getting important jobs done and exciting things started. Whether it's initiating city-plot gardens, setting up paper, glass and aluminum recycling centers, or reaching the schools with demonstrations and projects to bring organic living ideas into the classroom, the clubs are with it.

They're right in the thick of a dozen environmental endeavors, too—leading battles to halt pesticide spraying, to put city wastes back into the soil, to make organic foods available and to wake up more farmers, county agents, colleges and legislators. Now numbering nearly 150 across the U.S. and up into Canada, the Organic Gardening Clubs—first organized in the early fifties—have always been comprised of dedicated, enthusiastic people, eager to share gardening know-how and to help conserve our natural resources. Today, they're teaming with ecologists and students, city officials, farmers and grocers to put more movement into the local scene.

Start with a look at what's happening at just a few.

"Our club is coming along nicely after only two months of operation," writes Ruby Louis, president of the newly-formed Dirt Daubers O.G. of Odessa, Texas. "We are running a weekly column in one of our local newspapers and the response has been very encouraging. The director of the United Fund in our area has expressed a sincere desire to help us in any way possible. In fact, the club has booked a downtown recreation room for the next meeting, and we are expecting a cross-section of people to attend our Get-Acquainted Program. We will have three guest speakers—one an organic gardener, one a nutritionist, and one a district secretary for a chain grocery store." The Dirt Daubers have already launched an organic consumer campaign, surveying local supermarkets to find out which are selling organic produce and encouraging every family in the city to buy those products which help to improve health and the environment. And they're at work on securing city- or privately-owned land to set up a gardening center.

LONG-ESTABLISHED CLUBS

That's quite a beginning for a young club—but don't sell the longtimers short. The South Jersey Organic Gardeners and Farmers Club—organized in 1950 at Haddon Heights—recently completed a one-week educational display at the Cherry Hill Mall, where the group captured the flower show's first-prize blue ribbon. Louise Smith, who's had the program chairman job for 20 years, writes that J. I. Rodale, Phillip Wells, Ehrenfried Pfeiffer and other early organic leaders "were the backbone of our venture. Now," she adds, "the younger generation is beginning to wake up, take an interest and learn the how of it all."

Meanwhile, out on the West Coast, the long-established Santa Monica Organic Garden and Nutrition Club—which boasts a membership of 1,100 stretching cross-country—stays mighty active. As Maria Wilkes and Kay Rogers report via the club's bulletin, now in its 17th year, the southern California group has built an educational program on organics and health open to the public, is in the midst of legislative conflicts and efforts, and is trying to "spark other clubs" throughout the state.

ATTACKING ENVIRONMENTAL WOES

In Colorado, the High Altitude Gardeners at Colorado Springs are actively opposing a transportation plan which will cut freeways through the Black Forest. Club president Earl Anderson notes they're also maintaining an organic flower garden near the community center and preparing a booklet on methods for growing vegetables at a high altitude. At Columbus, the O.G. Club of Central Ohio is at work convincing city officials that "a public compost be made with the leaves they've collected."

There's increasing evidence that social action aimed at tackling environmental problems on the community level has become "standard operating procedure" for O.G. Clubs everywhere. The Peninsula Organic Gardening Club in California, for example, is engaged in anti-fluoridation legislation. It gives free tours of local spring water facilities, and explains to visitors what happens to water when it is processed and fluoridated. The Boyne Valley O.G. Club of Boyne City, Michigan, is helping to run a glass recycling project. They're also working with three towns in Michigan to establish a community compost pit for leaves, tree trimmings, and other green wastes. Boyne City has already made its city sewage sludge available to the public for fertilizer.

CLUBS IN GARDENING

Involvement with research by experiment stations represents another significant action front. The Tacoma, Washington, O.G. Club's project achieved just that by way of an experimental plot to test natural pest-control methods at the Washington State University Department of

Agriculture, Western Washington Research Extension Service in Puyallup, Wash.

Organic gardeners in mid-Illinois are holding their own against chemical farmers. It's big farming country there, and chemical farmers made "Nature's Acres" comparison test plots last summer. (They usually compare a chemical field with a worn-out chemical field —"Nature's Acre"— left untended. The latter is supposed to be organic.) Mrs. Russell of the Hartland O.G. Club of Decatur visited one of these plots and was infuriated by the unfairness of the tests. After telling the farmer in charge of one set of test plots (who is the owner of a chemical testing firm) that he hadn't given the poorly kept organic plot a fair chance, he challenged her to a public debate. So she took him up on it, and defended the organic method on T.V.

From Xenia, Ohio, a note penned by Pauline Pidgeon, who heads the Greene County Natural Foods Club, tells us, "Last summer a club member offered to take orders for trichogramma wasps. He did it to save money on a large-quantity order. Those of us who used trichogramma in our gardens and on fruit trees were very pleased. Not only were codling moths scarce. but we had no corn earworms. We want to go into this activity on a larger scale. And we think we could start a move to innoculate our whole area with milky spore disease, not that organic gardeners have problems with Japanese beetles—but wouldn't it be absolutely funny if ecology groups could stop the Japanese beetles without chemicals when the whole voluminous USDA can't stop them with an arsenal full of carbaryl, malathion, chlordane and such?"

O.G. CLUBS AND YOU

Join an O.G. Club if there's one going in your locale. If there isn't, why not help get one started? Just write Organic Gardening and Farming, Clubs Dept., Emmaus, Pa. 18049, for suggestions and guidelines. (Please enclose a self-addressed envelope.) We've heard from quite a few more folks eager to organize from Houlton, Maine to Laramie, Wyoming. And one of the biggest requests we've been receiving from many clubs is for information and material for organic gardening courses. We've put together an outline for an adult education class and will be glad to send it to you as soon as we know that you want one.

There's strength in unity—the strength to accomplish so much that needs doing today. By all means, get with an O.G. Club—and get active!

—M. C. Goldman

A New Generation of Organic People

Think how healthy you could be today had you realized when you were young the benefits of good eating habits, vitamins and minerals, exercise, and freedom from drugs and other harmful substances! Your arteries would be more clear and healthy, your muscles would be firm, and you probably would be a lot further away from the degenerative diseases that are the major causes of illness and death. Of course, it is never too late to start a healthful way of life. But a head start on a lifetime of health consciousness would be a great advantage to have.

The sad fact is that most people don't start working for health until age creeps up and takes away the glow of youth. It's a safe bet that almost everyone reading this can look back on an early life of relative non-interest in health. Youth, almost by definition, is a time of health and strength. Eyes are clear and sharp, nerves calm and muscles strong. You can abuse your body when young with the certain knowledge that in a day or two you will be as healthy and vigorous as ever. Sure, young people have physical worries. They think about pimples on their faces and whether they look good in a bathing suit. But they don't worry much about heart disease, stroke, cancer and diabetes—the chronic diseases whose seeds are planted by improper living habits established early in life and mature into overpowering illness if continued through middle age.

Of course, all of us were taught a certain amount about health in school. We learned the importance of washing our hands, brushing our teeth and a few basic facts about our bodies. But the health education of the past was largely slanted toward hygiene, which meant cleanliness and avoidance of the germs that caused contagious diseases. Today, those germ-caused illnesses are not the major health problem. Degenerative diseases, the things that creep up on us little by little over a series of decades, are what we have to be concerned about. And the childhood health education of the past paid little attention to those chronic diseases, because when we were educated they weren't even a serious problem for adults.

HEALTH EDUCATION NEEDS

Although health education in schools today is a far cry from the minor part of the curriculum it was 20 or 30 years ago, children still aren't learning all they need to know to be healthy adults. Now the big stress in school health courses is on the problems of the day for young people, namely sex education and the problems of tobacco and drugs. Schools still aren't teaching kids what they really need to know to live a healthful life. The emphasis is still on getting them out of school and into the work force in healthy condition, and then letting them figure out what to do to try to avoid degenerative disease.

Of course, trying to teach real, lifetime health to children is immensely difficult, because the subject simply isn't relevant to them. A teenager can experience drugs and sex and cigarettes, but he just can't comprehend how a 50-year-old person with angina or emphysema feels. And even those young people who do have a glimmer of understanding feel that the problems of aging are decades away, so why worry.

Now, despite all that's been said about how young people aren't directly interested in health, the young people are really doing things about health. In the coming years, if Americans are able to live longer and feel better, we will have our young people of today to thank. And on the contrary, if in 10 or 20 years our world is racked with sickness and pain far worse than we experience today, then we will know that our young people have failed to grasp the opportunities that are now within their reach. For there are clear signs that youth today has the desire and the will to change many of the bad elements of our lives that older people have been conditioned to endure. It is clear to me, at least, that a better level of health for all can result from those changes.

A NEW VIEW OF HEALTH

Young people today are in revolt. They are not marching under the banner of health (many of the most revolutionary are actually destroying their bodies with drugs), but they are expressing vigorous dissatisfaction with the money-oriented, polluted, selfish, unpleasant, technological society that has spawned them. They can see—perhaps more clearly than you—that if they do what the older people in society want, keep their noses clean, wear white shirts, and climb the executive

ladder, that they'll end up living a kind of life that is worse than anything anyone now experiences. Young people can smell the air getting
dirtier and can see the garbage piling up around us. Because they are
not yet plugged into a job and family, they can stand back at a distance
and see American life in perspective. Many don't care for what they
see.

Frankly, we sympathize with them, particularly with those who
have taken a back-to-the-land turn. Increasing numbers of them are
deserting the city streets for the countryside in an effort to return to
a natural kind of life that is impossible for any wage-earner to achieve.
Natural foods have become a major goal of young revolutionaries. Some
of them are gathering in communes in the country to try to produce
natural food together. Others are seeking ways to establish permanent
natural homesteads in the country. Escaping the pollution of soul and
body that afflicts today's city dwellers is their goal, and they see the
production of natural, unpoisoned food as the means to that goal.

What these young people are doing is carrying the organic system
to an intensity of fulfillment that older people just wouldn't be able to
accomplish. A central tenet of the idea is to shun foods that have been
processed in factories and to limit what you eat and drink and inhale
only to the most natural and purest of substances. Doing that completely and without exception is enormously difficult, unless you live
in the country and can grow and process your food yourself. Older
people have children to educate and jobs to occupy them. They have
had a taste of the easy life of an automated society and try to compromise—hoping to offset the bad air they breathe and other pollutants
with an enlightened selection of health foods and the other aids to
health. In a way, the synthetic, unnatural world that bugs the mature
is the same cynical, hypocritical, polluted society that longhaired young
people want to revolt against. You may be revolting in a mild way by
boycotting synthetic foods and dangerous drugs. Some of the young
people are going much further by pulling up stakes completely and
trying to live close to nature.

Not only are the young people of today willing to make bigger
sacrifices for health and natural living than older folks, but they are
willing to tackle the general threats to health that you may be passive
about. There are certain bad things about modern American life that
nobody can escape while still being "plugged in" to a job and perma-

nent home, things like polluted air, pesticide residues floating in water
and the futility of trying to retain individuality in a world run by com-
puting machines and punched cards. While older folks would like to
escape those things, they aren't likely to take to the streets over them.
Young people are willing to, however, because they aren't as bashful
and reticent as we are.

Wisconsin Senator Gaylord Nelson knows pollution and health problems better than most Congressmen, and he is also tuned in to how
young people think and act today. Nelson is convinced that youthful
protest about conservation and ecology is an important national force.
"The new generation is not satisfied with coming out on the losing end
of man's drive for progress and profit," he says.

THE MOVEMENT TOMORROW

The youth protest movement still has a long way to go. Our society
continues to get more technological and more hypocritical, and those
are the basic factors which spawned the rebellion. Where it will lead
and what it will accomplish we can't predict with utter certainty, but
young people today who are willing to explore new ways of life are a
valuable national asset and can help us find new ways of becoming
healthy. But we should try to work together. Just as young people were
surprised to find out that health-minded, organic people thought out
the natural living idea 25 or more years ago, we should not be surprised
to find out that experimentive young people can come up with some
new and worthwhile ideas.

Though many of their ideas are misguided or just plain juvenile,
they certainly have worked out effective new techniques of getting the
world to pay attention to them. They managed to get everyone from
college authorities to national legislators to take their protests seriously.
And if the world of the future finds the will and the means to clean up
our food, air and water, you can be sure much of our better environment will be due to the fact that the young people demanded it.

—Robert Rodale

Classrooms For Organic Living

School days are here for lots more people of all ages who want to learn
about living organically. Classrooms everywhere are going organic.

Courses, workshops, seminars, lectures, independent-study programs
—educators are seeking ways to channel the tide of organic-learning
ambition into the system. Right from kindergarten through a dozen
grades of public school, on up to collegiate, post-grad, community-
group and even senior-citizen level, the call for organic-living know
how is creating change.

More than 7,000 New Jersey elementary school children each year
are learning all about organic gardening, preparing healthful organic
food snacks in their classrooms, and even having fun with a new type
of exercise program developed by Rodale Press in cooperation with
New Jersey's Technology for Children Project.

T 4 C, as it is called, is a special learn-by-doing interdisciplinary
approach to education covering the area of social studies, science, math
and language arts. It got started when the project directors wrote us:
"We are interested in any curriculum materials dealing with environmental education that would be appropriate for grades K-6. If you can
suggest any courses of study covering the numerous problems that are
facing us today, it would be of tremendous assistance to our teachers
in Project Technology for Children, which numbers several hundred
—involving thousands of school children."

We went to work, preparing special materials and teaching aids and
conducting a two-week workshop for Technology for Children super-
vising teachers. Through a series of more than 30 projects contained
in a special kit, these teachers learned the philosophy and principles
of organic living. They participated in making compost, testing soil,
recycling wastes, planting seeds, sprouting grains, making peanut butter, granola and other healthful snacks—even participating in a special
kids' exercise session. Each teacher was given a kit containing background information on the projects so that he could pass it on to other
instructors in his school district.

Today more than 143 New Jersey schools are teaching the basic
principles of organic living. But Rodale Press and Technology for Children are going one step further. Cafeteria personnel in one T 4 C school
are being taught how to serve and prepare organic food lunches. At
another school, teachers and children will be planting an organic garden. These schools will serve as demonstration centers for teachers from all over the state to come and learn the organic living principles.

IN THE EAST AND IN THE WEST

The Board of Education of the City of New York has a feasibility study under way to determine whether it should "introduce into the curricula of New York City High Schools a course of study which would prepare students for careers in the natural food industry." That's a significant breakthrough, to say the least. Milton Rogers, the board's Project Director for Natural Food Careers, initiated his drive for the course by contacting Rodale Press.

Rogers' idea centers around the conviction that organically grown foods—and everything connected with providing them—are the coming thing. He's convinced, too, that businesses will need and want qualified workers in every phase of the trade. Based on that, his recommendations have zeroed in on the vocational opportunities in growing, distributing, marketing and preparing natural foods.

From Mercer Island, Washington, high school student Dave Ransom writes: "I'm working with the Island's environmentalist, one of the district's elementary principals and an architect on an organic gardening program for Mercer Island . . . One acre of land will be cultivated, planted and grown organically by elementary and possibly junior and senior high school children. Supervised by adults and interested younger people, each enrolled student will have his own plot of land nine-by-nine feet in which he may plant what he wishes. Besides each student's plot, there would be acres for a natural garden, a cornfield, possibly an orchard, flower beds, ponds, benches and, of course, compost and mulch piles . . ."

ON THE FARM

A learning approach somewhat different from the formal classroom is planned by cattle-raiser Lawrence M. C. Smith of Freeport, Maine. It's an idea with a lot to recommend it, one that might well be followed by other large-scale farmers, orchardists and livestock growers. Smith says he'd like to start with a small group of college students in the area. They would summer and put in part of the winter at his Wolf's Neck Farm, then return to school on a continuing basis, gaining both instruction and first-hand experience over successive seasons in raising feed by organic methods, haying, taking care of the animals and preparing them for marketing.

As a long-time pioneer in organic agriculture as well as in popularizing naturally raised meat, Smith sees an urgent need for thoroughly training interested young people in the fundamentals of good farming and livestock production. He thinks others should recognize this and extend similar opportunities. Under his alternating college-to-farm system, youths would not interrupt their regular studies, but would be housed and paid wages while becoming skilled in producing foods organically. Three other New England farms which Smith has under contract may follow the new plan once it gets going this year.

ON THE CAMPUS

The college scene is unquestionably the one that's come alive strongest in the organic-education field. Alert, concerned students, professors and others have dug into ecological problems, recycling, pesticides, land reclamation. Young people in every college community of the country have led the switch to natural foods, to healthful changeovers in cafeteria menus, to organic food co-ops, shops and restaurants. Young people (and plenty of older ones) have let it be known that they want to learn how to farm and garden with organic methods. They've shown that they want more than surface treatment of subjects connected with the environment, with recycling wastes, halting pollution, improving the quality of life. And they've displayed a phenomenal determination to learn much more about nutrition, organic foods and the whole world of vibrant health through proper nutrition.

At Ohio State University, an educational exhibit and field work carried out by student members of the Earthday Society represent another remarkable example of what can be done. Backed by a grant from the National Science Foundation for a Student-Originated Studies Program, they staged an imaginative display at the Ohio State Fair, aimed at informing the public and getting people involved. OSU student David Pelzer described it in *The Conservationist.*

At the fair booth, a video tape gave visitors a view of natural predators attacking harmful insects—ladybird beetles eating pests, parasitic wasps laying eggs within insects for their young to feed on. The tape also covered experiments with viruses found to be natural disease agents to control target pests. A second part showed a three-acre field test made by the group that used crop positioning, beneficial insects, the *Bacillus thuringiensis* insect disease and hand-weeding to curb corn earworm and other problem bugs. "Our earth has always had biological controls," said Dave, "but this old concept is in need of revitalization."

One way his group is going to keep working at it is through a new series of 30-minute programs on WOSU educational television. With another National Science Foundation grant funding it, the project will concentrate on explaining the phenomenon of biological pest controls, comparing them to conventional poison-spray methods, and citing advantages and disadvantages of both. One goal is to explore the reasons for "such an upsurge of interest in biological controls," adds Dave.

WITH NEW MOMENTUM

It's worth noting that National Science Foundation grants totaling almost $1.5 million have been awarded to 97 colleges and universities throughout the country. More than 1,100 undergraduate students expressed in productive ways their concerns for the environment by conducting student-directed research. Some of the more interesting projects include: "Relationship of Environmental Quality to Human Health and the Quality of Life" at San Jose State College, San Jose, California; "Chemical, Biological, and Economic Studies of Municipal Garbage Composting" at Northwestern University, Evanston, Illinois; "Links Between Life Style and Environmental Expression in Building, Past and Present" at Tulane University, New Orleans, Louisiana; and "Nutrition as Related to General Health Status of a Segment of the Greater Boston Community" at Massachusetts Institute of Technology in Cambridge.

The campus momentum to learning organic ways can be illustrated by what's happening at scores of other colleges. The few we've described are typical. Word of new developments and more classroom action reaches us just about every day. Courses, programs, seminars or outdoor projects are underway, for instance, at the University of Massachusetts, Iowa State, Florida Presbyterian College, University of Washington, Cornell, Sarah Lawrence, Oregon State and Mauna Olu College in Hawaii.

Then too, there are the earlier "breakthrough" classes—the pacesetting University of California, Santa Cruz Student Garden Project that captured the country's attention and led to an accredited course, plus an organic food-choice line at the school's cafeteria; the University of California at Santa Barbara and Berkeley community-garden and ecology projects; the pioneer farm-scale elective courses in organic agriculture long made a serious part of the curriculum at Ambassador College in Big Sandy, Texas; the highly popular extension classes given at several California colleges by Dr. Bargyla Rateaver who continues to crack "convention" barriers and bring lively organic-method know-how to many students.

A new, exciting chapter in organics has opened. The challenge is to make education for organic living a reality—along with everything that life-style makes important. It's a challenge we all intend to meet head on—and successfully!

—*M. C. Goldman*

2

And Where We Are Headed

Who Controls Agriculture?

"After prolonged and careful analysis by experts, the government was advised that U.S. beef was not safe to eat. Accordingly, the government has proclaimed that American beef, regardless of USDA inspection, may not be sold to citizens of this country."

Can that happen here? Why not? It has happened in Sweden!

Not only Sweden, but twenty other countries have outlawed diethylstibestrol (DES)—a growth hormone used in raising U.S. beef. Denmark, Norway, Finland, Ireland, Switzerland, New Zealand, Australia, and the European Common Market countries have banned DES-fed beef, primarily on the grounds that growth hormones have induced cancer in laboratory animals.

Can the American consumer afford to brush aside the arguments of these other nations while our U.S. Department of Agriculture and Food and Drug Administration maintain that American beef is safe to eat? Can we continue to feed our families meat produced in the United States, disregarding the substantial questions raised by all these other advanced, industrialized nations?

As American consumers, we rely upon food grown in the U.S. We have the right to raise questions about the safety of the food we eat, and we should demand honest answers to our questions. Up to now, our questions have been met with counter-charges, or else pooh-poohed and disregarded.

If we want good food, we have to learn to specify how we want it grown. If we want the government to stop administering questionable agricultural policies, then we will have to learn to ask the right questions.

It is essential that at least 20 or 30 per cent of U.S. consumers become interested in agriculture, food producing, processing, and marketing. For those who are over 40 (and with reasonably good memories), it is overwhelmingly evident that modern technology and progress have produced a situation wherein the less we consumers understand about our world, the more questionable practices and materials are introduced into it.

Our ignorance about the workings of this complex industrial society seems to have coincided with the emergence of a new stratum of policymakers. Groups of "experts," in agriculture as well as in other areas, have broad discretionary powers that can affect our lives without our having much to say about it. The old adage, "Let the buyer beware!" applies more today than ever. It is becoming apparent that food-regulating is too big a job for government to perform for uninformed consumers and that uninformed consumers present too much temptation for agribusiness and its "regulators."

WHO'S REGULATING WHOM?

The "questionable practices" we should be concerned about are not confined to contaminating food with chemicals or to using cancer-inducing hormones or to employing food additives and food spoiling preventatives.

Questionable practices also include the government's involvement in a broad spectrum of agricultural codes and regulations, market orders and other price-support mechanisms, not to mention regulatory boards which permit the "regulated" to do the regulating. Most of these government-supported food growing and processing mechanisms have contributed to an agriculture in which the big farmer gets bigger, the small farmer drops out of the picture, and the food buyer's choices become increasingly limited.

What we have is an industry which is constantly telling us what we want, and how we want it. Some agricultural codes specify which two sizes of fruit are acceptable; and if you want to buy small apples, or oranges in mixed-size lots, or unsprayed nectarines with a few thrip marks on them, that's too bad.

The agricultural code doesn't say why—it just says that they can't be shipped across the county line—it's "against the code."

Until insect and sizing tolerances are adjusted more reasonably, environmentalists and organic food buyers are almost talking to themselves. The average farmer won't gamble on a crop which might be rejected at the county line.

It might be, when all is said and done, that most consumers would prefer to buy oranges, for example, which had been sprayed, and sized, and artificially colored. Currently, however, consumers are not permitted to express this choice, and no one has bothered to ask them. As a matter of fact, supermarkets operate on the principle of *calculated acceptance;* in the case of oranges, this means that two sizes or types of oranges will be displayed in the market and that represents the extent of the buyer's choices.

Calculated acceptance is the art (sadly it is almost a science) of controlling choices; and the point here is that when supermarkets place their orders, a "movement" is created. This movement does not reflect what food the farmer has available, or what the consumer would like to buy. In fact, "movement" limits both the consumers' and the farmers' options regarding the supply and demand of various commodities. The farmer either has to supply what the movement will support, or starve. And the consumers' range of choices isn't much greater.

District Agricultural Advisory Boards, made up mostly of growers, are supposed to make judgments about the movement of commodities. Their job is to maintain price supports for particular crops by establishing "quality levels" and "volume controls"—within the limits established by state and federal agricultural codes. They might suspect that consumers would prefer something other than what is sent, but they are guided more by their own needs as growers, and by the orders placed by supermarket chains and food processors.

These Advisory Boards were originally created to divide the market among all of the farmers growing a particular commodity—a commendable goal. At harvest time, they figure how much demand there is for apricots, for example, and then compute that the market will support 70 per cent of the crop in one area. Seventy per cent of each grower's crop is then harvested. This may sound fair, but it doesn't offer any inducement to growing higher-quality apricots. If each grower is guaranteed an equal share of the market, at a specified price, then his main concern is with keeping his costs down. And if this policy leads to the production and distribution of tasteless, green apricots . . . the grower could care less!

FEW FARMS, LITTLE CHOICE

Controlled choice and our agricultural codes combine to be the all-time buck-stopper. The shape of the food industry is controlled by these two mechanisms, and farmers and consumers alike find themselves confused and powerless, on the outside looking in. Thirty years of codes, market orders, and advisory boards have welded together a rich and solid agribusiness which now rigidly insists upon one form of agriculture. Why does there *have* to be just one agriculture . . . one chemical agriculture? Why can't there be an alternative for consumers who want to specify otherwise? This is a question which informed consumers are reaching past "controlled choice," and market orders, to talk directly to farmers.

Yet another questionable government practice involves property tax structures which work against the family farmer. We are losing, by a conservative estimate, 100,000 farms each year! The plight of the family farmer is the plight of the average consumer, and as the family farm dwindles, so does our opportunity for alternatives. The family farmer and the consumer are more or less in the same boat. Both pretty much have to accept what is offered. Both are required to pick up the tab and support a status quo which enables super-corporations and speculators to eliminate one and conform the other. What is the future for the average consumer-citizen in a large country where fewer than 500,000 own and control the food resources?

Time is running out. If as informed consumers, we do not specify soon what kind of agriculture we want in this country, five years may be too late. The "land of opportunity" will become history, and consumers will buy food like they now buy cars and television sets—from an ever-smaller number of ever-bigger and ever-richer super-corporations.

Health Foods Tomorrow

A man in California who buys fruit and vegetables for 1,500 supermarkets all across the U.S. called with a serious problem recently. On a test basis, he had been offering organically grown produce in a few supermarkets in Denver, and now the test was a success. People were buying unsprayed carrots and other food so quickly it was causing a strain on the supply. "I can't buy enough organic food to keep these stores stocked," he said, "and I want to expand the program to other cities. Where can I get in touch with more organic farmers?" We are trying to help this man, and I'm sure that within a year or two organically grown food will be available in many more places.

Then a few days later, a lady called saying she worked for one of the largest brewing companies in the country, and this company wanted to diversify into health foods. She wanted information about the scope of demand for natural foods and other market information.

These are only two of many similar inquiries we have received in the past few months. A big change is taking place in the way people think about naturally and organically grown food. No longer are you an oddball or a faddist if you buy or sell an apple that hasn't been sprayed. Everybody is concerned about pollution, and many people now believe that food is one thing that we should be able to get in unpolluted form. People no longer have confidence that the government has the backbone to keep harmful chemicals out of food, and they became suspicious of the quality of standard, brand-name foods long ago. So there is only one place for the average person to turn right now, and that is to the health food store and to people selling natural, organically grown food.

HEALTH FOOD STORES

There are about 3,500 health food stores in this country now, and they are doing more business than ever before. New stores are opening every week, and both the old stores and the new ones are crowded with people of all ages seeking better things to eat. The image of the health food store has changed, too. No longer is it a place primarily for people with diabetes to get sugarless food. No longer is it the haven only for old people looking for some kind of food or supplement that will clear up their arthritis or cure their internal aches. Health food stores are now entering the age of natural, organic foods that have a built-in appeal for everyone, the young and the old, the sick and the healthy. The health food trade is on the verge of seeing demand for its products increased to fantastic proportions.

Some health food stores, however, seem to be slow to get into the new and larger field of catering to the basic food needs of people. They are doing so well selling food supplements, herb teas and speciality foods (which are valuable and needed products, of course) that they don't want to go to the expense, trouble and risk of trying to compete in the basic food market. The distributors supplying health food stores are having difficulty getting supplies of raw materials, because the demand is so great. There are signs, therefore, that the health food industry is not able to serve the rapidly expanding demand for better food. Particularly in the area of organically grown food is there likely to be a crisis in supply in the near future. Prices for food known to be produced without chemical fertilizers or pesticides and grown on composted soil are likely to be going up, simply because many more people want this kind of food.

RESPONSE OF THE GIANTS

The large food companies are not interested seriously in stepping into the health food market for the sake of trying to improve the general nutritional level of the American people. Until very recently, the grocery industry took the position that health foods simply didn't exist. If they had admitted that there was such a thing as a health food, then by implication the bulk of their products would be considered unhealthy foods. That admission would have been too much for a big-time food executive to stomach.

Events of the past two years have convinced almost everyone, however, that health food is not a mirage. First came the national study conducted by Dr. Arnold Schaeffer of the Department of Health, Education and Welfare. That investigation showed that the meat, potatoes, pizza, soft drink diet of many people—rich and poor—was creating dietary deficiencies. Then came the cyclamate affair and other revelations that harmful additives were being allowed in food. People began to wonder who really was watching the store and if the cooperation between food industry representatives and government regulators might really be a conspiracy as alleged for years by health food industry spokesmen. Finally, the explosion of interest in pollution and the environment caused many young people to take a new and critical look at their jitterbug diet and to wonder if perhaps a natural system of eating might hold out for them a better alternative for health and satisfaction.

Because large numbers of people now believe in the value of health foods, a big market for these products exists. There is now much more money to be earned in the health food trade, and the prospect of profit is what interests the large food companies. Supermarket chains and even large brewing companies are willing to investigate a field they formerly scorned and derided as the preserve of misguided faddists.

The big food companies have a tremendous problem, however, when they attempt to enter the health food market. We must not forget that the junk food concept to which the supermarkets and processing plants have been wedded for many years has great momentum, starting all the way back at the farm. Our agriculture experts and scientists know practically nothing about organic methods of farming. The farmers know only how to grow things with chemicals, except for the small minority of organic farmers. Billions of dollars have been invested in machines to take the germ and the minerals and the vitamins out of wheat and other grains. In every city and town of this land are food plants turning out junk foods, laced with additives and depleted of much of their food value. Many plans are on food industry drawing boards to make even more synthetic and imitation types of food. In short, there is a great investment in convenience food which American industry is not about to abandon just because a growing minority of people are willing to buy health foods.

TWO DIRECTIONS

The food situation in this country will proceed in the future in two directions, and they are almost opposite directions. Unfortunately, there will continue to be growth and expansion of synthetic foods, simply because it will always be possible to fool many people about the quality of food by adding artificial colors, flavors, and additives that give body and substance to food fibers that have been beaten and flailed in processing plants. There is money in such synthetic food, and the things are going we may see the day in a decade or so when the bulk of food sold in supermarkets will be the imitations.

At the same time, the natural food and health food segment of the market will also thrive. People who want real food and who are willing to pay something extra to have natural quality will go for their food to separate stores (like delicatessens or health food stores) or to "real food" departments in conventional supermarkets. I think this natural food idea will expand rapidly, largely as a form of protest to the increasing artificiality of modern life and especially in reaction to the growing synthetic character of most food. Even the farm may eventually be mobilized (at least in part) in support of real food products, because when food is sold in natural form the farmer tends to get a larger percentage of the retail dollar. The synthetic food industry is going increasingly to non-farm raw materials—like oil and coal—to supply the foods that farmers by rights should produce. So farmers will probably be more willing in the future to listen to people who are asking them to grow organic foods. The land, after all, is the only place where organic crops *can* be grown.

Even if the supermarket people give only a small portion of their energy to the natural food trade, they can soon mount an effort that will surpass in volume the business done by health food stores. Consider the problem of fresh fruit and vegetables, for example. Health food stores have largely ignored this type of food. But the supermarkets have vast experience in buying and selling fresh produce, and they know that people who are interested in health put a high value on fresh foods. Supermarkets already have the refrigerated shipping and storage facilities and the special bins to display fruits and vegetables. Without too much trouble the supermarkets could develop highly successful organic food sections in their fresh food departments and put a gloss of higher quality on their entire stock of food.

The health food stores must recognize the potential of competition from supermarkets and must do something about the competition now or be willing to accept second place in the industry they pioneered. And if the health food stores lose out, the public will lose out, too, because I think the health food merchandisers are the only people in the food trade now who even begin to understand basic principles of nutrition and who have the strength of character to protect the concept of organic and natural food from abuse. The idea of organic food is a fragile thing. There is no universally accepted definition of what organic food is. Of course, we know that organic food should not be sprayed with poisons or be grown on soil fertilized with soluble chemicals. But how much humus or organic matter should be in the soil, and how many years should pass before a chemically treated field is classified as fully organic? Those questions are unsettled and are important. Rodale Press is grappling with them in establishing a model farm certification program. But if the health food trade doesn't help to decide them now and enforce those decisions, the big food companies are likely to make the decisions to suit their own interests.

There is also the question of processing of organic food. Can you treat it with the preservatives and still call it organic? The commercial food companies are likely to try to do just that. Health food stores should take a firm stand against all food additives and against any processing which isn't absolutely necessary. Too often in the past the health food industry accepted products like artificial sweeteners because they believed the science-fiction that those chemical products contributed to health. The time for compromise is past. There *is* no compromise with natural and organic food. Only the purest, most natural, best tasting foods belong in the channels of the health food trade.

INDIVIDUAL ACTION

We must all act together to take advantage of the potential demand for unpolluted food that now exists. If we all sit back and wait for the opportunity to buy more good food to come our way, we are likely to be sadly disappointed. We must use all our voices to make the true extent of the demand for health food known to the people who are able to bring more health food to the American table. Here are some key actions.

1. For a start, get to know your health food store better. Tell the owner and the clerks what food they are selling that you think is good and where you believe their stock could stand improvement. If you have an organic garden, invite the store owner to your home for a dinner of organic food. Bring him or her some samples of organic food to taste, and do that over and over again. Most important, tell the people in the health food trade what organic food is. Surprisingly, some still don't know.

2. If you live in a farming area, visit local growers and tell them that you want and are willing to pay for fruit, vegetables, and other food that is grown without the use of chemicals. Talk to owners of

local farm stands and tell them about natural and organic food. Small, specialty fruit markets are likely to be interested, too. Keep mentioning the fact that people are concerned about pollution and that they don't want polluting chemicals in their food.

3. Write letters to all the people you can think of who you believe are influential in food distribution channels. Write to your health food store, to your local market, to nearby farmers and orchardists, to your County Agricultural Agent, to the manufacturers of health foods and regular foods. Tell all these people about organic food. Tell them you want to be able to buy more food that is not contaminated. Letters like that have an important effect—more than most people realize.

Now is the time to act, because the climate is right to win a victory in the war against junk food. If you have ever wanted to do something to help yourself and other people be healthier, the time to fulfill that desire is now.

—Robert Rodale

Organic Food Legislation

There are still places in this great land of ours where a farmer can still fudge about how organic he is. Cut down a little on the poisons and the chemical fertilizers, say "I'm organic" to the public and start charging more for the crops.

That's the way the organically grown food game is being played far too often, as you know if you read the newspaper and magazine articles about sham in the health food shops. No matter where people talk about organically grown foods these days, they're asking: "Is it really organically grown?" Thus, the days of the casual approach to organic farming for profit are rapidly coming to an end.

When some so-called organic growers monkey with what the words organically grown really mean on a food label, they're taking on more than just the hard core of the health food movement and some organic gardeners who want to buy better food during gardening's off-season. They're trying to pull the wool over *everybody's* eyes.

That fact is clearly apparent to Representative Edward I. Koch (D.-N.Y.), who recently introduced into Congress a bill calling for a national inspection and certification of organic farmers. If enacted

—and Ed Koch thinks the chances are excellent—the days of confusion and doubt about the real meaning of the words "organically grown" could be over for good.

Here are the basic provisions of the Koch bill, which I believe every serious and dedicated organic person will want to support:

1. The term organically grown is defined precisely to mean "food which has not been subjected to pesticides or artificial fertilizers, and grown on soil whose humus content is increased by the addition of organic matter." "Organically processed food" is also defined. It means "food, whose ingredients have all been grown organically, including meat and poultry, which has not been treated with preservatives, hormones, antibiotics or synthetic additives of any kind."

(Believe it or not, there are still elements in the health food trade who say that the word organic on food today can mean something other than organically grown as defined above. Since the word organic is magic commercially, they want to plaster it on *anything*, without regard to how it was grown.)

2. The Secretary of Health, Education and Welfare, in conjunction with other government and state officials, and consumers, shall offer regulations that will set a standard for a minimum humus and mineral content of the soil of organic farms, and set standards for maximum permissible residues of pesticides, herbicides, fungicides and chemical fertilizers in the soil, the produce, and the water sources of the farm.

3. All farmers intending to produce organically grown food for sale, the Koch bill continues, shall register with the Secretary of HEW on or before December 31 of each year. That registration shall include his or her name, place of business, and farm or farms operated. The Secretary shall make available to anyone the list of registered, commercial organic farmers.

4. Finally, the Secretary is instructed by the measure to design an "organically grown" seal which shall be the only acceptable seal designating foods as organically grown. Each separate marketable unit of the produce grown by a registered organic farm shall be stamped or marked in some way with the seal, and with the name and address of the farmer.

5. The cost of operating this federal organically grown food certifi-

cation program is to be borne by the farmers certified, who will be required to pay a fee based on acreage or units of production. Violations will subject farmers or merchants to penalties in keeping with similar violations of the Food, Drug and Cosmetic Act, which the Koch bill seeks to amend.

I had a chance to visit with Rep. Koch before he introduced his bill, and Floyd Allen, Jerry Goldstein, Lee Goldman, Jim Foote and others working on the Rodale Press certification program studied the bill in detail. We made a few suggestions for changes in the first draft, and most of our suggestions were accepted.

Now that the bill has been introduced, you can study it also and offer your own comments, preferably to your representative in Congress. Enacting this bill into law will take at least a year, and there will be hearings during which people directly connected with the commercial production and processing of organically grown food can have their say about its provisions.

Whether the bill actually gets to the hearing stage, though, depends to a large extent on how much interest in the measure is brought to the attention of Congressmen. If your Congressman doesn't get much mail or personal contact on the organically grown food bill, he's going to give it very little attention. Bills become laws because of pressure from some special-interest group or the public.

When I first heard about and read the Koch bill, I had two reactions. First, I said to myself, "By golly, this bill really tells the organically grown food story the right way." It defines organically grown food correctly, leaving little room for doubt. And it encourages the addition of natural fertilizers to the soil, which is an important often overlooked part of the organic method.

My second thought, though, was a feeling of reluctance about the federal government getting intimately involved in the organic farming business, which has traditionally been carried on in direct opposition to the government farm policies. In many ways, growing food organically is a subversive activity. We want to show the world (which includes the government) that growing things without expensive and harmful poisons and fertilizers is better. It's quite a feeling, after that tradition of rebellion, to think of yourself carrying a seal of the United States Government.

Like it or not, though, the only real alternative to someday carrying that seal may be chaos and a tearing down of the whole organic concept. We need government help, because what used to be our little, private—natural—way of growing food has become big business and has the promise of getting even bigger. The words "organically grown" are a potent sales tool on food labels, and as such are too vulnerable to cheating and fraud to be used without a foolproof certification program to back them up.

To me, the proof that the Koch bill is worth supporting will become clear to all organic people when the opposition lines up: the chemical companies, the scientists on their payroll, and the big food companies who specialize in making "food" out of additives. Our traditional opponents will not want this bill passed, because it will help to build a strong foundation under commercial organic farming.

That will be proof that we need this law, and proof, too, that we have to get on the ball politically to counteract those attacks. We have the numbers of people on our side—all the millions who are interested in better food. The problem will be to get them to speak out to their Congressmen and to their Senators, since a companion bill has been introduced in the Senate.

Should this bill pass and be signed into law, it will put out of business the certification program now conducted by Rodale Press. The Koch bill specifically says that government certification of organically grown food shall be the only kind of certification allowed, and that's reasonable and proper. We support that provision of the bill.

In the meantime, though, we are going to proceed with our own program of offering testing services to organic farmers who are selling their produce under the organically grown label. The need for that certification is so great right now that it can't wait a year or more until a government program could take effect.

So please support both the Koch bill and the Rodale Press certification program. We need all the help we can get to fight the organic phonies!

—*Robert Rodale*

The Social Significance of Organic Food

A whole generation of Americans has grown up without any personal communication with the producer of their foods. The supermarket checkout clerk has been the closest human contact, as the food goes from shelf and freezer into shopping basket for transfer to closet and freezer. The television screen gives the clearest picture of where the food came from before it got to the supermarket.

Organic foods have the ability to turn this all around. The consumer can identify the farmer, and the farmer can identify the consumer. The human identity of each can surface and interrelate. The money spent for food—for its production and consumption—can become a real economic force for societal and environmental objectives.

Part of each dollar spent for organically grown foods should mean:

1. Less money spent on pesticides and artificial fertilizers—consequently, less production of chemical pollutants and contamination of the environment.

2. More money for the farmers and farm workers who make their homes on the land—thus more profits when land is used for producing food instead of for residential and industrial development.

3. More jobs with adequate compensation on farms growing crops by labor-intensive organic methods—thus less forced migration to city ghettos.

4. More economic incentive to bring composted organic wastes from the city onto farmland where it builds up humus content.

5. More economic support to the *small* entrepreneur—the family farmer, the mama-and-papa grocery store and the *local* brand name.

6. More demand for personal services and less for mass-distributed environmentally hazardous products. That means more money for the man who is educated to advise on how to recycle wastes back to the land and less for the chemical fertilizer salesman whose product is supposed to be a cure-all for everything (except the pollution it brings to waterways from runoff.)

When J.I. Rodale started a small magazine with a handful of subscribers back in 1942, neither he nor anyone else could predict its role 30 years later. In fact, even today, only a handful are still aware of how his ideas on organic gardening and farming relate to the very core of many environmental solutions today.

Yet in this post-Earth Day atmosphere, the simple ideas of J.I. Rodale's organic method have taken on a new aura of social significance.

Without stretching the imagination or overglorifying the compost heap, we can develop the relevance of the organic idea to such problems as land reform, human nutrition, overcentralization, and waste disposal. Organic methods in agriculture put an economic base under city planners' dreams of open spaces around urban areas. For city people to get high-quality, inexpensive organic foods, city people need country people on small farms. A good many of those farms should be close to the city. Every city in America faces a crisis with garbage disposal; local farms know that garbage can be useful once it's returned safely to the soil. The organic idea lets everyone understand how everything interrelates.

Of course, if organic foods are to have all the relevance implied above, tremendous demands are put upon the buyers of those foods. You constantly must ask (often more than once) where does the food come from—whose farm, what growing methods, who knows the farmer—and have you given him a chance to know you?

If the food is expensive, you should find out why. Has the grower's harvest been drastically reduced by insects or disease? Or is it that the food has come several thousand miles, or that one or more links in the food distribution chain are taking excess advantage of your desire for organic foods?

When you buy organic foods, you consciously should realize that you are using your food dollar to encourage change in American agricultural methods. For years, American farmers have been led to believe that food is no different than any other product. Churn it out in assembly-line fashion as fast and as cheaply and mechanically as you can. Just like we do with cars. Or envelopes. Or wigs. Or any other product.

But now you are taking your food dollar and you are dissenting. You are saying that all food is not equal in quality regardless of how it is grown—not equal to the consumer, not equal to society, not equal to the land, not equal to the water, not equal—period.

By wanting to buy organically grown foods raised by a family farmer who is not supposed to be able to make a living on the land, you are helping to reverse a trend that has driven people off the land and made farming an old man's profession. By buying organic foods at a mama-and-papa neighborhood store that is not supposed to be able to compete with supermarket chains, you are helping to change the make-up of America.

I believe millions of Americans are saying important things when they buy organic foods. Things like "land ethic" and "decent wages for more farm workers" and "a way for the little guy to compete" and "I don't want everything to look alike—especially my food."

It's amazing how far afield we can go by buying organic foods. All of us together are trying to create a new change in the philosophy of American agriculture. It's far more than the negative side of not using dangerous pesticides and polluting fertilizers. It's far more even than using natural fertilizers, soil conditioners, and rotating crops.What we together are trying to show is that there is a rapidly growing trend for food grown with more man-power. Sure, we know that eggs produced by chickens which are allowed to run around will cost more than eggs produced by chickens that are penned four to a cage. But those organically produced eggs will get and deserve a higher price. Part of that higher price will provide decent wages for more farm workers—right now those farm workers of the future may be sweating it out in some urban tenement.

Does that mean organic foods are always higher-priced and only for the upper middle class? We think not—but time will tell. Many environmentalists including organic gardeners have been worried that industry is trying to isolate them from labor and the poor. Statements that organic foods are only for the rich, that antipollution costs force layoffs and claim funds needed to eliminate poverty are seen as an effort to set workers and the poor against environmentalists.

Groups like the Rural Advancement Fund have shown the relevance of the organic idea to small farmers and rural poor. They have shown the vital necessity to use organic foods as a way to relate the farmer to the consumer and to what is wrong in the city with what is wrong on the farm. Organic foods can help to solidify the coalition between the needs of sharecroppers and small farmers and the environmentalists concern for land use.

And the really great part is that when you get all through with the philosophy, the food tastes great!

—Jerome Goldstein

Doing the Impossible

Organically speaking, the sky's the limit. Because people are beginning to think organically, they are beginning to see their true place in nature.

We can now do many organic things we always have dreamed about but thought were impossible.

Here are a few examples.

Dr. Bargyla Rateaver of San Francisco long had a desire to teach organic gardening. Over a period of months, she asked for the support of several colleges, junior colleges and even county school districts but was turned down. Eventually, she took her plan for organic gardening classes to the University of California and was accepted. Now she has 150 students, and 50 of them are getting academic credit for their work. Dr. Rateaver is planning to expand her class schedule and even to set up an extension course for "urban gardeners," who will be shown how to grow things organically in cans and on apartment rooftops. Interest in classroom study of organic gardening will continue to grow, because many people are thinking ecologically. And ecology leads right into organic gardening.

Have you ever thought that your organic plans were frustrated by neighbors who spray and allow it to drift on your garden? Now chances are those neighbors are anxious to quit the hard-spray habit and are looking for advice on how to garden organically or even on how to dispose of their unwanted poison packages. Organic gardener Mrs. Pamela Welton of Port Coquitlam, British Columbia, recognized the problem of safe disposal of unwanted pesticides and decided to do something about it. She and her husband organized a pick-up campaign, which was highly successful.

NEW ATTITUDES

Gardeners are willing to change. If we organic gardeners will tell them how simple organic methods are, they will listen and will use these methods. At a hearing on a proposed Pennsylvania bill to license all people who apply pesticides, such as farmers and exterminators, testimony was taken from chemical sellers, farmers, ecologists and spray applicators. It was fascinating. How different now is the general attitude toward chemicals than it was 20 years ago! The chemical suppliers and users are now on the defensive—constantly trying to justify their affection for poisons. They are in a false position. And if we do a little better job of demonstrating the effectiveness of organic methods, the "impossible" will be within our grasp.

The members of the Pennsylvania Agriculture Committee had

probably all heard about organic farming, but they didn't quite put two and two together and realize that the acknowledged impending bankruptcy of chemical farming concepts is literally forcing everyone to at least move toward organic methods. They realized that many farmers were in trouble because sprays are less effective than they used to be (insects develop resistance) and because the harm that poisons do to the environment is becoming more clearly known each year. But these fine men hadn't quite gathered that the people who want a pure environment also want pure food and that the end of farm poison will lead to a new era of farm purity.

We have to explain these basic organic truths to the people who lead us and who are faced with making decisions that will change the quality of our future environment. I testified to that committee in the afternoon, bringing in a bag of organic vegetables from our storage house. Plunking down a cabbage, turnips, beets and carrots on the hearing table, I presented graphic proof that food *can* be grown without pesticides. Perhaps even more important, I read off the records of yields of feed grains from the Organic Gardening Experimental Farm, showing that for almost 30 years we have produced as much grain as the average production for our district—but without the use of any chemical fertilizers or pesticides. Hopefully, this kind of testimony will continue to mount in volume before our legislatures and congress.

RENEWED EFFORTS

Yes, we can do the impossible, if we keep trying. A crucial but "impossible" task may be convincing the American housewife and consumer that small marks and insect bites on food can be signs of purity, meaning that the food hasn't been sprayed. The vegetables I brought to the hearing as evidence weren't marked, but many commercial growers are hesitant to try growing fruit and vegetables organically, because they can visualize a whole crop lowered in value by superficial insect markings.

Dr. Francis Trembley, an ecologist from Lehigh University, told the hearing that in many countries the insects we look down our noses at are considered to be good food. It's all a question of how you've been brought up. Trembley himself learned to eat insects as a child and feels that with a little encouragement the American public can overcome the current morbid fear of bugs. On a youthful dare, Trembley once ate a cherry that contained a caterpillar grub. Finding it not too bad, he went back for seconds and thirds. Eventually, he got to like cherries with grubs better than "plain" cherries.

You may not *want* to get to like insects. That is your privilege. But the story about Dr. Trembley and the bugs proves that we can do things we thought were impossible. We must not let ourselves be limited in our horizons by false constraints. In a world changing as fast as ours is now, the limits are changing too.

UNDERSTANDING NATURE

Did you realize, for example, that we organic gardeners and farmers have a much clearer understanding of the real problems of living today than almost any scientist or "expert" you can name? By wanting to live in tune with nature, by trying to produce pure food, by returning our wastes to the soil, we have involved ourselves intimately with the natural world. Scientists today tend to be so specialized in their studies and expertise that they seldom understand clearly what other scientists are doing and are even further removed from the actual conditions and problems of life, in a broad sense.

We organic gardeners are more ecological than ecologists. "The current myth among a majority of scientists is that ecology is a science and that their practice of it as 'ecologists' is what ecology is all about," wrote Ron Warnick in *Earth People News*, published in Logan, Utah. Ecologists, he continued, "have constructed valid ecological descriptions of the world as totally interrelated, but they don't feel themselves to exist this way. Their feeling of objective identity is alienation from the world rather than interdependence with it. They look at it and describe it objectively, but never become a part. Consequently, scientific ecology becomes just another way to manipulate a separate world, as if the world were not a living organism, but an inert stage upon which man plays out his actions." Quite a challenging thought.

You and I, with our hands and feet in the earth, are really involved with the web of life. We are putting our wastes into compost heaps, then back into the soil. We are eating natural food, the only sane kind of food to eat. We are not poisoning ourselves by spraying our roses or cabbages with chlorinated hydrocarbons or organic phosphates. Most important of all, we comprehend that all these "organic" actions have a meaning to life, and we know what that meaning is. We understand that trying to manipulate the environment with technological tricks does not work, and we are proving in our own gardens and on our farms that organic, natural methods do work.

There was a time when I thought that convincing everyone of the soundness of organic ways was an impossible task. Now I am sure that it is possible, because I know that people are receptive and want to learn. The emptiness of the chemical-technological way of life has convinced them that there must be a better way.

We have that better way, and it's so simple, so easy! But we have to get some of the spirit that R. H. Conwell described in his famous talk "Acres of Diamonds." We don't have to look any more for help or salvation from the chemical laboratories or for tricks from science's magic black box. If we are willing to try, we can do the "impossible" ourselves. Under our feet are acres of diamonds. We can see them, and now we have to make sure that other people can see them, too.

—*Robert Rodale*

Index

Aamodt, Marjorie, 184, 185
Aamodt, Norman, 184, 185
"Acres of Diamonds" (Conwell), 333
Adams, Robert, 181
Advertising Age, 9
Agene, 21–22
Agricultural Testament, An (Howard), 56
Agriculture
  artificial fertilizers, 4–5, 7, 10, 11, 13,
    48–49, 70, 84–85
  available land, 236–239
  codes, 315–317
  corporate farms, 70
  crisis in, 63–67
  economics, 69–70
  family farms, 317
  food surpluses, 70
  fumigants, 47–48, 74
  organic, 3–4, 5, 7, 13, 67–72, 75–76
    beginning of, 13, 56–57
    bio-dynamic method, 58–59
    fertilizers, 54, 83, 85
    problems of, 73–75
  Organic Grower Certification Program,
    44, 195–205, 325, 326
  pesticides, 12, 44, 45, 47, 68–70, 74, 198
  property tax structures, 317
  regulations, 315–317
  rice, 68
  soil, 4, 10, 12, 50–54, 64, 71, 198, 238
  technology and, 70
  See also Organic gardening
Akikiyu tribe, 35
Albion Laboratories, 53
Albright, Nancy, 257–258, 261
Alfalfa, 165
Allen, Floyd, 197, 199, 202, 203, 325
Allen, Harold B., 18, 23
Allen, Richard C., 185
Allergies, 42–43
Alum, 23
Aluminum sulfate, 23
Ambassador College, Texas, 313
American Medical Association, Council on
  Food and Nutrition, 293

American Medical Association Journal, 49,
  291
Amino acids, 31, 169
Ammonium chloride, 22
Anderson, Earl, 303
Anderson, Jack, 202
Anemia, 41, 292, 294
Animal feeds, additives in, 190–192
Antibiotics, in animal feeds, 190–191
Apple pie, 22
Apples, 20
Arasan 42S (Thiram), 68
Arizona, 237
Arkansas, 238
Artificial coloring, 23, 24, 27, 71
Artificial fertilizers, 4–5, 7, 10, 11, 13,
  48–49, 70, 84–85
Ashmead, Harvey, 53–56
Atwater, Wilbur O., 31

Baby food, 277–279
Bacillus thuringiensis disease, 99
Backyard gardening, 76–77
Barley, 153
Barnes, Carlton, 184
Barry, Thomas, 181
Bean flour, 170
Bean sprouts, 165, 170
Beans
  cooking, 167–170
  See also, names of beans
Bear, Firman E., 51
Beef
  buying, 186–194
    antibiotics, 190–191
    DES, 21, 191–193, 314
    eye-check for quality, 189
    grading and inspections, 189–190
    supermarkets, 187, 194
  organically raised, 183–186
    availability, 183–184, 186–187
    consumer information, 184–186
    standards for, 188
Beetle larvae (grubs), 93

Index